JOAN

JOAN

BY JOAN HANNINGTON

**EBURY
SPOTLIGHT**

1 3 5 7 9 10 8 6 4 2

Ebury Spotlight, an imprint of Ebury Publishing
20 Vauxhall Bridge Road
London SW1V 2SA

Ebury Spotlight is part of the Penguin Random House group of companies
whose addresses can be found at global.penguinrandomhouse.com

Many of the characters in this book are composites of real people
and in some instances names and locations have been changed.

Originally published with the title *I Am What I Am* by
Headline Book Publishing in 2002
This edition published by Ebury Spotlight in 2024

www.penguin.co.uk

A CIP catalogue record for this book is available from the British Library

ISBN 9781529913149

Printed and bound in Great Britain by Clays Ltd, Elcograf S.p.A.

The authorised representative in the EEA is Penguin Random House Ireland,
Morrison Chambers, 32 Nassau Street, Dublin D02 YH68

Penguin Random House is committed to a sustainable future
for our business, our readers and our planet. This book is made
from Forest Stewardship Council® certified paper.

To my son Benny Hannington (aka Benny Banks), my daughter Debbie, my granddaughter Olivia Hannington, to Buster Hannington and all the Brighton family and, of course, Rosie, Prince and Nelson – my beautiful furry family. I love you all to eternity and back. To my agent Lucy Fawcett who's a right pain in the arse and is forever correcting my grammar. Thank you for 17 years of loyalty. Too many people forget to respect their agents. Well, I respect and love mine, thank you Lucy. And finally I'd like to pay a tribute to a special Irishman from Belfast who has lived and worked in England for over 30 years, Martin (Marty Mo) Mulligan, 1956–2024. RIP old friend, you were the hardest working Irishman I ever knew. Condolences to your wife Linda, daughters Sheila and Mary Ellen, sons John, Martin and Billy and all the Mulligans, too many to mention, in London and in Belfast.

CONTENTS

CHAPTER ONE

The Art of Stealing Diamonds

When I grew up I became the best at what I did because I was dedicated to the art of stealing diamonds. I knew one of the ways not to get caught was to work alone, because then I only had myself to worry about if it came on top – if I got nicked. Swallowing diamonds was my life, my buzz, my drug. It was the only thing that I really liked doing. Like I said, it was an art – and I was the artist. I couldn't read or write properly but I could be skint one minute and fifty grand richer the next. All I had to do was get in a jewellery shop and swallow a couple of rings or switch some loose stones. I knew people who robbed banks, held up Securicor vans, sold drugs, sold themselves, but even when I went to jail I never met anyone who'd done what I'd done. To me, I had a gift. I'd spend hours getting myself dressed up to look like a model or a well-to-do lady – because if you're gonna nick a diamond that's worth fifty or sixty grand, then you've got to look like you've *got* fifty or sixty grand.

Then off I'd go, down to a jeweller's in Bond Street to take a look in the window.

The rings could be anything from twenty-five grand up to three hundred, four hundred thousand pounds. But I wouldn't want to go for the highest. I'd think, *Oh no, that's a bit too much*. Instead, I'd pick a ring for around fifty thousand. A single-carat heart-shaped diamond, say. Then I'd go to Hatton Garden and tell the jobber I want the same ring made up – only it would be a fake diamond in a real gold or platinum shank. (A 'shank' is a gold band, to us in the jewellery trade.) The stone would be glass, which at a glance looked genuine and was OK for what I had in mind. In my early days I couldn't judge a diamond or its size just by looking; I'd have to go in and try it on. And while I did, I'd be asking the assistant how big the stone was, what the grade was, how much it weighed, and I'd ask him or her (usually him) to write down the details so I could show my husband, 'as obviously it's rather a lot of money . . . . Oh and we will of course be paying by banker's draft', blah, blah.

Let's say there was a choice between a single diamond and the same carat's worth of diamonds in a group of stones – a cluster. Even though both rings have got the same weight content, I'd want to nick the single stone because I know the fence would prefer to have just the single diamond, which is easier to get rid of.

I didn't always agree with that way of thinking. If I was a fence I'd rather have the cluster ring; I'd take all the stones out it and have new shanks made up. Instead of having one ring I'd have eight rings, and that way I'd make more money.

Two or three days later I'd go to the Savoy Hotel or the

Dorchester and book a room for one night. From there I'd make a point of phoning the particular jeweller's I'd visited and telling them I'd be along later that day to try on the ring again – 'Oh, and by the way, have you got such-and-such an item in stock and could you phone me back at my hotel and let me know . . .'

The reason for this, of course, was to impress on the shop assistant that I was staying at a high-class hotel – and there'd be no suspicion towards me if they'd had to call me back there. What they didn't know was that I'd be staying at this fancy place under a different name, that I'd be in disguise and I'd have used a fake-tan cream to look like I'd just come back from holiday or was a tourist. If I chose to be a tourist, it would usually be an American one. They were the only ones who could afford the posh hotels in the seventies and eighties. Also I could do a really good impression of an American, especially a New Yorker. They're like us Londoners: very loud and very direct and know what they want.

I loved playing those parts. I loved locking myself in the hotel room with a suitcase full of expensive wigs, worth several hundred pounds each. Long blonde ones, redhead ones, short styles, curly locks – you name it, I had it, a wig for all occasions. Fur coats, too, expensive handbags, good-quality shoes and always gloves to match the clothes I was wearing. In fact the gloves were just a ploy, because when I tried a ring on I always kept my right-hand glove on; that way I'd never actually touch the counter with my bare hand, so my palm prints or fingerprints were never on the glass. If I'd left any prints behind it wouldn't have mattered if I was in disguise or not; they'd have had me bang to rights.

Finally I'd be ready and I'd phone down to the hotel reception asking for a car out front in ten minutes to take me shopping. I'd be very relaxed, looking a million dollars, speaking with my New York accent. I used to get such a buzz transforming myself in front of the mirror. Then I'd pick up my fur coat, drape it over my shoulder, and I'd take to the stage. From the minute I'd left the hotel I was a different person. I was a model, I was a doctor's wife – I was whatever it took to get in the jewellery shop and nick that lovely big ring: the bigger the diamond, the bigger the buzz.

We'd pull up outside the jeweller's and I'd make an entrance. I wanted the whole world to see me coming. The driver would open the car door and I'd make sure he got an eyeful of my legs as I got out, like Lady Muck, because this usually guaranteed that he'd open the door to the shop, all part of the act. It looked good – this well-dressed American bird coming through the door. I'd have some nice tom on, too (tomfoolery: jewellery), so they'd be looking at me and thinking, *Yeah, she looks the part, limo outside, chauffeur, the works.* And when I entered they'd all be standing there like a load of vultures waiting to pounce.

Usually it was the men, they'd fall over themselves trying to help me. I'd stay so calm and make a point of throwing my fur coat casually over a chair like it meant nothing to me. I'd sit down at a table and they'd offer me a glass of Perrier water; all nice and easy and I'd be playing the part. When you go into these shops you've got to be aware that there's cameras on you from every direction. First thing through the door, I always spotted them in the ceiling. And they're zooming in, right into your face, so if you're nervous and you're twitching, if you're doing anything you shouldn't be doing, those cameras are going to pick it up and anyone watching in the back room will see you sweating.

Don't be too quick, don't be too slow; don't be too enthusiastic.

I'd get them to bring me the ring I'd seen a few days before, and they'd put a bit of cloth down on the table in front of me. And as I'd be going through the motions of trying on the ring, I'd be saying, 'Oh my Gawd, it's just so *gorgeous* . . . but it's so expensive' – and how I'll be the envy of all the other wives back in America. I'd be giving the assistant total eye contact, flirting openly with him the whole time so he was never sure whether he wanted to sell me the ring or fuck me.

The longer I'd spent in the shop, the bolder I'd get. Then I'd say, 'Can I just look at that ring on the other tray? No, not that one – *that* one,' pointing to a ring and leaning over so he could get a good look down the front of my blouse. (I never had big tits but to make them look bigger I used to stuff socks inside my bra so they pushed mine up; just add a half-cup Wonderbra . . .)

By this point I'd have the assistant so worked up and totally in my confidence that the moment would be right to make my move. I'd pretend to try the ring on again, but would slip the real one into my other hand and switch it for the dodgy one, which I'd now put on my finger. Then as quick as you like I'd throw my head forward and let out a sneeze, shielding my face. While doing that I'd swish my tongue round my mouth to make saliva . . . swallow the ring, lift my head up and say, 'My Gawd, I'm so sorry! I must be getting a cold from your British weather.'

I'd still have the ring (now the dodgy one) on my finger – the assistant could plainly see it. But by this time he couldn't give a fuck if I buy the ring or not, he'd just want to play with my tits. I'd give him back the ring, still flirting, still putting him on a promise, and he'd return it to the pad. He wouldn't have sussed it out because the actual shank would be gold; it'd have the markings, the assay mark on it. He wouldn't even check it closely because he'd be too busy thinking about the five-grand commission or whatever it is he might get. But I'd take my time, let another ten, fifteen minutes go by, no rush, no panic.

Once I'd seen the dodgy ring go back in the window, I'd tell the bloke, 'Look, darling, I can't make my mind up right this minute. Maybe you'd like to come to my hotel tonight for drinks . . .'

By this stage the bloke behind the counter would be sweating and flapping all over the place. I'd let him help me on with my coat and would give him my room number. One of the assistants would open the door as I made my exit, still smiling, still acting larger than life. The driver would be standing there waiting by the car and in I'd get, as cool and sexy as you like.

Back at the hotel I'd give the driver a big fat tip and tell him I'll ask for him later on that day when I go out. And that'd be my work finished. And I'd be £50,000 better off. Or at least I would be when the ring passed through my system.

Best bank in the world, is your tummy. Best safety-deposit box invented.

In my hotel room I'd get my things together, go downstairs and out the main door to a black taxi and get the cabbie to take me to a particular road. I'd pay him and watch him drive off. When he was out of sight I'd flag down another black taxi and get him to drive me home – but never to the front door. I'd walk the rest of the way, put my key in the door and only when I was safely inside did I punch the air in triumph . . .

God, it was always such a good feeling, such a rush to the brain. It was better than sex. *This is what I done – this is what I do!* To me it wasn't crime. Yes, it was an art and I was the artist – the best bloody artist in Europe. And no one knew, not even my husband Benny. Maybe he knew I was going on a job but he never knew what or where. He'd probably be out somewhere at an antiques auction. (We didn't have mobile phones in those days, and even if we had we would never have used them; too many people can listen in on the calls, especially the police.)

Once I'd safely locked myself in the house, I'd pull off the wig, take off all my clothes and roll a big fat joint, pour a gin and tonic, put on some Bob Marley or Burning Spear and lay back in the bath and get stoned. God, I loved it. I loved it so much. *This is what it's all about*, I'd tell myself.

Those within my circle knew me as an antiques dealer or a jeweller, but never as a jewel thief. Women didn't do those things. Women were considered stupid or we were supposed to stay home and make babies or cook nice dinners. Well, not Joan Hannington. I'd tried that and the system fucked me. Now I was fucking the lot of them, only they didn't need to know. I didn't need pats on the back. I just needed to be a diamond thief and no one could stop me.

It wasn't easy – I wouldn't say it was easy, not if I got caught; I just never got caught.

I'd finish my bath and put on my jeans and a Man United football shirt, Doc Martens boots, a baseball cap on my head, and I'd be Joan again, happy-go-lucky, only now a nice few grand richer. People expect you to live a certain way when you've got a lot of money. But I was still just Joan. I never changed, people around me changed. When they got money they'd feel they had to be rude to people just 'cause they never had money or weren't thieves. I tried to treat people I came into contact with the same, whether they were in the crime world or in the straight world. To me it was all part of the act. I didn't need to be in front of a camera and well-known, like a pop singer, a model or a film star. I always liked the quiet life. I'd much rather sit at home watching the football or thinking about my next jewel theft. For me, when I was out working, that *was* my social life. I'd be wearing the best of clothes, driving the best cars, eating in the best restaurants in the world, pretending to be all these different women.

To me the world was my stage and I played my roles to perfection. I never got the Oscar – I got the diamond instead. Every time and with no regrets.

CHAPTER TWO

Uncle Dan

From when I was born, in April 1957, until I was about four I lived in a prefab with my family in North Acton Road, London. It was one of those buildings with a tin roof, and when the rain came down it used to frighten the shit out of me.

We lived in front of a power station and a park, and if you stood in our garden you could see the big chimneys. I don't know who it was, but someone used to tell me stories about how when those brick chimneys were being built men used to fall inside them and be boiled to death by the steam. From then on I just know I hated them.

My mum and dad came to London from southern Ireland in the late thirties or early forties (I don't really know). I'm the youngest of seven children. My oldest brother was called Tony. He died before any of my other brothers and sisters were born. The eldest now is Michael, then there's Irene, Denise (the lady of the family), Trisha, and then Barry, and then yours truly (the Bleached Blonde Gangster's Moll, as I've so often been called).

I don't mind telling you, I hate that title. I was never a

gangster's moll. I was just a girl who came from nothing and tried to better herself.

Then we moved to a great big house, Edwardian I think, in Park Road West, South Acton. It had upstairs and downstairs and so much space, and I loved it. From the early to middle sixties we had what you'd call a nice home, and my mum and dad both went out to work. My mum was so beautiful I thought she was a princess. She always had her make-up on and nice clothes. When her and my dad used to go out on a Saturday night she used to wear those dresses that look like ball-gowns, the ones they wore up until the late seventies on *Come Dancing*. I used to think, *Please, God, when I grow up I want to be just like my mum.*

Even from a young age I hated Christmas because of the fights. My dad used to stay in bed most of the holiday and go into a deep depression, and the only time he'd get out of bed was to come down and kick the shit out of one of us or my mum. I guess I was the lucky one in those early days, because I was probably too young to really give a good hiding to.

People often ask me why I'm so fearless and not frightened of anything. I tell them that if they'd had a father like mine, they'd know why.

We were considered lucky because we lived in a house and not one of the high-rise flats that were going up all around us. There never seemed to be any hot weather. It was always raining and there was always smog in the air, and it always seemed to be dark outside.

Next door we had a family called Francis. The only way I can describe them is they were like the Alf Garnett family in *Till Death Us Do Part*. I can't remember any of their names except one: April. Her dad was a coalman and he used to wear a cap, and he was tall and skinny like my dad. He used to keep pigeons and every morning you'd hear him at the crack of dawn calling those fucking pigeons and rattling his poxy tin of seeds. It always fascinated me how he knew every single one by name (considering he couldn't remember his children's names half the time).

It was a dreaded ritual that my mum would call one of us into her bedroom in the morning to open the curtains, and then she'd take out her glass eye and give it to you to go and wash under the sink. God, how I hated that job. (None of us knew why she had a glass eye – all I knew was I had to wash the damn thing every day, along with her false teeth and empty the spittoon!) Anyway, one day I'd done the ritual and then gone back to my mum and gave her the eye. It was the middle of winter, and when I looked out of the window the next-door garden (the other side, which was the Dingles') looked like Kew Gardens – there was every single flower in the whole world in full bloom. There must have been 200 different flowers. I couldn't believe it, it looked so beautiful. I thought, *God, when I grow up and get married I'm going to have flowers like that in my garden.*

It was only when I went downstairs later that I realised all those lovely flowers were plastic. I don't know what was more stupid, plastic flowers or the fact that one of the Dingles had actually got up in the middle of the night and stuck them in the ground one by one. Did they really think that anyone would believe they were real? I ask you! Well, this little girl did, and I've loved flowers ever since – real ones of course. But there's a reason I hate anything snide in my adult life, and that's got a lot to do with my poxy childhood.

I do remember my dad and the Dingles' dad had a fight. I knew then that my dad was a weak bastard and could only hit my mum and us kids, because he never even threw a punch at the man next door but he still fell on the floor pretending he was hurt. I was in an upstairs bedroom, watching what was going on out of the window and praying that old man Dingle would kill my dad.

• • •

There's one thing I've always hated and was scared of, and that's swimming. I hated the water. The reason being that when we were very little my dad used to bath us more often than not. Barry and me would be in the bath together and my dad would put Vosene shampoo on our hair and we weren't allowed to close our eyes, so the shampoo would be going in our eyes and the stinging was unbearable. What with the carbolic soap as well, it was sheer hell (I've never used that soap or shampoo since the day I left home). Then he'd put his big hand over your soapy face and push you under the water for a long time. You weren't allowed to struggle, because if you did he'd hold you down even longer. What was going through his mind when he was doing that to us? We were babies – little kids who hadn't done anything wrong – and our dad was treating us this way.

And if that wasn't bad enough, when we'd get out of the bath we'd have to line up in front of him for nail inspection – and if you'd been biting your nails (which I always did) then he'd smash you straight across the knuckles. Somewhere inside I just knew this wasn't the norm. I didn't know what the norm was, but I knew this wasn't it.

• • •

While we were living in South Acton my mum's brother came to live with us. His name was Dan and we all loved him so much. He used to play with us and tell us stories. I don't think he had a bad bone in his body. Uncle Dan was a lot younger than my mum; I remember him having a big quiff in his hair and a long nose and wearing winkle-picker shoes. He used to drink in this pub down Acton on a Saturday afternoon and we'd walk past, hoping to see him standing outside so we could get sixpence off him for fish and chips. Then once we got the money off him we'd give him a load of lip. God, how we loved him.

Another reason we loved him was because he protected us from our dad. When Uncle Dan was in the house he'd never let our dad hit us.

One day Dan came home and my mum started crying over something he told her. It wasn't until a few weeks later, when a van came to pick Dan up, that we found out he was going back to Ireland and that's what my mum was crying about. I was eight then and that's the first time I knew what a broken heart was. I thought I would die. With Uncle Dan gone all I could think about was all the good hidings we were going to get now and no one there to protect us. Eight years of age and to know such love and then such fear.

I think that's when I learned to hate the sight of my father. I hated his face, his hair, his skinny body, his thick-rimmed glasses, his voice, but most of all I hated his hands. He had the biggest hands I ever saw. They were like shovels. I used to pray he'd get them chopped off so he couldn't hit us any more.

The sister I got on best with was Trisha. When I was little, Trisha would always let me borrow her clothes and would brush my hair and make it look nice. I knew then that Trish would make a good mum. She wasn't spiteful. If I got a good hiding off my dad, Trisha would always kiss and cuddle me. If Trisha had a sweet, she'd give it to me before she'd eat it herself.

One time, me and Trisha were in the bedroom and she started plucking my eyebrows. For us this was a big deal, because we weren't allowed to do things like that – wear perfume or make-up or anything – and my dad would have murdered us. Anyway, she did one of my eyebrows and we heard my dad coming up the stairs, so we quickly stopped and pretended to be making the beds or something. I had shoulder-length hair at the time, right wavy, which I hated, but it was long enough to hide my eyebrow. My dad did eventually notice one eyebrow was different from the other and once again I got a good hiding. But I said I done it myself so at least Trisha never got a clump.

Another time, me and Trisha was having a ding-dong fight in our bedroom, really knocking the shit out of each other (although I was getting the worst end of the deal). In the middle of this fight, my dad opens the bedroom door. Neither of us had heard him coming and we froze on the spot, still clinging on to each other's hair and waiting for him to lay into us. But he never did. He just turned round, closed the door and walked out. We were so shocked we just started laughing, and cuddling each other. I don't even know why we were fighting in the first place, because Trisha wasn't a bully and never mistreated me.

There were a few funny things in my childhood – things that weren't funny at the time, but that I can't help but laugh at when I look back now.

Like when we were sent down the shops and told to get

a quarter of Lyons Red Label tea and a pint of gold-top milk, or maybe half a pound of New Zealand butter. In those days, those were the best items and not many people could afford them, so if someone saw you buying them they'd be impressed or jealous because they couldn't afford them. The fact was, when we bought the expensive tea or milk and butter, we didn't have bread in the house to go with the butter, or sugar to go with the tea, or even cereal to go with the milk. But no, that didn't matter. The fact that my dad was very seldom in work didn't seem to matter either – after all, he was Mr O'Leary and everyone respected him.

I don't know much about my dad's childhood. I do know his dad died young and that his mum was a wicked old cow, so maybe my dad wasn't taught about love and affection. I can't blame him for that. He could have run away and left us (I used to wish he would), but as bad as he was he never did that or put us in a home. There has to be something said for that.

• • •

I can't say why my dad was so bad. I do know you only have one real dad. Mine was called Richard O'Leary, and he came from Black Rock in Cork. I don't run away from it any more; I have to forgive him. And I think I finally do – otherwise what is life all about? He never let me love him, but I did love him.

CHAPTER THREE

Creeping Jesus

We moved to Old Oak Common Lane, East Acton, when I was still at junior school. I can still remember how beautiful our street was – all you could see were trees in full bloom with pink blossom, and there was a wide grass verge before you got to the path of our house. I thought we were in the country, it was so pretty and clean. The house had a front garden, and a back garden that was like a football pitch. We were all so happy moving into that house that it's hard to imagine how much I was going to hate it, and hate East Acton, in years to come.

I noticed how life changed for us O'Learys not long after we moved. Our house needed decorating and new carpets and we never had money to do it. My dad didn't go to work any more. All he did was sit in a chair all day, smoking his John Player's ciggies, waiting for one of us to come home from school so he could play with our brains for a while and then kick the shit out of us.

We were never allowed to play with other children because my dad said they were common. Also my dad would say, 'Why do you need friends when you've got brothers and sisters?'

Across the road from us were two big families. One was called White and the other was called Slater. I became great friends with Anita White. Her mum was Spanish and her dad was from Liverpool. His nickname was Chalky and I used to love listening to the different accents. They weren't a rich family, but whenever you went in their house there was always a nice happy atmosphere, not like ours. In our family we didn't go in for saying how much we loved each other. We weren't allowed to speak at all, half the time, and I can recall just rare occasions when my dad showed any kind of emotion towards his children except violence.

He used to do such cruel things for his kicks. My mum was on night work, and on Friday night, say, my dad would send one of my sisters down the shop to buy seven Crunchies, seven Mars bars, two bottles of cream soda and two bottles of Tizer. It didn't take a lot of working out – one each of both chocolate bars for us kids and one each for my dad, and drinks all round. So we're sitting there, with our mouths watering, and my dad eats the fucking lot right in front of us. Then drinks the Tizer and marks the bottle so we can't have any. I knew then that he was a sick bastard. Another of his tricks was to offer one of us children some sweets and not the others, so that the one who got them would feel such guilt when they ate them.

You might well imagine that this man hitting his children means they must have done something wrong. I can assure you we didn't. We were too scared of him. In those days a lot of children from big families got hit – whether it was a shortage of money or no work I'm not sure. I do know that Irish people were treated like shit, and the fact that there was trouble in Northern Ireland in the seventies didn't help the Irish living in this country. I remember going to school and not a day went by that I didn't have a fight with some boy or other because he called me an Irish slag. I could never go home and tell I'd been fighting, because I'd get another good hiding.

Every time I think about my dad my legs go all funny and I get goose pimples. For most of my adult life I've done nothing but condemn him for the physical and mental torture he inflicted on all my brothers and sisters, not just me. But as bad as he was, as I get older I realise he taught me a lot of skills I didn't know I had until way into my adult life. He taught me how to accept physical pain without crying out (because if you cried, you got a harder hiding). He taught me mental strength and a code of silence that even Hitler couldn't have broken. He taught me how not to believe that everything the English said was right or that everything the Irish said was right.

• • •

My mum was a hard worker and our home, however humble it was, was always spotlessly clean. As much as I hated my dad, I have to say that he gave us great training in how to be good housewives. We had to scrub the floors every single day and polish everything, and that training has stayed with us all our lives: me and all my sisters are spotless to a point of obsession. That I'm thankful for, because now I don't reckon I could be dirty if I tried.

One time I had an operation on my eye for a cast, but while I was in there I got glandular fever and had to go into isolation for a couple of weeks. The day I came out I thought I was going to be picked up by my mum, and I'll never forget how disappointed I was when my dad turned up in his Crombie overcoat. (I will say one thing about my dad: he wore his clothes well, and, although he didn't have many clothes or shoes, the ones he did have were class and quality and you wouldn't be ashamed of him in that way.)

Anyway, my dad came and got me from the hospital and took me home on the bus. I don't think we exchanged two words. When we got home, my sister Denise was there. I really loved Denise, she was so pretty and slim and had such beautiful hands. My dad said he was popping down the road. The house was spotless, so me and Denise were in the kitchen, just talking. She'd just finished putting drops in my eye and I couldn't see very well, it was all blurred, and in walks my dad (we used to call him Creeping Jesus because you never heard him come in – maybe the old bastard thought he'd catch us doing something we shouldn't be doing, but all we ever did was clean). He walks straight over to the fridge and says to Denise, 'What's that?' pointing to something on the fridge (it was supposedly a hair).

She couldn't see anything, and told him so, so he smashed her in the face and grabbed her by the hair. She had such lovely hair, really curly and long, and he just wrapped it round his hand and started swinging her round the kitchen.

I was just standing there, at eight years of age, skinny as you like, and I was too scared to move – and I pissed myself. All I could think was, *I wonder if he's going to hit me?* I didn't have to wait long to find out. He let her go and said to me, 'Come here, Joan, can you see that on the fridge?'

Well, of course I couldn't. I'd just had my eye drops in

so my vision was blurred. When I said I couldn't see it, I got the shit kicked out of me. My big sister was trying her best to protect me, but even at that young age I had so much pride I wouldn't let him see me cry. Inside, though, I was crying and screaming. I just wanted that bastard to drop dead at my feet.

Another time, my sister Trish and I had done something wrong – I think we'd been down the launderette with his overalls and they weren't dried properly or something. He told us to get undressed to our knickers and then he sent my brother Barry out to the garden. We had a coal fire, so there was always plenty of wood or sticks in the garden, and he told Barry to get the longest and thinnest piece of wood he could find and bring it to him (obviously, the thinner it is the more it will sting).

Well, Barry went backwards and forwards about six times because my dad said the sticks weren't thin enough. When Barry finally got the right stick, my dad made me and Trisha stand up straight in front of him, with our hands by our sides, and he beat us black and blue. We had welt marks all over our body, and then had to go to bed. It was one of the very few times in my life when physical pain really hurt me. I thought I was going to die. Me and Trisha couldn't even cuddle each other in bed because we hurt so much.

• • •

At mealtimes in our house we'd all sit round the table, my dad up one end and the rest of us down the other like fucking puppy dogs. We never ate the same food as my dad; basically he ate the cream and we ate the crap. Us kids got Irish stew (which I've never eaten since I left home) and boiled bacon and cabbage. I could never understand why my dad always got steak (porterhouse) or big lamb chops and we got sausages or bread and dripping.

I used to say that when I grew up and had children they'd eat the same as me; if I have steak then they'll have steak – and thank God I've been able to do that most of my adult life. I also promised myself that my children would never ever wear second-hand clothes or shoes. I don't remember ever going to a shop and having new clothes. I only ever wanted a pair of real leather shoes and a velvet dress with a beret to match, but I never got them. All I ever got was my sisters' hand-me-downs or stuff from the Oxfam shop.

I've made up for it since, I can tell you – there's not a designer label I haven't had, or a fur coat or a diamond. I'll die knowing I've had the very best of everything, but I've also paid the price.

• • •

One of my biggest hates in life was when my dad would come home from the pub with all his pro-IRA mates and get us out of bed to sing the IRA songs in front of them.

Armoured cars and tanks and guns
Came to take away our sons.
But every man will stand behind the men behind the wire.

I used to feel so embarrassed. But at least there was some happiness in the house, however short-lived it was.

I do remember that my dad was a good talker; in fact he was rather a clever man. I don't think he ever went to a concert of any kind, but he knew so much about music and we used to listen to Strauss and Mozart, Richard Tauber and Deanna Durbin. (In the sixties we had a lodger called Mark who was the manager of a record shop in Acton. He was gay, but my mum and dad said it didn't matter, it was none of our business who he did the dirty deed with – and him being a 'fecking Catholic'. Oh no, what mattered was that Mark and his boyfriend Michael would both steal whatever records my dad wanted.)

My dad had a massive collection of fine music, especially Italian opera, and I loved listening to Mario Lanza singing *Ave Maria*. I don't get much chance to hear it now, but when I do hear it I think of my father and cry. I'm not sure who I'm crying for, him or me.

My love of sport, especially boxing, also comes from my dad. He was just making his name as a trainer and promoter in Dublin before the TB, or consumption as it was called in those days, got him and robbed him of a lung and half his body weight. It affected him very badly, but it didn't stop his passion for boxing. When Muhammad Ali boxed or spoke poetry, my dad hung on to every punch and every word. A Black boxer from America was the only person who could make my dad smile, and when my dad smiled we all smiled; he'd be so happy, he wouldn't be kicking the shit out of us for once, which made us happy too – and it was all because of Muhammad Ali. (I had always hoped I wouldn't die before seeing Ali. I wanted to be able to tell my mum that I met him and he put his hand on my head, just like the Pope. Only I didn't want the Pope, I wanted Ali. Sadly, Ali died before I ever got the chance to receive his blessing.)

In another life my dad might have been a nice person. I never realised until he died just how much people liked him. What you have to understand is that although he was a rotten bastard at home, in front of his friends and workmates he was a fucking superstar.

We had an aunt, her name was Lena, and she was really my mum's cousin but as children we had to call her Auntie Lena. She was a wonderful person, big and fat and such a jolly woman. Whenever she came for a visit she always brought us cakes and sweets and made a right fuss of us children, and every now and then one of us was allowed to go back and stay with her for a week or so. She lived in Stockwell. Her husband had recently died, and I was still quite young on one of the occasions that I stayed with her. She was a really good cook and made me lovely dinners. She'd read to you before you went to sleep, or tell you a story, and when I used to sleep in her house I'd think that was how it should be for a child: nice food, lots of laughter and plenty of kisses and cuddles. I used to call her the Angel from Heaven.

The strangest thing was that Auntie Lena really loved my dad. She and he got on so well, laughing and joking, and my dad would be so nice to us when she was there. I don't think she had a clue what we were going through – if she did, she didn't let on. I just know that of all the people I've met in my life, Auntie Lena was the one I wanted to be like when I had children.

Sometimes my mum went to stay with Lena for a weekend. On one occasion that I can remember to this day, my dad spent all weekend playing with our heads, using us as his little slaves, trying to turn one child against the other, sending us out to the garden to pick all the weeds out of the earth. The garden was like a football pitch and the weeds were there in their millions. As fast as you pulled one out, another one grew. With the sun belting down on you, you weren't allowed to cover up your body so as not to get burned, or to get a drink of water. It was sheer hell. I reckon some children would have probably become ill or got sunstroke, but we never did.

When it was time to come in, something happened to upset my dad; I don't know what, but his anger was directed at my brother Barry. He took his belt off and, using the buckle part, he beat the shit out of Barry. I can still see my brother, who was so lovely, crawling across the floor in agony, his body all bare and red and sore from the sun, and there was my dad belting and kicking him like he was a punch-bag. Then the blood just spurted out of Barry's knee. It was awful, and when my dad saw it was a serious cut he seemed to just stop. His bottle had gone and he realised he'd gone too far.

My mum was due home from her weekend away. We all had to sit on the settee and not move, and my dad was telling us not to tell my mum what happened or we'd get worse. Then he was making Barry rehearse what story he was going to tell my mum about his split knee.

I was just switched off by then. I totally switched off. I'll explain what I mean when I use the expression 'switch off'.

When my father was playing with our brains, making us call him 'sir' or continually hitting us, you could actually see his pleasure. I don't know why or how, but I had the ability to block the pain out, or not hear the sound of his voice. It's like I was in the room and all these terrible things were going on around me, but I wasn't really there and it wasn't really happening to me. I knew from a very young age that I had an unusually strong mind and an even stronger will.

Like I said, we all had to sit on the settee, so when my mum came in, there we all were watching television. Barry had to sit on my dad's lap, and my dad was cuddling him in such a way that his hand covered Barry's cut. We looked like the perfect family.

How I hated it. The only thing that kept me going as a child was the knowledge that I would one day grow up and be able to leave.

CHAPTER FOUR

Welcome to Bloody Twyford

I went to Twyford secondary modern, on Uxbridge Road, Acton. You could get a number 7 bus all the way, but more often than not my dad made us walk. It was about three or four miles, I'm not really sure – I just know it was a bloody long walk. There was a school just down the road from where we lived, but my sisters had gone there and by all accounts they had built quite a reputation for fighting. So when Barry and I were old enough to go there, the head-mistress wouldn't accept us because we were O'Learys and might be the same as the other O'Learys. That's why we had to go to Twyford.

I remember queuing up for school dinners on my first day there. In those days if you were on Social Security and got free dinners you were given a white ticket and had to stand in a separate line. I remember how degraded I felt in the 'skint members' line, as they used to call it. There was just no way I was going to do that, so I got in the other queue with the kids that paid. I was doing OK until I got right up to the front and the dinner lady asked me for my one-and-six and I told her I forgot it and I'd bring it tomorrow. In a right loud voice one of the teachers said to me, 'Your first day here, girl, and you forgot your dinner money?'

Everyone looked at me – then this teacher spotted the white ticket in my hand and asked, 'What's this, then?' and held up my hand with the ticket so everyone could see it. 'What's the matter, girl, do you think you're too good to stand in the free-dinner line?' and everyone started laughing.

I just wanted the floor to open up and swallow me up. The teacher then asked me my name. I said, 'O'Leary,' and she said, 'Speak up, child,' so I said it again, 'O'LEARY,' – and I got a crack right across the back of the head.

Everyone fell silent. I guess they were all waiting for me to start crying, but I never did. I just held my head up high and kept total eye contact. *What a bastard, a total bastard.* She then said, 'You're not Michael O'Leary's sister, are you?' and when I said yes, she says she should have known. 'Your brother had a chip on his shoulder, too. Still, we've got four years to knock yours off,' she said, and then told me to get in the free-dinner line.

Welcome to Twyford, I thought. *Welcome to bloody Twyford*.

• • •

I was no different than any other child when I was eleven. I wanted to get a good education, leave school and get a good job, etc., etc. But to me school was no different from home: always getting picked on because I was an O'Leary, always getting dug out by the teachers because I never had

PE kit or the right pen or pencil, or couldn't go on a school trip because we couldn't afford it. Always fighting with the boys because they kept taking the piss out of the Irish.

I'd never back down. It was when I was at senior school that first year that I realised my own strength, not to mention that I was quick on my feet and in my reflexes.

These boys in the fifth year – they were about fifteen or sixteen years old – used to pick on me every day for one reason or another (I think my brother Michael had given one of their brothers a slap in the past so they thought they'd have a go at me). The school had three main buildings; two were modern-type blocks and one was an old house. The house was beautiful, and stood in its own grounds, a fine old place with a great big staircase and all original features, like fireplaces, picture rails, high ceilings and so on. We had art lessons there – and music sometimes, too. Other kids used to say it was haunted and wouldn't go to the toilet on their own, but I was never frightened. I loved that house and couldn't wait to do art or music just so I could go into it (if you weren't taking lessons, you weren't allowed to be in there).

This particular day, as I was going up the stairs, these three boys who used to pick on me were on their way down and blocked my path. If I moved to the left, they'd move to the left. If I moved to the right, they'd move to the right. Then one of them says, 'Say please and we'll let you go past.'

Well, I wouldn't. I couldn't. I could feel myself getting all tight in my body. I was so frustrated. I just wanted to go to my lesson; I didn't want any trouble with anyone (I'd get another good hiding at home if it got out).

This boy, the so-called ringleader, started singing this song, 'One, two, three, O'Leary'. Des O'Connor had made a record by that name and everyone used to sing it to me when it first came out, but after a while the joke was running thin. Now here am I, eleven years old, skinny as you like and quite small in height, surrounded by three wankers singing this song to taunt me. I can't say I was frightened; I reckon I just got angry at the situation. It didn't occur to me that there was three of them and one of me. Then all of a sudden one of them, the ringleader, started poking me with his finger. It didn't hurt me, it just humiliated me and I thought, *I get this bollocks at home from my dad. I don't have to take it at school from strangers.*

As he was poking me and generally being nasty, I just switched off and suddenly lunged at him.

I tried to stick two fingers in his eyes (I think my brothers taught me that trick). By all accounts I put up one terrible fight with these boys and they couldn't get me off one of them. I remember two teachers dragging me across the playground and up to the headmistress's office. No one seemed interested that I was only eleven and three fifteen-year-olds had picked on me. All they could talk about was how I was just like my brother, and how I'd probably end up in borstal by the time I was fifteen.

I could never understand it. I wasn't a rude child at school or out on the street and I never answered my teachers back in a cheeky manner. I always respected old people, and on the odd occasion we got a bus home from school I always willingly gave up my seat to an adult without being asked. So why would I end up in borstal? It just didn't make sense.

The only thing good to come out of that fight was that no one at school ever picked on me again. Without realising it, I had gotten a name for myself, and a certain respect, and of course everyone wanted to be my friend.

But I hated having a reputation as a fighter. I also hated the way other kids wanted to be my friend just so they knew I'd stick up for them if they were in a fight. All I ever wanted was to be like the other kids at school. I loved English, I liked art and I loved games. I was good at running – no one, but no one, could catch me when we played rounders or netball or five-a-side football.

In the gym I could climb up a rope like lightning, yet I never got picked to be on any of the school teams. I knew it was because one of the teachers who particularly disliked me saw to that. How I hated that old bastard. When our school was in competition with another school and teams were being picked, all the other kids used to say, 'Pick Joan, sir, pick Joan,' and in my heart I wanted to be picked. But he'd just look at me and, as always, find an excuse to say no.

He probably got his kicks out of having that power over me – I was the child and he was the adult and the teacher and whatever he said was right.

• • •

Once, when I was about twelve, I was walking home from school and on my way I had to walk past Trisha's school, which was much nearer where we lived. As I went past, about four or five girls came out of the gates. I didn't know them, and they were probably fourteen or fifteen. They noticed I had a Twyford school uniform on. Most children at the time would fight about whose school was harder.

What a load of bollocks. But that's the way it was.

These birds blocked my path and one of them, I assume the ringleader, stared me in the face and said, 'What's your fucking name, you Twyford slag?' and I wouldn't tell her. They surrounded me and wouldn't let me pass. I knew I was going to get a clump and yet all I could think about was being late in from school. My dad wasn't working and I knew he'd be home, watching the clock, hoping one of us would be late so he could give us a hiding.

Another thing was that I didn't want her to know my name was O'Leary. By that time the trouble had kicked off in Northern Ireland. I wasn't frightened of being a Catholic; I was frightened of the fact that I was Irish and in London it felt like everybody hated the Irish – even the London Irish, like me, were disliked.

However, I had to get home, so I just said, 'Joan O'Leary.'

Well, this bird nearly had a heart attack. All of a sudden she blurted out, 'Are you Patsy O'Leary's sister?' (She meant Trisha of course.)

When I said yes, she went right the other way and said how sorry she was, said she didn't know I was Patsy's little sister and, 'Please don't tell Patsy.' By this time the other girls had floated off and this one was nearly crying. I just told her to fuck off and ran all the way home. When I got home my dad wasn't in but Trisha was, and when I told her she went like a nutcase.

The next day I waited for lunchtime to come and borrowed the bus fare from someone and went down to Trisha's school. She was waiting for me at the gates and I had to point out the girls from the day before; my sister did the ringleader and made her apologise – which she did, no messing about.

I felt really proud that day because one of my older sisters stuck up for me.

It probably sounds silly now, but in those days none of us knew much what love or affection was. But I did when it came to Trisha. It was no secret that Trisha was my favourite sister. I really did love her and wanted to be like her. She never tried to be anything she wasn't; she was kind, very funny and generous with her time and her possessions. I always thought she was so pretty. She had the best hair out of all of us, and her eyes were two different colours – one was green, the other brown. I'd love watching her put her make-up on when she was going out, and if she needed a tissue or dropped something I'd rush to get it for her.

Denise was pretty too; I was the ugly one. I had a dodgy right eye and always squinted in the sun. I'd had the operation, but I wouldn't wear my glasses because they were NHS ones. In those days there were only two choices of glasses for children on the National Health and of course I had to have the shit ones, with a band-aid plaster over the right lens.

CHAPTER FIVE

The Whisky Run

My mum had a job in the Western pub, just down the road from where we lived. Her title was Head Cook and Bar Manageress – in short, she made pub grub for the snack bar and when she wasn't doing that she was a barmaid. My dad used to go down and drink there. Anyway, around that time things began to change. Her and my dad were fighting even more. It was the norm in our house, which was a pisshole by then anyway (though still clean because we were always cleaning it).

Even though the house and the furniture were scruffy, we always had lovely net curtains up at the windows. I guess this was another ploy to let the neighbours think we had a nice home – Jesus, talk about top show. (Years later, when I was with Boisie Hannington and we were burgling a place, we'd never pick the houses with the nice clean net curtains. We'd go for the dirty curtains; that way you could always guarantee getting the prize. The people with long-established homes full of valuable possessions were more likely to have older, dirty curtains than those like my family who had nothing but were trying to keep up appearances.)

My mum and dad were at the pub nearly all the time now, my mum working, my dad drinking, and we were always at home, never allowed to go out, never allowed to have friends in. Her and my dad got very friendly with a man called Ned who ran the off-licence that was joined to the pub. He was Irish and a nice enough person. My dad used to send me down to Ned to get Teacher's whisky. I used to hate it. He'd come home pissed as a newt and I'd be fast asleep in my bed, and he'd come and get me up to go down the road at ten or eleven o'clock at night in my nightdress with my coat over the top.

I used to be so scared, because I was only little, and I'd have to run all the way. My dad used to time me. Let's say it would usually take ten minutes to walk there, two minutes in the shop and ten minutes to walk home again. My dad used to give me five minutes there and back. I'd like a pound for every time I nearly got hit by a car when I was running across the A40 to get to that pub. I should have been a runner and gone to the Olympics; I wouldn't have needed a trainer – I had my dad.

Ned had the biggest German shepherd dog. I reckon he fed it on leprechauns, because it was huge and everyone was petrified of it. I never was, though. It never barked at me, but it barked at everyone else and used to jump up at them if they taunted it. But it couldn't get over the counter because it was chained up. Young as I was, I used to wonder what was the point of having a guard dog that's chained up – because if someone tried to rob Ned the dog couldn't get free to bite them or whatever.

Anyway, I'd have to do the three-minute mile, running down Old Oak Common Lane, past the toilets and past the church. I'd get so scared because it was so dark, and I'd be sure that someone would grab me just as I ran past the toilets. I used to hold my breath, close my eyes and put my feet into top gear. Sometimes I'd run so fast I thought I was going to take off. *Right, that's OK . . . I'm past the toilets now . . . next I've got to do the run past the church . . .* I thought a ghost would jump out and get me there. Mind you, I was only a kid then. I'm not frightened of the dead or ghosts now; it's the bloody living you've got to worry about, because the dead can't hurt you.

Sometimes I used to stay a bit at the off-licence and jump over the counter and kiss and cuddle the dog – then I'd run home even faster. On one such occasion, I knew I'd been more than five minutes so I was running like the clappers and fell arse over tit and I dropped the bottle of whisky. I thought the world was coming to an end. Not only was I late – I'd broken the fucking bottle and I knew my dad was going to kill me for sure.

All the way home, stinking of whisky, I was trying to think of a story to make my dad feel sorry for me and not kick the shit out of me. I came up with one: I told him some boys outside St Aidan's Club had bullied me and in the struggle the bottle got broken.

My little story fell on deaf ears; he knocked me from one end of the house to the other and accused me of spending the money. Where in the name of God was I going to spend the money? It was late at night, and in 1967 there were no corner shops open till midnight.

• • •

One time, one of my sisters was making a sandwich and she used the same knife for the butter and the peanut butter. My dad brings the dirty knife in and wipes it all over her face and made her sit holding the knife with her hands behind her back for hours.

God, what a bastard. He used to get such pleasure out of humiliating us.

My sisters all had big tits and none of them were allowed to wear a bra. I don't know why, I guess it was just one of my dad's sick mind games. The funny thing is, I used to pray to God not to give me big tits in case I too wouldn't be allowed to wear a bra and would be embarrassed at school. In those days we wore nylon blouses, and I could imagine myself dying of shame if I had tits and no bra on. I just knew the boys at school would give me grief and I'd end up fighting.

Well, God answered my prayers. Now I've got to go and pay five grand for a pair!

I wonder sometimes why my father was the way he was, and I wonder if maybe he was mentally sick or something. In my heart I know he wasn't, though – he really was just an evil bastard. Since his death I don't really talk about him much, but I do think about him. I wonder what I'd be like towards him now if he was alive, and if I'd still be scared of him.

But I'm glad I've never had to find out. When I die, if I get to go to heaven, I know I won't bump into him, because if there's any justice in this world my dad went straight to hell.

He used to have this vision that all his daughters would grow up and become hairdressers and eventually have a shop together – except he didn't ask us our opinions about this. When one of us girls became old enough to get a Saturday job, he'd send her off to work. When each of us left school, we went straight into an apprenticeship – which would be fine if you like doing people's hair, but I hated it and so did my sister Irene. By the time I was old enough to get a Saturday job, Irene had left home and Denise and Trisha had already started their apprenticeship. They both loved their work, and to this day are still hairdressers.

The sad thing about those days is that I'd see Denise and Trisha work their butts off all week, come home on a Saturday night and hand their wages over (I'll never know why, because none of us ever got a cooked meal or any washing or ironing done) and as fast as they put it in one hand I'd be given it with the other and told to go down and buy whisky. My poor sisters worked so hard for their money, and it was all just fucking drunk.

There was no way I was ever going to let that happen to me. I had about as much interest in becoming a hair-dresser as Mother Teresa had in becoming a brass. I always loved jewellery. When I was young I didn't know anything about its worth or anything like that; I just loved rings and bracelets because they glittered. I guess it was no surprise that I ended up in the jewellery trade eventually.

• • •

I used to hang around with a girl from across the road whose name was Lyn. I loved Lyn and I loved her mother, Joyce. In fact it was her mother who taught me what my periods were all about. I was round there one day and I went to the toilet and I just started screaming – I saw all this blood and didn't know what it was, so I thought I was bleeding to death.

Lyn's mum came running up the stairs to see what the commotion was about. I must have looked a pathetic sight, but to my surprise she burst out laughing. The more she laughed the more I cried.

Once she'd sorted me out, she took me downstairs, sat me down and said in her rougher-than-rough cockney accent, 'Well Jo-Jo, you're a woman now, so watch your fucking step, girl. Keep your hand on your ha'penny and your knickers pulled up.'

Although I said I would, I really didn't have a clue what she was on about. I can't believe I was so green. I mean, I'm one of six children, with three older sisters, yet I didn't know about periods.

. . .

I do try and remember nice times as a child, but I just can't. I wish I could tell you about holidays and nice birthday parties, but they never existed. I'd like to say that our circumstances were normal, that we just never had the money because we were poor, but that wasn't the case. It was because the money was all spent on drink. I remember when we were all still young, my mum and dad used to go down the pub at weekends and leave us at home with all the warnings: don't get out of bed, don't touch the phone, don't eat any of the food out of the fridge, etc., etc. – in fact the only thing they never said was, 'Don't breathe.' But of course we'd all go to bed like little angels. Then Michael, who was always allowed to stay up because he was the oldest, would tell me and Barry to get up as long as we behaved, and we'd go like fucking loonies, running round the house, playing the records, dancing. Michael, who was a brilliant dancer, would try and teach us how to dance and it used to be so exciting.

But there were the odd occasions when my dad would play sick mind games and sneak back home; he'd look through the front-room window and catch us. He'd come in and grab the first one he could lay his big hands on and bounce our heads off the wall or take his poxy belt off and whip the life out of us. I can't believe how one of us was never killed or maimed for life. Then, as calm as you like, he'd go back down the pub and carry on drinking. I often wonder what kind of a mind someone must have to do that to their own flesh and blood; but like I said, I guess that in a sick sort of way all the things my dad did to us helped me in years to come.

CHAPTER SIX

Snake Tattoo

I met Raymond Richard Pavey when I was thirteen. It was the end of the sixties, out with rock 'n' roll and in with PVC and platform boots. Women wore heavy eye make-up and always went to the hairdresser's on a Saturday. It didn't matter if you were from a rich background or a poor background: women went to the hairdresser's and men went to the pub or to football matches (working-class men, that is; the upper-class men went to play golf, the toffee-nosed gits).

My mother was no exception when it came to going for her hairdo on a Saturday; and my dad would go to the pub then on to the betting office, where more often than not he lost all the housekeeping money. Then he'd go back to the pub and carry on drinking on tick. (The Irish pubs always gave the Irish customers their drinks on tick if they had run out of money 'cause it was a sure way of knowing they'd come back the next time they got paid, pay off their tick and start drinking again, and so on and so on.) Then he'd go home and fall into bed all afternoon. It wasn't only my dad who lived that way, or just the Irish. The English did too, and the West Indians, the Polish – it didn't matter who, that's the way it was. I remember one occasion when my mother came back from the hairdresser's and my father was fast asleep after losing all his money in the betting office. I was told by my mum to go down the pub and ask the barman, who was my mum's friend, how much my dad had lost and how much his tick was. (I never really knew why she made me do that. I can only imagine it was something she could throw at my father during one of their rows over money or drink.)

So, it's about six o'clock in the evening and off I go down the road. I knocked for my friend Lyn and she came with me. I can't remember what I was wearing but it doesn't matter 'cause we were all paraffin lamps (tramps) and more often than not I'd be wearing something that one of my sisters, if not all of them, had worn before me.

I should explain that our house was only a stone's throw from Wormwood Scrubs Prison. The surrounding area had various estates that housed the prison officers or ex-offenders. The main pub was the Western, which was our local and was also handy for the criminals finishing off big sentences. There was an area called the hostel block, which was outside the prison but inside the main gates, where the men who were soon to be released lived. They were allowed out to go to work, Monday to Friday, but had to be back at the hostel by 10pm, and they could go home for the weekend, too, provided they returned by the same time Sunday night.

It wasn't that girls like me wanted to mix with criminals; we just didn't know any different. If you went to the local pub there were men there from all over the country, some from up north and from north and south London. It was instilled in us from day one that you never asked them their business. But the cons and ex-cons were easy to spot 'cause they always left the pub around 9:30pm, which gave them time to walk up Old Oak Common Lane, turn right into Du Cane Road, stop off and get fish and chips or a Chinese, then carry on to the prison gates, where they had to sign a book to prove they had returned to the hostel block.

So, on this particular night me and Lyn walked in the pub, thinking we were all grown up, and bumped straight into Lyn's mum and dad. It was so funny – Lyn's mum was at one end of the bar and her dad was at the other and they were slagging each other off. 'You ugly bastard, I don't know why I married you.' 'You ugly cow, you can't cook, you've got no fucking teeth and your tits are sagging.' 'Yeah, and what about you, you smelly old bastard, you ain't had a bath for ten years and then it was only 'cause one of the boys was getting married.'

The slagging match went on and on, and the last thing I heard him say was, 'Oh yeah, and you can't fuck either.' I just carried on walking round to the other part of the pub, where my mum's friend was working. Before I even opened my mouth he shouted out, 'And I suppose, young Joan O'Leary, that your mother's sent you to find out what that blaggard of a father of yours has spent. Well, you go home and tell your mother his tick in here is sixty quid. And tell your parents they'd be better off buying you some clothes or a good meal. Look at you, you look like an urchin.'

I couldn't believe what this bloke was saying (even though it was all true). I mean, why's he having a go at me? And that's when I heard someone say to him, 'Oi, mate – leave the kid alone or I'll chop your dick off and shove it in your mouth!'

The whole pub goes quiet. It's like time stands still for a few seconds and you're waiting to see if a gun gets drawn or a bottle gets smashed in someone's face, or if a blade gets drawn and someone's arse gets slashed.

I looked round to see who had said this and there he was: Ray Pavey. He was about five foot seven, very slim, and had the best set of pearly whites I'd ever seen. He was so handsome, with shoulder-length black hair. As I'd never seen him in the area before, I just assumed he was from the prison. He looked about twenty-five and he had 'RAY' tattooed on his neck with a snake underneath it. He was wearing dark-green Oxford bags with one-inch turn-ups and platform shoes that made him look taller than he really was. I often wonder if it was him or the Oxford bags I fell in love with – a fine white stripe running through the bottle green. He also had a full-length, double-breasted suede patchwork coat on which must have cost a bomb. Yes, to a green thirteen-year-old kid he really did look the business. And I thought, *How come he's sticking up for me when I don't know him?*

Well, there wasn't a fight. The barman came over to me and said, 'Sorry, Joan, I was only joking. You know your mum and me are great friends really.'

I told Lyn I was going home to my mum, but not before Ray made himself known to us, telling us his name and asking if we'd like a drink. I said no, I had to go, and all the time he never took his eyes off me.

I found out later he was living at the hostel in the Scrubs after finishing a five-year sentence for armed robbery. He came from Canning Town and had no proper family. He was adopted by a very old couple and ran away from them at a young age. Not long after I first met him (a matter of weeks), Ray was late reporting back to the hostel and had to finish his sentence behind bars. He was in prison another nine months, which is when I started writing to him.

CHAPTER SEVEN

Leaving Home

I was thirteen when I left home – or ran away, I should say. I remember the reason so well. I had been asked to go down the off-licence for the usual bottle of whisky. On my way I bumped into a boy called David who I knew. David was older than me and had already been in trouble with the police and been in DC (detention centre). He used to be into nicking cars. I'd always got on with him since I was a little kid.

Anyway, he asked me where I was going, and I told him, and he said he'd walk with me. When we got to the off-licence he said, 'Come in the pub.' (My mum had long since stopped working there by this time.) I told him I couldn't because I had to be home in five minutes, but somehow he managed to get me in there.

I can still remember that day as if it was yesterday. The jukebox was playing 'Mack the Knife', which was quite appropriate because five minutes later one of the local plastic gangsters started a fight and cut a bloke's ear off, then all hell broke loose. All the girls started screaming, there were chairs being thrown everywhere, tables going through the window, and all this time 'Mack the Knife' was belting out on the jukebox. The smell of stale beer and smoke was making me sick and dizzy. The fact that some poor bastard had just had his ear chopped off really didn't affect me whatsoever. After all, I was used to seeing fighting going on at home. Obviously my dad never chopped any ears off, but I do remember him taking a red-hot poker out of the fire one time and doing damage with it.

I guess fifteen or twenty minutes went by and then I realised I should have been home by now, so I looked for David to walk up the road with me and he'd gone. I went to the off-licence to get the whisky, but they'd closed it because of the trouble. There were police everywhere. Then all of a sudden I got pulled or pushed back in the pub and told to sit down; I knew a lot of people in the pub and I think they was just trying to protect me. Someone put a fag in my hand and gave me a drink – I'd never had a fag or a drink in my whole life and there I was, sitting in the Western pub at thirteen years of age with all these people. Some I knew, some I didn't.

By now I'd forgotten all about the time. I happened to look out of the window of the pub and there was my dad, standing outside. Well, I just froze. I'd still got the fag and the drink in my hand. I couldn't move. I knew I was surely going to be murdered. I put my drink down, dropped the fag and walked out of the pub and up to my dad.

Well, he just landed his fist straight into my face, and after the first punch I never felt the rest. He was kicking, punching and beating me all the way home. I pissed myself and vomited and kept getting knocked down. But I wouldn't stay down. I kept trying to get up. Both my lips were cut, I had big bald spots on my head where he had yanked my hair out, and my vagina was sore from where he kept kicking me between the legs.

It seemed to go on forever, but somehow we got home. As soon as we got in he told everyone I was a dirty fucking whore, I was drinking and smoking and mixing with the scum. I don't remember much after that. I can honestly say I'd gone past the stage where I felt pain. I just wanted to get out of the house and run away.

If you can imagine someone grabbing you by the stomach and squeezing the life out of you, then that's what he did – literally, with his big, fucking, stinking Irish hands. He held on to me and dragged me from the kitchen to the front room, up the stairs (still squeezing my tummy). For the first time in my life I really did think I was going to die – and the funny thing was that I didn't care, as long as I never had to look at my dad's face ever again. Well, as luck would have it, I guess my dad could see how hurt I was and he seemed to come to his senses. He stopped hitting me and just told me to go to bed, he'd deal with me in the morning.

The next morning, my mum walks in the room. There was blood all over the sheets from my nose and my lips, and my mum just said I done wrong and let's just forget about it. (Funny, I'm too young to drink or smoke, but I'm not too young to buy whisky or get my face smashed in.) I was looking at my mum and hating her so much, because she was sticking up for my dad, and the door opens and in he walks. He came straight at me, grabbed me by the hair and yanked me out of my bed. My mum did try to stop him, but he was too quick. He twisted my hair and pulled me over to the door. My mum was screaming but he didn't stop, and he bounced me off every stair while he dragged me downstairs. And when he got me downstairs, I had to sit on a chair in the kitchen with my hands behind my back while he gave me the third degree about the night before.

I told him, in between getting smacked in the mouth and getting hit in the shins with a cricket bat, what had happened in the pub. (I forgot to mention that one of my dad's favourite punishments was to make you sit on a chair with your hands behind your back and your legs stretched out in front of you, and then he'd smash a cricket bat on your kneecaps or your shins – it doesn't matter which, really, as either one of them would hurt you like nothing on earth.)

I didn't cry or scream; I didn't try and defend myself. I just took it like a man. Which ain't right, because I wasn't a man – I was a thirteen-year-old girl, a bloody child. But this monster was not going to take my pride, he was not going to make me cry in front of him, and my father knew this and it made him hate me more.

This punishment of his could go on for any length of time – five minutes, maybe, or an hour sometimes. He'd tell you to sit there and not move while he'd go and have a fag or just walk out of the room. Every now and again he'd come back and smack you in the mouth or punch you in the stomach. Well, on this occasion it was about half an hour into this punishment that he walked out of the room and I heard him go upstairs to the toilet.

Without thinking, I jumped up off the chair. I nearly passed out when I put the full weight of my body on my legs. I was in agony, but I just switched off and opened the back door and ran out. I didn't even stop to open the front gate. I jumped over it and just kept running and running. I

48

didn't stop until I'd run from East Acton to South Acton, which was about four miles.

I finally stopped when I got to Acton Park, and I just collapsed in the park in such pain. I kept telling myself, *I'm not hurting, it's not hurting*, but the truth is I really thought I was going to die, and for the first time in years I did cry. I couldn't stop this crying. I wanted to kill my dad, and the hatred was deep in my soul. I had no money, I was covered in blood, my hair was all ripped out. I felt ugly, dirty and so degraded, but I was free, as free as a bird. I didn't know where I was going or who I was going to turn to, but I knew I wasn't going home – not then, not ever.

CHAPTER EIGHT

Runaway

I went to a couple of schoolfriends' houses. One of my friends' mums wanted to call the police and get him nicked, but I kept saying, 'No, no. It's my dad. I can't get me dad into no trouble. He'll kill me.' I was really frightened and I forgot about the pain I was in. I had a bath and my friend's mum started crying when she saw me undressed. My body was black and blue all over. She said she'd never seen anything like it and that she must call a doctor. But again I managed to persuade her not to. (It wasn't like today, where if a child gets abused by their parent they can pick up a phone and get help; when I was thirteen years old it didn't happen that way.)

I mean, we were Mr O'Leary's children. We couldn't go saying bad things about Mr O'Leary. He was wonderful. The life and soul of any party. You couldn't go getting him into trouble just 'cause he drank seven days a week and kicked the shit out of kids or messed with their innocent little brains. No, no, we were only children, and I'm afraid adults came first. We were just the baggage and it was our fault we were born. I don't think a day would go by in my life at home when one of us wouldn't be told that we were a noose around the neck. I used to hate hearing those things but I'd never show it upset me. I just knew that one day I'd cut that fucking noose and never go back. I just didn't know it would be when I was thirteen.

Now here am I in my friend's mum's house, down South Acton, and I can't go home and she wants to call the police. She keeps saying, 'Joan, how long has your dad been hitting you?' But I won't give anything away. I just keep saying, 'It's my family's business and we can't chat outside the house about what goes on inside the house. We just don't do that.'

I left my friend's mum all clean and with borrowed clothes on. She gave me £5, which wasn't a fortune really but it was to me. I'd never had £5 before.

I walked from her house back to East Acton. I didn't know anywhere else at that time, just East Acton, Ladbroke Grove and Notting Hill. I went round David's house. I'd been there loads of times with him. He was going out with a girl from Acton Vale. I knew her from school and we all just kind of hung around together. David's mum, Jean, was in. I think her husband was in prison at the time, and Jean used to let her kids do what they wanted. She never seemed to hit them or bully them. I liked her a lot and felt safe in her house. She was so tiny and pretty.

I can't remember how long I stayed at David's house – maybe a few days, maybe a week. I do remember that while I was there Jean used to cook nice dinners and would let me wear her clothes. Jean just looked after me. She knew my sisters so she knew what kind of life we all had. She put herself right on the line by letting me stay there, and then someone found out and went and told my dad.

• • •

He did find me, but he didn't get me. It was late at night and we were all in bed; when I heard my mum's voice I thought I was dreaming. One minute I was asleep, the next there was yelling, and when I got up I heard my mother's voice downstairs. It probably didn't help that my father was there too, pissed as a skunk, talking all posh to the coppers, but they weren't having any of it. The police came into the bedroom. There was me, David, his sister and their little cousin – all sleeping top to toe in our pyjamas – and this policeman asks which one of us is Joan O'Leary.

I was taken in a car to Acton Police Station, still in Jean's pyjamas. I was really scared. I'd never been in a police station before and I kept thinking, *What am I going to tell the police when they ask me why I left home? And where am I going to say I've got all these bruises from? And what about all the bald spots on my head? How am I going to tell them that my dad done it the week before? I can't. I just can't and I won't.*

But the police didn't want to know anything about my bruises. They just kept on saying, 'Do you think you could be pregnant? How many boys have you slept with?' And, 'Do you think you've got anything nasty down below?'

I was thinking, *What are they talking about? What do they mean how many boys have I been with and do I have anything nasty down below? What's fucking going on?* I was scared and I was angry with the police and this other bloke who I found out was a doctor. I kept getting told, 'Just tell us the truth and you can go home.'

Then I started crying. 'I don't want to go home. I'm not going home.'

But I wouldn't tell them why – and, let's face it, in 1970 how many young girls of thirteen would have got up and said, 'My dad has beaten me up every day since I can remember, and if we tell anyone outside the house he'll kill all of us.'

I was taken into this room where I was going to be examined. I thought to myself, *I'll say some boys beat me up, that's how come I got the bruises and bald spots – and I don't want to go home 'cause I don't want me mum and dad to see me like that and that's why I was round David's house.*

The man told me to lie on this bed and relax. I was so scared, but I did it. After all, he was a doctor and at my age I had no reason not to trust a doctor. But when he asked me to take my knickers off I became like a nutcase. I wouldn't. I jumped off the bed, screaming for my mum. I panicked. I felt trapped and there were all these policemen running backwards and forwards.

I said, 'Why have I got to take my knickers off, mister? I ain't done nothing.'

Then the police were telling me it was for my own good and that the doctor just wanted to make sure I didn't have anything nasty down below.

'What do you mean?' I kept screaming. Tears were running down and my face was sore and swollen. *'What do you mean?'*

I wasn't aware about sex when I was thirteen. I'd never seen a willy or even kissed a boy. Every night when we all went to bed we had to give my mum and dad a kiss. (The fact that I hated kissing his whisky-smelling face didn't come into it.) They were the only people I'd ever kissed. So why did I have to take my knickers off? There was no way. I put up such a struggle that the police told the doctor they would put me in a cell for a while and it might quieten me down.

The only crime I'd committed was running away from home, and now I was in this cell 'cause I won't take my knickers off for the doctor. I was so scared. I just switched off and closed my eyes. I never even took in my surroundings. I knew I was in a cell at Acton Police Station. I knew I was on a hard thing like a bed, and I was given a blanket that smelled of piss.

I don't know how long I lay in that cell. I know I was numb. My mind was racing. Later, very reluctantly, I let the doctor examine me. There was just me, a male doctor and two male policemen. One was a police constable and the other was a sergeant. I had to lie back on the bed, pull my knees up and relax. But when he told me to open my legs I started crying. I switched off again then. I opened my legs and he pushed something into my vagina and I thought I was going to die. I now know he was actually giving me an internal examination to see if I had VD or anything, or if I was pregnant, or at the very least to see if I was still a virgin.

Well, not only did I not have VD and not only was I not pregnant – I was also very much a virgin. The doctor and the police seemed almost disappointed at this news. I didn't have to be humiliated in that way. I didn't know at the time that the doctor should certainly have had a nurse or a social worker – female, of course – at his side when I was being examined in such a private area.

Maybe the doctor and the police had seen it all before, but I hadn't and now I was in fucking agony from where the doctor had been examining me. I was bleeding a bit but the doctor never took any notice. He just told me to put my clothes on and that the police would take me to a place of safety until I appeared in court . . .

'But I ain't done nothing! Why have I got to go to court?' Then the sergeant is shouting at me that if I don't want to go home then I got to go before the court and they'll decide where I go, but in the meantime I have to go in a home.

I couldn't fucking believe it. But on the other hand, anything was better than living with the O'Learys.

CHAPTER NINE

Acorn House

I've been in here a week today
I've really got a lot to say
The food is bad, the kids are worse
I think they need a fucking nurse.
They sleep all day, they fight all night
My mind puts up a terrible fight.
I know I ain't committed no crime
I know my virginity is still all mine.
I don't miss my sisters, I don't miss my dad
I don't miss my mother, or even my brother.
But I'm locked up in here
And I ain't got no choice.
So tell me Lord, oh tell me please!
Why you locked me up with these?
And help me Lord, oh help me please!
To get myself away from these.
Only you Lord
Only you know
Why I am here
And when I can go.

I wrote this poem after I'd been in council care for just seven days. My social worker at the time wanted to put it in the newspaper. I said no and ripped it up, but I never forgot the words I'd made up about that pisshole of a place.

I didn't know where the police were taking me that night, I just knew it was a children's home in west London. We didn't get there until the early hours, and once they'd put me in the care of the woman who opened the door, they went. She was nice and made me some toast. I was starving and I think she made me about eight slices and a cup of tea, and then put me to bed with all these other girls in the same room. I wasn't scared, but I found it strange that there were other girls in the same room – I mean, I wasn't even related to these girls. I'd only shared a room with my brothers and sisters; now I was in a room with a load of strangers.

In the end I fell into a deep sleep that must have been the best sleep I'd had in my whole life.

When I woke up it was late afternoon. No one woke me, apparently because the police brought me in so late in the night. The staff told the other children not to disturb me and they didn't. I'd never laid in bed before till so late in the day and it was such a blessing that I didn't have to wake up to hear my father demanding his tea and toast and getting me to empty his spittoon (a can that he used to spit into all night and day). No, I might have woken up in a children's home but it was a small price to pay not to have to look at me dad's creepy face and skinny body and those hands.

To think those hands would never be able to hit me again. *Yahoo.*

I spent about three weeks in the home. I couldn't handle the other kids. Some of them had been sexually abused. Some of them used to take pills. I kept myself pretty much to myself and fitted in as much as I could.

I wouldn't say the staff were nasty, I just think they didn't understand any of the children's needs. We were made to feel so worthless. We weren't allowed to voice our opinions and nobody really wanted to know what our problems were. 'We must be grateful that we're here 'cause plenty of other girls and boys would like to be where we are.' Were they *sure*, or what? We were only there because we were being abused by our parents – some sexually, some physically and some mentally – so what have we got to be grateful for?

Besides, all the carers were single or posh. They didn't have a clue about working-class kids. How could they? I quickly sussed that only one or two of them were married or even parents, yet they all thought they knew what was best for us children – and I soon found out why!

I'd been at this home for a couple of days. It wasn't homely, it was a new building and all very clinical. There was a flat at the top of the building where three or four seventeen-year-old girls lived – but they weren't allowed to take boys in there. Because I was so grown up for my age, the older girls used to take me up to their flat. We played music and talked about all sorts of things, but I'd never talk about my family, not in a good way or a bad way. On this occasion I'd been asked by one of the carers to go and get one of the girls, but when I got to the flat I couldn't find anybody, so I opened one of the doors and it's a bedroom. Just as I opened the door, one of the attendants pulled away from this girl so quickly that his willy was still hanging out. He was standing and she was sitting on the edge of the bed; and although I didn't know what a blow-job was in those days, I remember thinking, *He had his willy in her mouth.*

I can't say I was scared. I just got all embarrassed and shut the door quickly, then I got a touch of the nervous giggles. I thought back to when I was in the police station and the police and the doctor were trying to get me to tell them which boys I'd slept with and I shouted back at them that I'd never even seen a willy or kissed a boy. Now, in a secure children's home, not more than a few days later, I'd seen a willy – and the willy I'd seen wasn't some stranger's or one of the older girls' boyfriend's; it belonged to the very man the council had appointed to live in the home and look after us!

It all just seemed so ridiculous to me, and I knew one thing: 'I won't let him put his willy in my mouth, and if he forces me I'll bite the fucking thing off and I ain't fucking joking.'

I wish I'd had the courage to speak out that day, but I didn't believe or trust in the system. After all, I'd been abused by my dad (not sexually but still abused), and the only thing that stopped me from grassing this bloke up was that I knew I wasn't the only child who had had a rotten time at home. Loads of kids in my school and on the street I lived on got nasty things done to them, so why was I any different? Let someone else grass the bloke up.

I did speak to the girl about it, and she was threatening that all the other girls would beat me up if I told what was going on with this bloke. I had no intention of grassing on anyone anyway – but being threatened made my blood boil.

A few days later I jumped out of a window because all the doors were locked at night. I sprained my ankle but fuck it, I was out of the council system and officially listed as missing.

• • •

For the next few days I travelled all over London on my own. I used to go to the swimming baths in the day so I could get a wash. I had this obsession about being clean because in the home the girls never seemed to take a bath. I used to think it was because they were dirty bitches but now, more than thirty years later, I wonder if the reason they didn't take baths was because they were scared one of the male staff would come in and nonce them. Well, at the time I didn't know and I didn't care, 'cause I'd broken out and I wasn't going back.

I couldn't go back round David's so I just spent my days dodging the trains, usually the Tube. I'd ride from one end of the Central Line to the other and when I got off at a station I'd just run straight through the men collecting the tickets. I never got caught 'cause the guards were either too fat or too lazy and I was young enough to outrun anyone. I'd had plenty of practice running up and down the road to buy the whisky!

I was only away from the children's home for a little while. I got caught walking down Acton High Street at about nine o'clock one night when a police car pulled up and asked me if I was lost.

One thing led to another and I was quickly back in the children's home, only this time I was to be locked in a room on my own. I wasn't allowed any TV but I was given a colouring book and crayons. I couldn't stop laughing when they gave that to me. At that age, I'd probably seen much too much of the wrong things in life, and I just thought, *I know about drink and violence. I've seen a man with his willy in a girl's mouth. I've jumped out of a window, walked the streets. And now you give me a colouring book and crayons.* It just about summed it all up for me, and I knew I was going to run away again the first chance I got.

I was taken to Acton Magistrates soon after and my mum and dad were there. As I was taken into court my mum threw me such a look I knew I wasn't going to go home with them.

It was all grown-up people in the court and I kept my head down and my eyes firmly on the floor so I didn't have to make eye contact with my mum and dad. I wasn't asked many questions, but when the magistrate suggested that maybe I should go home with my mum and dad I started crying. So they called a fifteen-minute break and I was taken to a room with a social worker and told that if I didn't go home with my parents I'd be in a home until I was eighteen.

'Will I be locked up all the time?' I remember asking.

'No, you won't,' was the answer.

I told the social worker I'd stay in care until I was eighteen; I wasn't going home. As long as I wasn't going to be locked up, I knew I'd run away. Only this time I wouldn't get caught.

The social worker left me in this room on my own. She said she was just going to tell the official people we were ready to go back into court. While she was out of the room I got up and opened the door and I saw my mum and dad outside and they saw me. My dad took about three big strides towards me and I froze. I mean I couldn't move, I couldn't scream and I definitely couldn't run.

He's coming towards me in his best suit and his black cashmere Crombie coat. His blacker-than-black, combed-back hair and those awful thick glasses he wore. I hate this man so much. It's his fault I'm in this court today. Why does he hate us kids so much? We'd never done anything to him.

He's right in my face now. I don't say a word. Then he gives me a £20 note and tells me to run . . .

I couldn't believe it. But I didn't hang around. I took the £20 from my dad's hand without looking at him and just ran out of the room into the little corridor of Acton Magistrates. Out into the street and I never stopped running until I reached Acton Town station. I reckon I was in shock. Why did my dad tell me to run? Why did he give me £20? He'd never given me anything and now he'd given me an apple core (score). I just couldn't believe it, but there I was, sitting at the station, drinking a Coke and eating a bar of chocolate, thinking, *Even though me dad gave me £20, I still hate his guts.*

I never went back home after that. Well, not to live, anyway.

I found out later that in my absence I was made a Ward of Court until I was eighteen. This meant I was no longer in my mum and dad's care. I was in the care of Ealing Social Services. But they had to catch me first! Because as far as I was concerned I didn't trust the council, or the Social Services, especially after they gave me a social worker who always smelled of drink and looked like a Sergeant Major. I absolutely hated her. I can't remember exactly everything that happened. I think I phoned up my sister Denise. She and Irene had a place together, and they let me stay in their flat for a while. Eventually the council

put me in Denise's care and I got a flat upstairs from her
with permission of Social Services. There was no way on
God's earth that I'd have gone back into a council home
where some bastard would ask me to let him put his willy
in my gob, or where some woman who thought she was a
Sergeant Major would have told me what to do.

CHAPTER TEN

A Special Day

I met up with Ray Pavey again when he got let out of prison. Ray had done his apprenticeship, done armed robbery, done a five. It was funny to find myself with someone who had what I believed to be a bit of a reputation as a hard bastard. I felt safe, thought I was a big-time Charlie. In those days it wasn't drugs that were big-time; armed robbery was *the* crime – security vans, hijacking, bank robbery. It was those crimes hitting the country back then.

I was seventeen and eight weeks pregnant when we got married in May 1974. I now had an original East End husband, born and bred. Soon after, we went to live down in Hastings where we moved into a ground-floor council flat, which was a right pisshole. I'd never seen anything so dirty in my life, but we transformed it into the typical successful villain's home of the early seventies: flock wallpaper, York stone fireplace in the front room, stained tongue-and-groove wood, *Capo di Monte* ornaments – and of course velvet curtains, crystal chandeliers and wall lights. If you went into any villain's house in the seventies they all looked the same. Close your eyes and think of the drinking club in *Minder*, and the décor was just the same as your own home.

If Ray had money he always took care of me. I mean, he'd buy me nice clothes and nice cars. The criminals of the seventies and eighties, the married ones anyway, always seemed to put their money indoors; and with whatever was left over they went clubbing or took a tart out. In my eyes she had to be a tart to go out with someone's husband in the first place.

I could see my whole life mapped out in front of me. While Ray and his mates would be out twenty-four/seven, I was expected to be friends with the wives and go to their silly Tupperware parties that were full of sex-starved women talking about all the sex they weren't getting from their husbands but *were* getting from someone else's husband. I was wondering if that was including mine – but silly seventeen-year-old Joan didn't have a clue at the time. Even if he had been messing about with another woman and I'd caught on to it, I'd have been too scared of Ray to do anything about it. Early on I realised I was in for a bad marriage. I used to dream of running away to London – but where would I go? Back to the O'Learys? I don't think so. No, I'd made my bed and I had to lie in it.

• • •

After I gave birth I was sat there, looking at all the other mums in the ward with their husbands and their families visiting them. They would bring them flowers and fruit, chocolates, and I would feel jealous. They all got visitors and I didn't. It's not like today where you're in and out in a day once you've given birth. We had to stay in for ten days, which I think was a good idea, especially for young mums like I was, because the nurses taught you how to feed your baby and bathe her. They taught you not to keep picking them up if they cry.

I was the only mum who got into trouble, because at night they used to take all the babies away from the ward so the mothers could get some sleep, but I used to get up and take my Debbie back. I thought no one would notice if I put her in my bed. I just wanted to keep her warm, and I loved the smell of her head. I couldn't go to sleep because I thought I might roll over on top of her and she'd die.

Every day I was hoping that my family would come and visit me, but I don't remember I got a card, a visitor or a flower from any of them. I must admit I did feel very alone and sad. I wanted their approval, I wanted them to say she was lovely and all that, but they just never came.

Ray Pavey wasn't there when she was born. He came the next day. I'll always remember him walking on the ward in his pinstripe designer suit, shirt and tie and platform shoes (I thought he was the bollocks, so handsome). This was my husband and I worshipped him. At that moment the fact that he could be a right bastard didn't matter to me. He was mine and so was Debbie.

He came in and kissed Debbie and as he bent over I could smell the cheap perfume on him but I blanked it out of my mind. This was a special day and I wasn't going to spoil it by asking Ray if he'd been with another woman, was I? After all, he was a man and you just didn't get in your man's business, especially if your man was Ray Pavey. I was petrified of this bloke. As tough as I was I never ever hit Ray Pavey back in all the seven years I knew him. I'd hit anybody else, men, women, big or small, but not Ray.

The day I came out of hospital, I was so excited to be going home so all the neighbours could see my Debbie, and maybe, just maybe, my family might come down from London to see her. I remember walking in the flat with Ray (still in the same designer suit). I put Debbie down in her cot. Ray was in the kitchen, putting the kettle on, and there was a knock at the door. I opened it, knowing it was one of the neighbours come to see the baby. It wasn't. Just someone asking for Ray – some girl, a bit younger than me. I didn't know her so I asked her what she wants and she says, 'Is your brother in?'

I shook my head and said, 'Sorry, mate, my brother lives in London, and I don't know where my other one is,' and laughed, thinking she'd obviously knocked on the wrong door.

But she said, 'No, this is the flat—' and just as she said that, Ray appeared. To say he went white would be an understatement. The blood just drained from his face. He pushed past me, told me he'd be back and closed the door in my face. I didn't run after him, but my mind was working overtime, plus I was unhappy at being left just after I'd walked in the door after a week and a half in hospital. Ray came back about ten minutes later, still looking a bit white, not 100 per cent himself. I could only guess at what had been going on while I was giving birth. How it kicked off I don't remember, but I lost my head and went into one; I was screaming at Ray and him at me. By this time Debbie was awake and crying for her feed, and my only instinct was to take care of her. I tried to switch off from the pain – after all, I'd had plenty of practice at cutting out pain – and fix my mind on Debbie.

Ray must have gone out again as I just sat on the bed with this little bundle of joy and held her so tight I think I might have hurt her, and I promised her we would not be spending the rest of our lives with him. I was going to get away from him, and me and my Debbie were going to rule the world. (If someone had told me then that by the time she was four I would have lost her, I would have laughed in their face at the sheer thought of it.)

What a great start I'd made in my adult life. God, I was seventeen and married with a baby and already talking about running away from my husband.

At home – when he was at home – Ray would sit on his arse all day. It didn't really bother me, because I thought that's what married women's life was all about, taking care of the men and the children, and taking a lot of shit. I have to admit I was beginning to think, *I don't like this marriage game; it ain't all it's cracked up to be.* I used to look at Ray and want to be physically sick. I knew I'd made a terrible mistake marrying him, but I was brought up to believe that when you got married you stayed together for life. It didn't matter that you hated each other's guts or fought each other every other week. We were London Irish Catholics and we did not leave our husbands, no matter what. Divorce was a dirty word.

No, it wasn't love that kept me with Ray, it was fear – fear of him and fear of being a one-parent family, because it really did have a nasty stigma to it in them days; to be on your own with a child wasn't the British way, the way I was brought up. What a load of bollocks.

• • •

When Debbie was just a few months old, Ray had to go on his toes (on the run). He ended up in a forest for a few days in the middle of winter. Meantime the police diverted their attention to me and our home. I'd never seen so many Old Bill. They tore my flat apart, knowing very well there was nothing stolen. You could see they had the right hump with Ray. I think it was more to do with the fact that we were Londoners and the Hastings Old Bill didn't like Londoners like us in their silly little seaside town. I had the police sitting outside my door twenty-four hours a day. They were even behind me when I went out to the shops.

Ray was gone for months, and I was very unhappy in Hastings. I didn't have many friends. I didn't like Sussex people, I found them very cold, and they didn't like outsiders. The only person I ever liked was a girl called Wendy. She was older than me and married with children. She was a good laugh and wasn't two-faced like a lot of the other women I'd met. This was all very new to me, trying to be a mum, trying to make friends in a very hostile area, trying to deal with the Old Bill sitting outside my front door and making snide remarks every time I came in and out of the flat. And I heard that Ray meanwhile was in south London, and living the life of Riley I guess.

Apart from the fact that I hated Hastings, one of the reasons I couldn't settle in Sussex was that everyone was English white. There was no Black people, no Indians. They'd never heard of reggae or ska or any of the music I grew up with. There was one Indian restaurant. The owner was as white as me but used to tint his hair black and always have a suntan so he passed off as an Indian, plus his shit attempt at a Pakistani accent. All his food came from a frozen-food factory in bags you had to boil. I knew what a real curry tasted like, and it never came out of a fucking bag – it came from a tandoori on the Commercial Road or Khans in Queensway.

That first summer there was a carnival all along the seafront and everyone was saying what a great day out it was. Well, I knew all about carnivals. After all, I came from East Acton, which was only a five-minute car ride to Ladbroke Grove – and of course I went to the Notting Hill Carnival as a child. I used to love the West Indian food and all the costumes. We all thought we were big-time because we were puffing weed and drinking rum and black, listening to Bob Marley or Burning Spear on the pub jukeboxes, which would be blaring out all over Ladbroke Grove and Portobello Road, not to mention the Irish and the London Irish giving their versions of 'Danny Boy' or 'Mother Kelly's Doorstep'.

For the Hastings carnival I remember dressing my Debbie up like a princess. She must have had about thirty of these little hand-knitted cardigans in all different colours with hats, bootees and mittens to match; she looked like a doll. I used to love it when people would stop and stare at her and say how lovely she was. I was so proud. Other women used to think I was mad because I refused to buy her paper nappies – I wanted real towelling ones. I would wash them by hand and put them in a big steel bucket and boil them for hours so they stayed white. I just couldn't bear the thought of putting dirty clothes on the oh-so-beautiful child. I felt she was the only thing I had that was really mine.

On that day I wore these lime-green platform boots that made me about ten feet tall, silver-coloured stretch jeans and a gold-coloured bomber jacket, plus a pound of red lipstick and bleached blonde hair. I thought I was the bollocks, a Debbie Harry lookalike at least.

When we got to the seafront to watch the procession go past, I got the right horrors. There were hundreds of people, more or less local, and they all looked alike. And to make matters worse, everyone was related to everyone. No wonder they didn't like outsiders. All the blokes looked like and dressed like Benny out of *Crossroads*, and all the women looked like Rose West – and the joke was they all thought I looked weird in my platform boots and silver and gold clothes. Were they sure or what?

There was a raffle, I remember, and the winning ticket was going to be drawn by the town's beauty queen. All of a sudden we all have to be quiet as she drives by on some snide float. I couldn't believe it – she must have weighed twenty stone and that was only her tits. When she lifted her arm up to wave her wand at the crowd, she had right hairy armpits. Well, if she was Miss Hastings then I was Miss Fucking World.

As she went past me, I looked up at the sky and said, 'Beam me up, Scotty, I can't take this. Beam me back to London.' I knew there and then I wasn't the same as these people. I knew I wanted to go home. What I didn't know was that I had a few more years of this place before I got to live back in London.

CHAPTER ELEVEN

In the Cuckoo Nest

In the end, the police had nothing on Ray and enough time had lapsed that the heat was off, so he came back home. Ray, Debbie and I ended up moving into our new GLC two-bedroom bungalow on a lovely estate of smart new houses with garages and patios. All around were woods and trees, foxes and squirrels. I really liked it. To get to my part of the estate you had to drive up this long winding country road. It was always very dark and a bit scary.

Ray was out of work for a while so I had to get a job and pay someone to look after Debbie. To me this was unheard of. My mum and dad never paid people to look after us. And besides, Debbie was my daughter and I wanted to look after her, not leave her with some person I don't know. How did I know they'd feed her, or supposing they smacked her? I'm not sure how it came about, but Ray found out there was a job going across town at a mental health care home – Friday, Saturday and Sunday nights.

Well, there was no way I was going to work there. What did I know about mental health patients? Supposing one of them went off their nut and tried to kill me? I was strong and could have a terrible fight, but you can't hit people with mental health issues (let alone the fact they were a hundred times stronger than me). No, I definitely wasn't going there.

It was a home for mentally and physically handicapped people. I don't think anyone was there long term. The idea was to give the patients a couple of weeks of sea air and then send them back to their parents or whatever institution they came from. I did wonder at the time how come these people were hidden right out the way. How come this place wasn't on the seafront so these people could go in the sea and swim or play in the sand or go to the amusement centre? I suppose it's fair to say that people with mental health issues were locked out the way in those days.

You'd see them all walking along the road like a chain gang, holding hands, all ages, with right dodgy haircuts. They really did look a sorry sight. Their clothes were a joke – the men's or boys' jackets were always too small, their trousers looked like they'd had a row with their ankles and were trying to get away up their shins. My heart used to go out to them. People used to take the piss out of them and would never walk past the lane where this home was, because they were afraid of the patients.

My pleas fell on deaf ears – we were skint – and it was agreed he would stay home to look after Debbie at night till seven in the morning while I would go to work. The only good thing was that when I left for work at night she'd be sleeping and I'd be there in the morning when she woke.

My job as a night orderly was to sit and watch telly all shift, because the patients were in bed already asleep. You had to walk round the corridors and bedrooms every half-hour to make sure the patients were OK, which meant you couldn't fall asleep because you had to turn your key in the clocks and they'd check it in the morning. All the day-care people had gone and it was just me and another woman, the two of us sat in the front office staring at the telly and clocking on every half-hour. We could make tea if we wanted, or have something to eat, so it wasn't so bad. But I really was scared to work in this place. Every time I'm nervous I start giggling and can't stop – supposing I started laughing at one of the patients and they went for me? In those days, there wasn't anyone on hand if something did go wrong or if someone got violent. All these years later I still feel the fear I felt going to work in the mental health facility at night.

Anyway, this woman and me got this little routine going whereby we took it in turns; I'd do the rounds on my own for the first part of the shift while she got a few hours' straight kip, and then we'd change over. Seemed like a good idea at the time. I wasn't getting enough sleep at home because as soon as I got in from work I'd have to feed and change Debbie and get Ray's breakfast ready.

One night, the other worker went to sleep first and I was watching the TV. At about 1am I was off doing my rounds again. I'd been in three of the bedrooms and everything was OK, all the patients were asleep. I then had to climb the stairs to this attic room where there was a man who had Down's syndrome. I reckon he was about twenty-five but it's really hard to put an age to him.

The rooms were quite tidy, very clean, but they lacked atmosphere – there were nice curtains and carpets and so on, but the beds were hospital beds. This, I found out, was because most of the patients, regardless of their ages, were still pissing and shitting the bed, so they slept on rubber mattresses, which would be easier to keep clean. I really hated walking round this house on my own; it was so dark, and being an old house it creaked every time you walked up the stairs. And the fact that we were in the middle of nowhere didn't make me feel any better. I'd be thinking, *Supposing all the patients wake up at the same time and decide to come and attack me and the other woman?* (I have to laugh now when I think how scared I was in those days. I was green and inexperienced about a lot of things – mental health issues, sex, crime. I didn't know much about anything, and I had a lot of growing up to do and a lot of things to learn.)

Like I said, I was in this bloke's room. Because the clocking-on meter was above him in the corner you had to lean over his bed, and I was doing my very best to keep quiet so as not to wake him up. Just as I'm about to shine the torch on the clock to put my key in, I look down at the geezer and his eyes are staring straight up at me. I really thought he was dead. Then I saw the blankets moving and I pulled the cover back. I don't know why I did that, I just did. He had a teddy bear in one hand and his cock in the other and was wanking over the teddy bear. I couldn't believe it. I was so green at the time that I think I was of the opinion that the patients' sex drive would be suppressed by the medicine they were given. Even though I was married with a child and was having sex, I was still only a kid myself, and there I was faced with this geezer wanking over a teddy bear. What made matters worse was that he'd had a nappy on and he'd pulled that down too. I could feel my nerves going, and I was starting to laugh. I didn't even put the key in the clock; I just backed out of the room.

When I got down the stairs I woke the other woman up

and told her what happened. 'Oh, take no notice of him,' she said, 'he's harmless enough. He's always doing that. That's why he's at the top of the house, away from the younger patients.' Then she says, 'And as for the teddy bear, he takes it everywhere.'

'But he's wanked on it. That's got to be thrown away – it's disgusting.'

I don't know what upset me more, what the bloke had done or the woman's couldn't-care-less attitude. I remember going home the next morning and telling Ray what had happened and he thought it was really funny. I began to think I'd made a big deal about nothing.

Looking back on it, I reckon that bloke was probably more scared than me, because even though he was in his twenties I was told that he had a mental age of ten or eleven, which completely fucked my head up. I just had to put it out of my mind, and I told myself I had to get round Ray and make him see I could leave the job. I wasn't qualified to deal with it.

Not only did I not give the job up, but I also ended up getting more hours. That meant I started work two hours earlier and I had to have hands-on contact with the patients.

Starting earlier meant the patients were still up when I got there. I've no idea what their illnesses were – I didn't know the fancy medical terms. Once they were all in bed I had to look after them. Piece of piss, I thought – didn't even know what I'd been so scared of. By this time, I'd gotten over the geezer I'd caught having one off the wrist.

Once this little firm was safely asleep, everything would be as before. Well, yes – but trying to get them to bed was like happy hour at the Simpsons'. They'd all be washed and bathed and in their pyjamas and being quite well behaved. But when it was bedtime they'd lose it – screaming and shouting, smashing their heads against walls in temper, and you couldn't restrain them because they were just too strong. Maybe it was the medication: one way or another they were all on something. I didn't have a clue what to do. I'd be standing there, laughing my head off. I don't know why; there was nothing funny about trying to quieten down twenty mentally ill people. There was very little organisation. No one really gave you any orders – just 'Get them to bed'. It was like something off the telly; it was a joke.

What had I gotten myself into? I'd only been out of school two or three years. The only thing to do was just get on with it, and somehow getting on with it was what we did. We got them into bed at last without too much drama, and I used to feel right sorry for them in the end.

• • •

Not long after I got the extra hours at the mental health home Ray got a nice few quid, so I could leave the job – which I did. The only time that I ever thought about that place again was one Christmas when I was in Holloway Prison.

As a special treat we were allowed to watch two videotapes. One was called *Midnight Express* and the other was *One Flew Over the Cuckoo's Nest*. I'd never heard of them before that. Every time Jack Nicholson came on in that hospital with the other patients I'd burst out laughing, because it would remind me of the mental health home I'd worked in. Not the way they were treated or anything like that. It was the way they looked – dodgy haircuts (including Jack Nicholson's), dodgy clothes, all wanking under the covers. I wondered if the people in the home I worked in grew up to be like these patients, or whether one of them was grown up now and the director of this film.

Whatever, from my own very short experience of working in a mental health home, then having been in prison with the criminally insane, that film reminded me so much of my time at the mental health home, which had taught me a lot.

CHAPTER TWELVE

Gorgeous George

I began working in Rene's Night Club, shifts from 8pm until 2am. It was a small drinking club down in the town centre and was the in-place for the thirty-to-forty-year-olds. I loved working there because it got me out of the house and away from Ray for a few hours.

Sometimes this bloke used to come in who you couldn't help but notice because he was so good-looking. He was over six feet tall, had big broad shoulders, big blue eyes and natural white-blond hair, and I thought he was drop-dead gorgeous. A right man's man. He was very loud and a bit flash, but not in a nasty way. He was just a charmer and everyone used to like him, including me, and when he came in the club he always seemed to want me to serve him. He was always offering to buy me a drink but I never accepted because I knew he fancied me and that was enough for me.

I remember that when I used to serve him a drink I'd touch his hand when I gave him his change. The minute my hand made contact with his it was like a rush of electricity running up my arm; I couldn't give him eye contact because I thought he might guess I fancied him. I couldn't believe it – Ray Pavey didn't have this effect on me and I was married to him. But I was just too scared to get involved.

However, George (as he was called) continued to come down to the club occasionally. He'd be with people, usually men, but he always stood out because his mates looked like right plonkers in cheap leather jackets and two-bob suits.

After a while it seemed like George was not only coming down the club, but also wherever else I used to go – whether it was out shopping or going for a walk with Debbie. I didn't really think much about it. Sometimes I'd see him in a coffee bar and he'd always come over for a chat, drop me loads of compliments, tell me I looked like Debbie Harry (you know: all the usual old bollocks blokes tell girls when they want to get inside their knickers).

He said he was a car dealer and I reckoned that was about right – because he could talk non-fucking-stop, just like a car dealer trying to sell a shit heap to some unsuspecting mug.

I noticed George never seemed to pull a bird. I didn't flatter myself that he was saving himself for me, but he was so good-looking that loads of girls in the club or out on the street used to shout out to him. But he never used to go home with any of them and I found this strange. I didn't know if he was married. I think he was about twenty-five; I was twenty. I know I told him I was married and had a three-year-old daughter. It was obvious I came from London by the way I spoke. I had a cockney accent and the locals had country accents. George's accent was a cross between cockney, fake posh and country local.

He told me he was born in Eastbourne, which was

about twenty minutes away or more from Hastings. Other than that I never asked him about his business, because I just wasn't that way. It wasn't my place and I wasn't really interested enough, but I still fancied him; I wouldn't admit it, but I fancied him like mad.

But I just couldn't fuck him because I couldn't cheat on Ray. Don't think it was because I was Little Miss Innocent or anything like that. I mean, I knew I didn't love Ray Pavey any more, but he was the only man I'd ever really slept with, and sex wasn't important to me – not with Ray, not with George, not with anyone. I was a Catholic and I was married. It didn't matter that Ray wasn't the husband I deserved. No, that didn't matter. What mattered was that I'm a Catholic, and as a woman and as a married Catholic woman I couldn't cheat on Ray – and I didn't, whatever Ray did.

I respected myself too much to give my body up to George or anyone. I wasn't going to be a notch on George's headboard. For me, a pretty man like him came with a price tag. And I wasn't going to pay the price for a quick shag in the back of a car or a night in some cheap hotel.

What I didn't need is some bloke fucking me and at the same time telling me I look like Debbie Harry. For me, George could only bring me trouble I could do without.

For whatever reason, I stopped working in the club. So now I was home every night but Ray stayed out instead. He was always out a lot in the day too. I never really got involved with him much. We were married, living under the same roof, but I wasn't really in his life. He chose this period of time to inform me that he'd got a new girlfriend: he loved her and they wanted to live together. I can't say I minded – but I couldn't stay there. Well, where was I going to go?

I couldn't go to my mum and dad's – or I didn't want to. I had no friends in Hastings. No money. I was thinking, *This ain't right! I'm going to have strong words with God about this.* Because the way I saw it God once again was making me suffer and I don't think I called it on. I thought, *I'm a good Catholic, so how come I've lost my husband?* (Even though by then I didn't want him.) *How come I've got to move out of my home?*

Well, as usual, God – the only man I believed in – had let me down. So I told Ray I'd look for a live-in job or something like that, and that's about what happened.

• • •

I saw an advert in the newspaper. Basically it was a live-in job in a place called Sandwich in Kent. I rang the number and spoke to a man who turned out to be the landlord of a Tudor-style pub. He told me he'd run it with his wife until recently, when she ran off with a barman. He said it was a live-in job and he had room for one child. Well, that's all I had to hear, wasn't it? I didn't care what job I did as long as I could take my girl and I didn't have to live with Ray Pavey any more.

I went to Sandwich for a job interview. The landlord met Debbie and I at the station in his Jaguar. He was tall, and to say that he was skinny would be an understatement: I'd seen more meat on a fucking chicken wing. I swear to God if he stood up straight and turned to the side and poked his tongue out you'd think he was a zip. And he was so ugly – big nose, glasses and bald as an egg – and all I could think of was how not to laugh in his face, but I couldn't stop myself and when he was about five feet away

I broke into hysterical laughter. But at the same time I swung round and swept my Debbie into my arms and made out like I was laughing at her and not this lolly on a stick that's coming towards me. Somehow or other I managed to compose myself enough to turn round and shake this bloke's hand. But he didn't want to shake hands – he goes for the full bear-hug and throws his arms right around me and Debbie.

I couldn't believe it. I'm thinking: *I've only come for a job interview and this cunt's treating me like I'm a long-lost friend, and if he don't stop hugging me I'm going to knock him spark out.* I wasn't used to other men touching me; and besides, Ray didn't even cuddle me now, so why did this mug think he could put his hands on me? I didn't give a monkey's what job he was going to offer me; he could shove it up his arse if he thought I was going to give it up to him.

As I managed to put Debbie on the ground this bloke's telling me, 'My God, you're beautiful! You look like Debbie Harry. You look like a doll . . .'

Just shut up, you wanker.

He then turned his attention to my Debbie. 'Oh, and you – you're as beautiful as your mum.'

To which my Debbie promptly replied, 'Ain't your head shiny, mister.'

I wanted the ground to open up and swallow me, but this bloke just laughed it off and started to walk us towards his car.

He seemed like a nice enough man, only he didn't stop talking. We eventually reached the pub and went inside, and I liked it instantly. He started shoving me through the bar area and up the stairs to an equally pretty flat. Everything was on one level and there were loads of rooms, all

done out with original oak-beam ceilings and antique furniture everywhere. We went into the kitchen where an old
lady was peeling potatoes at the kitchen table. When I saw
her I kind of got a lump in my throat because she reminded
me of the people in London and where I grew up. All the
old grannies used to always be peeling spuds at the kitchen
table, not the sink. Nine times out of ten they'd have a fag
in their mouth and their hands never touched the fag. The
old grannies had it down to a fine art, peeling spuds and
smoking a fag at the same time without the ash dropping
onto the spuds.

I liked the old girl, the landlord's mother, straight away.
Since the wife left she'd come to live there, but the work
was too much for her and that's why he needed a woman's
help around the pub. She was about seventy years old, but
very together, very wise, and obviously loved living at the
pub with her son. She even got up to get my Debbie something to eat and drink.

At this point I get shown round the pub and its garden.
All very nice, but when do we actually talk about my wages
and hours, etc.? So far I'd had half his life story, a detour
round the flat, pub and gardens, tea with mum, but he still
hadn't mentioned what it was that he wanted me to do or
even asked if I want to work in his pub. Eventually we ended
up sitting at the bar, and I was just thinking I wanted to go
home when he finally said, 'Well, Mrs Pavey, do you think
you'd like to work here? I know I'd love to have you working
here and living upstairs with me and my mother.'

*I bet you would, you ugly old boot. And even if I do work for you
you've got more chance of getting a wank off the Pope than getting
inside my knickers.*

But of course I don't say that. I say, 'I'd love to work in

your pub, and will me and Debbie have to share a room or will we have one each?'

I asked him how much I get paid and if I'd get a day off, etc., and eventually we reached a deal. If I wanted the job it was mine and he was offering me a very good wage, and also I could use any of his cars on my day off. I said I'd think about it and let him know the next day. I told him the truth – that I got married young and was now getting a divorce, that my husband's met somebody else and I've got to move out.

By now it was early evening. I said I must go soon as I didn't want to be too late getting the train back, but he insisted that Debbie and I stay the night and have a meal with him and his mother.

It was then my mind started to do overtime. Because this bloke was acting so nice to me and Debbie, and because he kept going on about his mum and how he just knew if I took the job we'd be one big happy family and Debbie could easily get a place in the local nursery because he knows the headteacher there (he drinks in his pub), and on and on and on, I kept thinking that he reminded me of that bloke Norman Bates in the Hitchcock film *Psycho*, and I started to get a little nervous.

On the other hand it was a lovely pub. Lovely flat. The wages for then were fantastic, and in spite of the fact that this bloke was a plonker I thought his heart was in the right place. Also, I hadn't had a decent meal in weeks because we never had money for food.

So I think, *OK, I'll stay the night, and anyway what can happen? I've got my girl with me and the mum lives upstairs too, so yes, I'll stay the night.*

As far as I recall, his mum cooked a big meal upstairs

and after that I went downstairs with him and more or less started working behind the bar straight away. When the customers came in I was aware that I looked so out of place working in this pub. I mean, I was only twenty years old, I had a size-10 figure and pure-white bleached hair – and I was so particular that you couldn't see a dark root in it because then people would know it wasn't my natural colour. And, of course, bright-red lips and heavy eye make-up. But I never wore low tops. I thought that was tarty, and even from a young age whenever I saw a woman get pissed and start getting her tits out at a party, shoving them in some bloke's face, I'd want to die. I told myself that when I grew up I'd never dress like a tart. So even though I had the face and the body, I'd prefer to wear jeans and football shirts and Dr Martens boots. I also stood out because of my cockney accent, which I must admit I really used to over-exaggerate. It was my only proof to myself that although I didn't live in London any more I was still a Lon-doner, or a London Irish bird. It was so important to me not to lose my roots, and I thought that if I took this job I'd only take it long enough to save some money to take me and Debbie to London.

Well, I decided there and then, behind the bar in this pub while some country local was taking the piss out of my cockney accent, that I would stay and work there. I'd save enough money to go back home – all forty miles away – and once I left this place I'd never live anywhere else except London again.

CHAPTER THIRTEEN

Norman Bates

I moved into the pub with Debbie the next week. We were sharing the flat upstairs with Norman Bates and his mother. I was the live-in barmaid-cum-housekeeper.

I'd been there about a week, and it had been a long day and I was tired. Back in the room that was to be mine for my stay I put my nightclothes on. I liked to sleep in the nude, but to me this was not my real home. And of course I realised that this bloke fancied me, so I'd keep my underwear on under my nightclothes just in case. I knew I'd be uncomfortable, but so what – I was covered up.

I got into bed and pulled all the covers up and started to doze off. I was just falling asleep when I heard someone outside on the landing. I thought it must be the landlord going to bed. I heard him go into the bathroom and decided I'd try and stay awake until I heard him come out and go into his own room. I couldn't stop thinking that this bloke might turn out to be like Norman Bates. *Suppose he comes into my room and wants to fuck me? Suppose he kills me and Debbie? Apart from Ray no one knows I'm here* . . . God, I was really scared.

He must have been a long time in the bathroom,

because I did fall asleep, and some time later I was woken by a knock on my bedroom door. I pretended not to hear it. *Tap-tap-tap.* 'Can I come in?'

'Oh fuck me. Norman Bates is outside.'

The door slowly opened and the aftershave came in before he did. He was obviously trying to look sexy, because he didn't have his glasses on, and he couldn't see and was fumbling about in the dark. I was sat up in bed with my knees under my chin and the covers pulled up tight. He asked me if I was all right and I said yes, and he said, 'Can I sit on the bed?'

'What do you want? Can't we talk about it in the morning?'

The room was very dark and he pulled the curtains back so the street light from across the road came in. At this stage I could see what he'd got on, and even though I was scared I had to see the funny side of it and wanted to burst out laughing.

He was standing by the window, a tall, bald streak of piss. He'd got silk pyjamas on, a padded smoking jacket and a Paisley cravat round his neck, and leather slippers. Without his glasses his eyes were all squinty like a mouse. He moved back and sat on the end of the bed. He says, 'I'm sorry if I woke you up, but there's something I want to say to you and I think if I say it you'll think I'm mad.'

'No I won't,' I say, 'but please hurry up, mate, because I don't feel comfortable with you in my bedroom. My girl's asleep next door and I don't want her to wake up.'

He then starts to tell me that even though I've only just started working there he thinks I'm perfect for the pub. I was so nervous; I hadn't played these games before – I was only young and he must have been about forty-five, and what I knew about sex and boyfriends you could put on the back of a postage stamp. I'd had only one sexual experience before Ray, and after seven years with him, even though I was a mother, I was still very green when it came to hanky-panky. I still thought a 69 was a fucking bus.

And now it's 1am, I've got the ugliest geezer in the world sitting on my bed, and although he doesn't know it yet – but I do – if this character puts one finger on me I'm going to take one of his eyes out; and no, I ain't joking.

On top of which, the fact was that his aftershave, although good quality, was really beginning to make me feel sick. I was just about to tell him this when all of a sudden he just lunged at me: 'Oh Joan, I've fallen in love with you. I know it's crazy but you're so young and beautiful. You're every man's dream . . .'

I tried with every ounce of my strength to push him off me. I put my face close to his as if I was going to kiss him and when he relaxed a bit, still more or less on top of me, I let him have it. Pulled my head back and gave him a head-butt in the face. I was crying by this stage but there was no way on God's earth this bloke was going to get any closer.

By now we were wrestling on the bed. Somehow I got my fingers in his mouth and tried to rip the side of his mouth open.

He then tried to put his hand over my mouth. I don't think he was trying to hurt me but he was obviously thinking I was going to scream, and if I had done I'd have woken up his mum or worse still my Debbie. But what was I to do? It wasn't my fault his old woman left him and he hadn't had a fuck since. He wasn't fucking *me*; I was just there for a job and I didn't have to lay down with the governor. I wouldn't have cared if he had diamonds hanging off the end of his cock – I still wouldn't be blowing it.

At some stage we were both off the bed, and I took full advantage of this bloke not seeing a thing without his glasses by sticking my thumbs in his eye sockets. It was the only time he cried out. By now I knew I could do him; even though he was a tall man he wasn't aggressive really. I found enough strength that night to fight ten men.

The hall lights went on. This threw him off guard and he stopped straight away. I just jumped up so fast and gave him another head-butt he'll never forget. He went down like a sack of potatoes and I ran out of the bedroom and straight to where my Debbie was sleeping. I could hear the bloke in the background telling his poor old mum to go to bed, everything's all right now: Joan had had a nightmare and he'd gone in to see if I was OK. She asked him if she should make some tea, but he said, 'No, no, go back to bed.'

I wouldn't come out of the other room. I got into bed with my Debbie (who slept through the whole thing, thank God) but I couldn't sleep, I just cried into the pillow. Why was this happening to me? God, if I ever wanted to run away it was then – but where could I go in the early hours with a three-year-old child? I didn't have much money, no car, and where could I go anyway? I thought Ray probably had his bird in our flat, so I couldn't go home. And I couldn't go to London.

I had to get back on my feet. I had Debbie to consider. Eventually I think I fell asleep cuddling my Debbie, promising myself that first thing in the morning I'd nick fifty quid out of the till or anywhere I could find it and get the hell away from fucking Norman Bates . . . and from Ray. I wanted more than anything to get away from Ray. I just had to get away from him before I ended up like him.

CHAPTER FOURTEEN

Losing My Girl

Well, God must have heard me, but it wasn't the route out I'd dreamed of. I was in a bedsit in Hastings. By this time Ray and I had lost our council flat – none of the bills were getting paid, including the rent – and all our furniture and my jewellery were sold for cash. All I had was my clothes, but it didn't matter. I had Debbie. Ray was on remand at Maidstone jail in Kent for a bit of work and the cossers were on my back, offering me all sorts to grass on him.

The bedsit was on the seafront and it was always cold and damp. It had one bedroom, a bathroom and toilet that was very dirty and smelly, with the front room and kitchen in one, and no garden. Nothing like my lovely bungalow I'd lived in for the past four years. I'd been in this pisshole of a bedsit about three or four days and I was feeling very ill. I was scared to go to a doctor in case I had to go into hospital – who would look after my Debbie? I had no money and I didn't go to Social Security; I didn't know about such things, really – how to go about it.

Then the local police came round. They said

something like, 'You know, Joan, this is ridiculous. Everybody knows what's gone on, what's happened. Everyone knows you're frightened of Ray. Just tell us how he planned it . . .' *What?* I didn't know anything about it.

They wanted to help but they also wanted me to inform, and I wouldn't have informed even if I'd known anything. It's not that I wasn't scared of him – I *was* scared of him – but that's not why I wouldn't inform. You don't do those things, you just didn't. Where I came from in west London you didn't talk to the police in that way. But they wanted the full story from me, and they promised me this and they promised me that – we'll get you a counsellor, this, that and the other.

Three days later I was in bed – about two o'clock in the morning – and as I woke up someone was strangling me. Debbie was beside me but she didn't wake up. I was being strangled but I couldn't – didn't – fight, because I didn't want her to wake up. Then I was lifted by my throat out of bed and taken from the bedroom to the front room. I think I established there were three or four guys; one was at the door, as a look-out, and the others were holding me down. They burned my vagina with lit cigarettes, they burned my nipples with lit cigarettes, they put lit cigarettes under my tongue. But I wouldn't scream, I never made a noise. Basically, I was getting beaten because they were after Ray.

I honestly didn't know what they were talking about. I was married to a criminal but I wasn't involved in the crime world, not in any way, shape or form. I didn't have any dealings with Ray's associates. I was just a young married girl who wasn't involved in that side of things, in Ray's business. And they said to me, 'Next time we come it'll be for your girl.'

And I must admit, I was frightened. I took a very bad beating that night.

• • •

I was only a young girl, with a child of three and a half, and I was as green as grass. I had to grow up fast. I had a lot to learn about men – not just about my husband or blokes like Norman Bates. When the police were investigating Ray I found out that George was a fucking copper. I hated the police. I'd never forgotten what they did to me in Acton Police Station all those years before, and I knew never to trust them – not then, not now. I was wondering how come I hadn't known that George was a copper. How come all the villains used to drink with him in Hastings? Even my boss at the club used to drink with him, so someone must have known . . .

I never reported the break-in to the local police, or the beating I got from the three blokes. I did get someone to change the locks, but there was just no way I could stay in the poxy bedsit with Debbie. I phoned my mum and she said I could take my Debbie to London to her and my dad's place. By this time my dad had sort of mellowed out. He said I could stay with them as long as I never went back to Ray Pavey. I only stayed about three or four days because nothing had really changed there, except me, and I couldn't take it.

I went back to Hastings. That's when I asked the local Social Services for help. An appointment was made and I went with Debbie to see the social worker. It was her who said I looked unusually white in my skin colour and suggested that I go and see a doctor. I said I would but never intended to. I asked them to look after my girl until I got myself together.

I broke down and said, 'Will you look after my girl, 'cause I don't want her to go to my parents?' The social worker agreed it was the best thing for me until I found another flat; at no time did I ever think I wasn't getting her back.

I hadn't told them the whole truth; I just said I'd come out of a very bad marriage. I remember saying, 'I don't want my child to go into a home. I don't want her to go to people unless you really check up who they are—' I wanted to know that Debbie wasn't going to end up with sex offenders or what have you '—I have to see where she's going.'

They said that when they found somewhere for her they'd tell me.

They did find somewhere: a family living in a big mansion house in a village not far from Hastings. I was allowed to go and meet them, and I'd never been in a place like it. I'd never even *seen* a house like that, only on the telly. There was this long driveway, servants in uniforms, horses, the whole shebang. They were lovely people. She especially was so nice, very charming, and as soon as she saw Debbie she just fell in love with her. I thought, *Yeah, my girl'll be safe here.* They told me they had kids of their own, they didn't feel like having any more, but they felt they could give something back to society and they would like to foster a child.

So I said to them, 'It's not forever, it's just, you know, for a few weeks till I can get my health back and get myself sorted.' I told them I didn't want her in the system, and I kept saying, 'I won't lose her, will I? I'll give her to you and I'll sign and it's all official, but I won't lose her.'

The social worker reassured me: 'Yeah, yeah, it's all right, don't you worry.'

I was going to leave her there and I remember she was screaming. She didn't want to stay there and they gave her a rag doll. I didn't – I *really* didn't – want to leave her, but I didn't really have a lot of choice. When I was coming away she was still screaming and I was crying. Mentally, I was drained; I didn't have the strength. I was very weak, and I had no idea how ill I was.

I was scared, very naïve, so thick, so stupid and so green. I just couldn't believe I had to do this, leave her. I hadn't done anything wrong, I didn't cheat on my husband, and we ended up like this. But in my heart I knew it was the right thing, to give her to them, and I trusted them. I was allowed visitation rights. I came out of there, out of that house, and the Social Services brought me back to Hastings. I didn't have anywhere to live; I had the clothes I stood up in. I just remember walking the streets.

• • •

I fixed myself up with a flat in Brighton. I had relations living there, my dad's brother Michael and his wife Nelly. I visited my Uncle Michael, who I'd only ever met a couple of times before. He was nothing like my dad; he was about five feet ten inches in height with a mostly bald head, but he was lovely, totally dominated by his wife and so gentle with his children – all girls, five of them I think.

I have to say I didn't really know them that well. It wasn't like my mum and dad kept in contact with them that much. As little children we went to Brighton two or three times and they came to London about once, so you'd hardly call us close. But all those years later I found myself in Brighton, so obviously I popped in and said hello. (And into the bargain my aunt, like many Black women of my day, was a brilliant cook. She made spicy food and curry, which I loved. I never knew the names of the food she cooked but I ate everything she put in front of me.)

I didn't know anyone else much in Brighton – and I didn't stay long in contact with my relatives – so I was thinking about moving again. I went back to Hastings and stayed in a friend's house for a couple of days. I knew I had a visit coming up with Debbie and I didn't have a penny, but my friend had said that if I needed to bring Debbie to her place in Hastings she'd make sure she got well fed before I took her back to the foster family. I remember coming out of my friend's flat and there were loads of cars. I told myself, *I'll pinch a car, drive back to Brighton, get my stuff, then drive back to Hastings and sleep in the car until it's time to see my Debbie.*

And that's what I tried to do: I stole one of the cars, drove to Brighton and picked up my belongings. But just outside of town I was stopped, arrested and taken to Brighton Police Station. I was kept overnight and appeared in court the next day, remanded in custody to Holloway. The car I stole was an Austin 1100. I've forgotten what colour it was. I was twenty-one and knew no better. I guess all I was interested in was going to see Debbie, but I paid the price.

I stole a car and lost a daughter.

CHAPTER FIFTEEN

In the Nick

I was taken from Brighton Magistrates Court in a van to Holloway Prison. I was so upset about my girl, I kind of gave up. I was thinking, *That's about right now, that I've ended up here* – even though I didn't really know how it had happened. I couldn't understand it. I hadn't robbed anyone before; I wasn't a thief. I hadn't cheated on my husband or done him wrong – I'd taken seven years of marriage to Ray, and I hadn't grassed on him even though I'd had every opportunity: I was offered money, I was offered a home, I was offered everything, and I wouldn't do it.

When I went into Holloway my first impression was that they were all big butch women and I was very small, a skinny little thing. It gave me a terrible fright. You hear all the stories, like when they get hold of you the first time and all that. But they could see I was such a little nut and I wasn't going to give them any lip. I was crying but I didn't want their sympathy. My tears were for me. It wasn't because I was scared; it was for my girl. But I wouldn't give them my business.

The first night, they put me in a dormitory with five

other girls. It was dirty and there was one toilet. The next morning I couldn't get out of bed. I didn't say anything to anyone, but I just couldn't get up. The warders came in and tipped me off the mattress, saying I was play-acting. I know I had pains in my legs and under my armpits, but no marks whatsoever, and pains in my vagina. I was actually beginning to think it was in my mind, but I wasn't on drugs and I wasn't a drinker. I told the warden that I couldn't stand up, and she kept telling me, 'When you address me you call me "miss".' And I couldn't say it. I just couldn't.

I was trying to explain how I felt. I told her I had to get up in the night and I'd been coughing blood. She just said, 'Yeah, they all say that when they want to go down the medical room.'

So then I resigned myself to the fact that I was in prison. I thought, *No one knows I'm here, I'm not going to tell anyone I'm here, and I ain't well though I don't know what's wrong with me.* But I knew I had to keep my mind strong. I had to keep that strong and never mind the physical side of it.

Two or three days went by and I got these sores, and when I went to the toilet it really hurt. I was still coughing up and urinating a lot of blood. They wouldn't let me see a doctor or a nurse or anybody. I was just in the same dormitory with these other women, and there was a big Jamaican, in her forties, a real tough-nut from Stoke Newington. In the early hours I was really in pain, just in agony, and I wasn't crying even though I wanted to. I was too proud to cry but I must have been moaning. In the end this woman got the hump and she jumped up and started kicking the door, demanding that somebody come.

Then she came over and pulled the covers back, and she screamed when she saw my body. I hadn't even seen it myself – all these lumps like golf balls, and in the centre they were bright red and with pus coming out. You'd think I'd been burned, they were so awful and horrific. The one on my vagina was like a tennis ball. I was so scared. I thought I was going to die and that I was never going to see Debbie again.

Because it was night-time, it wasn't screws on duty, it was orderlies (this was over twenty years ago) so they didn't have a key. I was vomiting blood, and this bird in the dormitory – she was probably a junky – was saying, 'This girl isn't a junky. Look at the girl.' And then all of a sudden they all start; they're kicking doors, picking it up from one another. But they couldn't open the door, and all night long the Black woman was running cold water over a towel and wrapping it round me. She was so gentle. She was obviously a mum and she kept telling me, 'Don't worry, honey, don't worry.'

I kept on saying to her, 'What's the matter with me, what's the matter with me?'

She said to me, 'Did you take drugs? Are you a prostitute? Have you slept with any dirty men?'

I was horrified. I said: 'No, no, no, no. Don't do them things. I've been with one man for seven years . . .'

Eventually, the next day, they come and open the hatch so as those who are on medication can go and get it. The Black woman wakes up and she comes over and asks if I'm all right. Well, she can see I'm wet and I'm delirious. She goes to the hatch and starts demanding that someone helps me, and they just say, 'If she's ill, get her to walk to the door,' and she's like, 'She *can't* fucking walk to the door.'

So then this girl pulled the cover back. I didn't even have the energy to put my head down and look at my legs, but what I could see of my body looked awful. I thought I had a tropical disease. The screws now finally realised it was serious and told me to get up, but I said I couldn't. I genuinely couldn't get up. The screws came in – four big northerners – and they manhandled me. No sympathy, no nothing. They got me dressed, and I think they must have got a minicab, and they took me to the Whittington Hospital.

The minute we got there this doctor saw me and went berserk: 'Why wasn't this person brought in before now? Do you realise . . .'

They shoved me straight into an isolation unit. I don't remember much about it after that. I was delirious, I know, and because I was on remand the prison authorities were answerable to the court, and if you go to an outside hospital they have to come with you and sit with you so you can't get up and run away – as if I could have done!

The doctors gave me medication and kept asking me all these questions. *Have you had this, have you had that . . .* So many tests – so many this, so many that – and nobody could find a cure and I wasn't getting any better. Maybe a week went by, I'm not really sure, and one day they said, 'Joan, you've got a phone call, do you think you could get out of bed?'

Well, no, I couldn't, and when I asked who could be phoning me, they said this person wouldn't give their name but had said it was a member of my family. Because I couldn't get up, the nurse brought a phone to me and plugged it in in my room. At the other end this voice said, 'You gave me daughter away.' It was Ray Pavey, who carried on with a load of mouth and: 'How dare you put my child into care.'

I mean, not to mention I've got no home to go to. Not to mention he'd fucked off with his new bird. Not to mention who it was had worked to keep the family together. No, we don't talk about that, do we? But there you go . . . I was very sick and scared, and I became hysterical, put the phone down.

What I didn't know then was that Ray had been in touch with the Social Services, and because he was Debbie's father he'd been given visitation rights. He'd even been in contact with the foster parents. He told the Social, and he was very plausible, that he was quite annoyed. He told them that my father was an alcoholic and that I'd been a battered child – both of which were true, of course. He said there was no way he wanted Debbie to go to my family. He wanted custody. (There wasn't a hope in hell of him getting that.) He relied on the fact that I was frightened of him, which I was, because I thought he was going to cause trouble for me and for my family.

• • •

I was in hospital for about four to six weeks, diagnosed with TB. It's difficult to know how long, being in isolation, on drugs, in and out of delusions. I thought I was going to die because my dad had TB and had to have one of his lungs out. I was treated very well in there, though; I do know that.

My sister Irene's bloke came to see me in hospital. I think he felt sorry for me because I was so ill and I had no visitors. He never fancied me or anything like that, but he came nearly every day. Sometimes he'd stay for five minutes, sometimes a couple of hours. I still had to have two screws with me twenty-four hours a day. The fact that he came to see me and bring me sweets or food earned him nothing but respect from me. I also respected him because in all the years I knew him, he never tried anything on with me. To me he was my brother-in-law and that was that, let alone that he was someone else's husband.

My sister Denise came to see me too. She brought chocolate and offered some to the screws. I remember saying to her, 'You're not supposed to talk to them, they're scum on the other side.' Let it be known I've got a loathing of prison officers. I can understand a person wanting to be a copper and getting off on the buzz of catching the criminals, but for the life of me I've never understood anybody wanting to want to make a career out of spending all day locking people in then letting them out.

I wouldn't speak to the screws. And in fact – I have to be honest – they were really nice to me; they'd bring me fruit and flowers. But I was trained not to talk to that kind of people. All right, I was a cocky young girl, but I was ill, and I never abused them.

The worst thing was Denise saying to me, 'Why don't you let Mum have Debbie? It won't be like how you and me were brought up. Mummy and Daddy love Debbie, they'll look after her . . .' And so on and so forth.

And I was crying and saying, 'No, no, no, Debbie's coming back to me.' I think I realised then that somehow I had to get Debbie back before it was too late, but I knew I'd messed up by ending up arrested. What with that and the business with Ray Pavey, it was kind of a catch-22 situation for the Social Services. They'd been trying to do their best, what was right, but then I'd blotted my copybook by getting myself a criminal conviction. What I got, when I eventually went to court, was a conditional discharge due to the state of my health and a probation order for two years for TDA theft (Taking and Driving Away).

• • •

When I was released, they gave me some money – not much – and a travel warrant, and I went straight down on the train to Hastings. It was all arranged – I'd made an appointment – for me to go and see Debbie. It was several miles to the village and I walked it. I was about an hour-and-a-half late, but obviously I wasn't going to tell these people I'd walked it and haven't any money.

When I got to the house I think they were expecting me to have come in a taxi or something, and they were a bit concerned that I was going to walk back down this long driveway with Debbie – she was only a little girl, after all. It was a nice day, a lovely day. This driveway seemed miles long, but I walked Debbie down there and then I carried her. It nearly broke my back; she was all kisses and cuddles, hanging on to me. They'd done something to her hair. She had lovely hair, straight hair, and they'd messed it up. They'd put rollers in and it didn't seem right, a little girl having a bouffant hairstyle; she didn't look like my little girl.

As we were walking I was thinking, *Where am I going to take her? I haven't got any money, and I know when she goes back they're going to ask if I fed her and what she'd had to eat.* We went on walking, and we were playing, and I was so pleased just to have her. We carried on to the end of the drive and on a bit down this country lane. I don't know how long we walked, but down at the bottom of the lane there was an old lady outside this house. She smiled, like country people do, and we got talking, and before I knew where I was it was an absolute gift.

Obviously I didn't tell her what my business was. She said she never got any visitors and invited us in for a cup of tea, and from my point of view I'd had a right touch. I wouldn't eat anything but I made sure Debbie ate the biscuits and the cakes, so basically we'd had a good day.

It wasn't the sort of day you're supposed to give a child, but for me I loved doing it. It was like I'd never been separated from her.

I asked if I could have a photo of Debbie, and promises were made that next time I went down they'd give me some. But I never got to get them. That was so hard. At the time I put it aside because I had a lot to think about. But it's always tormented me.

CHAPTER SIXTEEN

A Spanner in the Works

In London I stayed with Irene, who had a little rented flat in Upper Street. She was going out with this bloke who I will not name (not because I'm frightened, but because he's a really nice bloke). He was so quiet and nice, I don't think in all the years I knew him I ever heard him shout or gossip. He just wanted an easy life.

Funny, although I had the bleached blonde hair and the red lips, I really didn't put myself about that much when I was young. I just wanted to earn money so I could get a flat. Within a week I went out and got a job. It was a clothes shop on Holloway Road and I bluffed my way in there. I knew I had to bluff it. I couldn't add up, couldn't read properly, couldn't write. But I got this job.

I wasn't flash; I was very quiet and nervous. I was on the run from Ray, still pissed with me about Debbie, and I was so scared of him finding me.

So I was at the shop, working for a wage and not

getting anywhere. I had to have money because the Social Services said that, if I had a job and got a flat and furnished it, I could have some visitation rights with Debbie and maybe bring her up to London sometimes.

• • •

I decided to go and see Debbie. The events of that day will haunt me for the rest of my life.

I got up early and took the train to Victoria station. From there I got the British Rail train to Hastings. The journey usually took two hours, three on a bad day – and I should have known then that it was going to be a bad day, 'cause the journey did take a long time.

In Hastings I took a taxi straight to where my Debbie was staying but soon as I got there I just knew something was wrong. At first no one answered the door, but I banged and banged so loud that in the end one of the maids came to a side entrance (like I was a bloody peasant or something) and informed me I was to go to the Social Services office, back in the town centre. 'But where's Debbie—where's my Debbie?' I could feel my eyes filling up with tears. The woman just closed the door and I had no choice but to get back in the taxi, and I guess about thirty minutes later I arrived at Social Services. I hated these people; I didn't trust them. But I knew I hadn't done anything wrong, so I told myself: *Don't cry, don't get upset. Wait till you see these people, it might be nothing.*

Yet in my heart I knew there was a problem. I can smell fear and I can smell trouble – especially fear, even if it's ten miles away.

The taxi pulled up outside the big Victorian building and with my heart racing I paid the driver, got out the car and walked in. I told the receptionist my name, and I was just about to say I didn't quite know who I was supposed to see when I saw a tall man coming towards me. I'd never seen him before, but he seemed to know me.

'Oh, good afternoon, Mrs Pavey, do come this way. I'm so sorry nobody told you that the arrangements have been changed.' The man was ushering me along to some room but I refused to go in.

'Who are you?' I say. 'And where's my girl?' I could feel my eyes filling up with tears and I could feel panic coming all over me . . . But I knew I mustn't break down or lose my temper. I had to play it the way these people said. I had to do whatever they told me to if it meant I was going to see my girl. After all, it should have been easy – pick my girl up, take her out for the day, let her know I'm still her mum and that she'd soon be coming to live with me in London, etc. Then take her back to her foster parents and everybody's happy.

So how come all I'm getting so far is treated like dirt? Yet I still haven't lost my temper. But half an hour later, when I was still sitting in a room all on my own, I was beginning to get the right hump. 'Where's my girl? What's going on?' I blurted out when someone finally appeared at the door. Three people came in: two men and this woman social worker, who I can still remember so well – she was a right bitch. There was no warmth in her eyes; she was as cold as ice. She didn't smile, she didn't want to make pleasant conversation with me, nothing.

I soon fell into the stiff mood of the atmosphere, and I remember her saying something like, 'We have decided, Mrs Pavey, that it would be in everybody's interests if you signed all parental rights to your daughter over to the foster parents. If, however, you do not wish to do this, then we may consider handing custody of Debbie over to her natural grandparents, Mr and Mrs O'Leary.'

My parents. Oh my God. No, never – not in this lifetime. Suddenly I felt my head spinning. I felt like an animal – a helpless fucking animal backed into a corner with no way out unless I attacked. But I didn't want to attack anyone. I just wanted to know why these people wanted me to give Debbie away for good. *Why?* Oh God, I thought I was going to explode. I didn't understand why they were trying to get me to sign these papers that meant I'd never be able to see my girl again. What did I do? I knew I wasn't perfect, but I didn't take drugs (in my day drugs meant weed or pills – anything else was for rich people, film stars and pop singers and all those fake people – but I didn't do anything); I went to work and went home to my flat every night, saving money so I could go and see my girl. Only now I was here and they wouldn't let me see her.

By this time I was trying to gather my thoughts. I was crying, I felt very young and alone. I couldn't believe that these people I'd trusted with my girl wanted to keep her. I started shouting, 'Why? Why?' and becoming more hysterical, shaking uncontrollably and tears stinging my cheeks.

The social worker tells me to stop crying and grow up. 'This is the very reason we feel Debbie needs an older mother – one who can give her a good education and more stability, let her live near green fields and horses. Can you offer her that, Joan? Can you?'

'But I love her,' I said. 'I love her. She don't need horses in London, she needs me and she's mine and I'll never sign your fucking paper, you filth pots, you dirty bastards.' The words were rolling off my tongue; I was spitting them out. I'd asked these people of authority to look after my girl and now they wanted to keep her. *This ain't happening to me. Lots of people live in London, why can't Debbie? I was born there, it's my home, why can't she live there with me?*

I asked them why they wanted to keep her down there, said she wouldn't learn anything there. I said she's got Irish blood in her – there weren't even any Irish people there. 'I want to take her home—where is she?' I screamed. '*Where is she?*'

'Calm down, Joan, or we'll have to call the police.'

'But I haven't done anything. What's the police got to do with any of this? I ain't committed no crime, I just want my girl.'

My eyes were now finally focused on the social worker. I looked her up and down, took in every detail. I can tell you, she looked like your stereotypical social worker of that time: knee-length tweed skirt, thick woollen tights, Crimplene blouse and snide-leather briefcase. I looked this woman straight in the eye and told her, 'I know I don't talk posh and I know I ain't rich but I trusted you. I trusted you. When you first took me to see the foster parents you was all nice to me and now that you got my girl you've gone all cold on me. What's going on?'

Well, she remained standing there with her arms folded. She then told me she'd heard I was stealing in London, and said my family actually *wanted* custody of Debbie. I got chills down my spine. Suddenly I had memories of my childhood at home with my brothers and sisters. God, I just got all these thoughts going through my young head, about all these terrible things from my childhood and how it now looked like my family were going against me. This I didn't understand. Seven years had passed since I left home at thirteen and went into care, and

I'd only ever seen them on a few occasions in that time so they didn't even know Debbie that well – never mind that Debbie shouldn't be left with them for all those other reasons.

While I'm listening to the social worker going on and on, and while I'm thinking about my childhood, somewhere in the distance I hear a woman's voice. I knew the sound of the voice – I could tell that west-London accent anywhere. The social worker then informed me that Irene, Denise and my mother were in the next room, with Debbie, that they'd come to try and talk sense into me. At this point I ask to see my Debbie, and that's when the social worker said: 'Yes, Joan, you can see Debbie once you sign the paper.'

Well, that was it. I mean I lost it. I was totally in control of my mind and was totally aware that I head-butted the social worker and tried to strangle her. I was telling her this is what'll happen to my Debbie. 'It ain't happening! It ain't happening—do you hear me, you fucking arsehole?'

By now the social worker was going from white to blue in the face. It looked like her eyes were going to pop out of their sockets, at which point I let go of her throat. I was very calm and she was coughing and spitting all over the place. (When I first got the news that they wanted me to give my Debbie up, the two men ran out of the room.)

I told the social worker that if my child went to live with my family I would come back one day and inflict all the punishment I suffered as a child on her. Then I'd blow her brains out.

I remember turning round, my eyes filled with tears, and looking that woman straight in the face. I said to her, 'You are the authority, you are the system, and I trusted you and you betrayed me, you fucking slag, you betrayed me.'

All of a sudden the door opened and in walked my family. I couldn't get over it. I couldn't work it out, why they were there. The long and the short of it is, of course, that they went to Social Services to try and persuade them they should get custody of Debbie. Everyone felt I was young and inexperienced and didn't know how to be a mum and all this. I don't know whether they realised it or not, but they just threw a spanner in the works for me. So now I had a criminal record, and my sisters and my mum weren't speaking up for me. And on top of that, my family had seen Debbie but I wasn't allowed to.

We all stood there, and none of my family would give me eye contact. God, I hated them all more than anything. I wasn't like any of them. I hated them but I would never hurt them; they were my blood.

I prefer not to mention every detail of that day. The only way I can describe the way I felt would be to say that all the physical pain and torture I'd experienced in the twenty years I'd spent on the earth – being held under water, thrown out of cars and through windows, beaten up with cricket bats, belts, whips, burned with cigarettes, all of it – meant nothing compared to the pain I was feeling then. My heart was busting open. I wanted my girl.

I just want to get my girl and go home!

I just didn't understand why I couldn't have her. Debbie's *my* child, I gave birth to her, I sat up with her when she was cutting her teeth, I'm the one who would put her in the car and drive her down the seafront in the early hours when she couldn't sleep and would be crying and Ray would be moaning 'cause he couldn't sleep. I got into such a state that eventually they agreed to let me see her. I kept saying, 'I want to take her, let me take her.'

Debbie came into the room and she just looked so different. She was different. I kind of realised I was losing her. She was used to being pampered in this big house, talking about her horse and, 'Mummy says I'm going to private school.' She kept saying 'mummy', and she didn't mean me. I didn't tell her not to; I didn't know how to deal with it.

She was drawing on this bit of paper, and when I asked her what the picture was about, because I couldn't understand it, she said something like, 'One day you were there, Mummy, and then you were gone, and now I have a new mummy.'

I didn't flip in front of her. I never flipped in front of Debbie. I just didn't know what to think, where to turn. I had my family against me, I had Ray against me. I'd handed her over because of circumstances, and I didn't understand what it all meant.

The social worker was there in the room, and I felt so awful because I thought, *Do they think I'm going to hurt her? I love this little girl.* I wasn't on drugs, I didn't have much money but I was paying my way and I was saving, just kept saving what I could. There's a Section 1 or something under the Child Act, which meant that my daughter had now been legally taken off me and was in care. And if I wanted her back I had to go to court. I realised not to go berserk. You know, thinking, *Don't lose your temper or you know for sure you'll lose her.*

Basically I never again got custody of my girl (I was to spend the next ten years trying to see Debbie, legally and illegally). I didn't understand the law or the system in the seventies. I was young and green and thought the only way to deal with things was with anger or violence. My world consisted of crime, dodgy coppers and dodgy crooks and a well-and-truly biased system. At the time, it still hadn't dawned on me that I was not getting Debbie back.

So now I sort of disowned my family, disowned everybody. I'd split up from Ray, been in prison, lost Debbie and had gotten over TB. I'd left Irene's and was living in Mildmay Grove in Islington, north London. I never went back to East Acton. I was still working, hoping to get Debbie back, trying to do all the right things. I knew that eventually I'd have to go to court to get her back – I had to fight this and keep fighting it. I just used to work, pay my bills and cry myself to sleep every night. I missed my Debbie so much.

I hate you, God, and I'm never going to church again.

Stuff your fucking church.

After that I became a non-stop thief.

CHAPTER SEVENTEEN

Cloud Nine

What I had learned was not to trust anyone when it came to crime. I trained myself to work alone (then you've only yourself to blame if it goes wrong) and to keep my gob shut. If I met someone in the street, I'd say I was going left when I'd probably be going right. It was just the way I was. I put up a wall and wouldn't let anyone in my head.

I couldn't read very well, and even though I'd had the operation to sort out my right eye I still couldn't see very well out of it. But I got myself a job in a right posh jeweller's in the West End of London. It was a straight job and for the first time in my twenty-two years I felt good about life, and I wanted to learn the gold and diamond trade. I knew I wasn't a thief in my own right; since I was fifteen I'd lived in Ray's shadow and it hadn't done me any favours.

The manager was a right sad case of about fifty, and as soon as I started working there he started trying to get hold of me. Every time he walked past me he brushed up against me. I used to feel sick. I knew I could have kicked him in the bollocks but that would mean I'd get the sack. I needed my job because I had to have my fares to go and see my Debbie out of London.

But as luck would have it another girl started working in the shop. She was a lot prettier than me, with big tits and a posh voice, and the manager soon stopped hassling me and started to leave me in the shop on my own while he took this bird out on long lunch breaks. I used to get right pissed off because I knew he thought I was thick. But I was loyal and always on time, I never took a lunch break and was totally honest. I wasn't interested in crime and it never entered my head to nick anything when the bloke was out of the shop. I already had a criminal record and knew it could fuck up my chances of ever getting my Debbie back. I just wanted to do my job.

After about four weeks I got used to the boss taking the posh bird out. (I think they used to go to the Piccadilly Hotel for a quick fuck before coming back to work.) But I did used to think, *Supposing someone comes in to rob me? Why should I protect this poxy shop? It ain't even mine!*

It soon came out that this boss of mine had been cooking the books. One day when I arrived at work there were people from the company head office waiting to see me and the other girl, and it didn't take them long to realise what had been going on. I think the shop manager had fallen head over heels in love with the bird and he'd been nicking stock to sell on to a couple of dealers. Then the girl started making demands on the bloke, saying he had to give her expensive presents and money if he wanted to carry on their so-called 'love affair', and apparently he didn't cover his tracks too well. (I think his brains were in his cock, ha-ha.)

I know the police came and the girl and my boss were taken away from the shop in handcuffs.

One of the company directors, some bloke with a right posh voice, told me not to worry: I still had a job and if I liked I could stay behind and help him with a complete stock-take. He told me there'd be three other people helping us and I'd get extra money in my wages that weekend. (In those days most people got paid weekly and usually in cash, and if you thought you were going to get an extra £10 in your wages it was a big deal.)

I think God must have been watching over me that day.

For the next five days the shop stayed closed and we had to check all the stock. Most of it was logged on a computer, but because this shop supplied four others we couldn't trace what was supposedly missing – as in nicked – or just out at other branches, so it had to be done by going through every piece of jewellery manually. And it was during this time I decided to nick some diamonds.

I didn't plan it. It just happened.

Late one morning I'm helping this other member of staff check through a load of stock, him calling out various items of jewellery and me ticking them off on a list, when the phone goes and he answers it, says, 'OK, I'll send her up with the trays.' He then tells me to go to one of the safes, take out the four trays with the loose diamonds in them and take them to someone upstairs. Apparently these 'rocks' are not on the computer, he informs me, so they're not sure if any of them are missing or not.

The shop had CCTV in operation, but only at the front of the shop – not in the rear, where the safes were located. In fact I'd never been to the safes before, because when the manager was there he'd said that junior members of staff were not allowed. So now I felt all grown up because these people trusted me.

Anyway, I went to the office where the safes were. They had about four or five of them, freestanding ones – big old bastards, but not the combination-lock sort of thing. These had solid handles and a long key, and it took all your energy just to open the door once you turned the key. I couldn't believe my eyes. There were all these trays inside, and I'd never seen such big diamonds and emeralds; I just thought, *Fuck it. I've got to have some of this.*

There was no time to think about it. I just did it. I found the four trays they'd sent me to get, and every one of them was full of loose stones. I lifted them out of the safe and turned to carry them out – and no one was watching me, but I didn't do it then. I was sweating like a pig and my heart was going ten to the dozen.

I had to go through two doors, then up the stairs to another office. I grabbed a handful of diamonds off each tray and swallowed them. It was very easy and they didn't get stuck in my throat. I was just about to swallow some emeralds but I thought, *No! Green's unlucky,* so I put them back.

I looked at the trays and said to myself, *Fuck it – it don't even look like I've taken any* . . . So I took another handful and threw them down my throat, and they never hit the sides. I remember making lots of saliva in my mouth so they'd go down my throat, and so they did.

Welcome to the world of crime. I didn't know at the time, but I'd swallowed about £800,000 worth of stones.

I went into the office and put the trays down in front of this man, who then asked me if I'd go and buy him a sandwich and a coffee. I never took my bag or coat when I left the shop, just the money from petty cash for his lunch. I got myself a can of Coke and drank it back really quick. I couldn't believe what I done; I hadn't planned it. How could I? I wasn't to know I was going to be in the safe that day. I didn't regret it and I still don't. I went back to work, finished the day off, and went home. Nothing seemed to have been noticed. Everyone was acting normally and yours truly was on cloud nine.

That night, I caught the train from work and got off at Highbury Corner and crossed over Holloway Road on to St Paul's Road, where there was a chemist that stayed open till about nine o'clock. I bought two bottles of olive oil and went back to my flat in Mildmay Grove. I drank a whole bottle of it the first time and just let nature take its course – which it did, about twelve hours later.

After a couple of hours in a bowl of gin they were as sparkly as when they were in the shop's safe. And now they were mine, only I didn't really know what I could do with them. People will tell you it's harder to get gear than to sell it. In my case this wasn't true. I found myself with all these stones (or 'sparklers', as I liked to call them) yet I didn't have a clue what they were worth. But I was more than happy with what I'd got, and once they were all clean I put them in a tin and buried them.

I knew that the only way I wasn't going to get my arse kicked was if I kept my mouth shut: hide the stones and not tell a soul about them. I remember thinking I'd go and tell someone, but wondering who I trusted enough. The answer was no one.

I never sold a single stone for about three months; I'd learned from living with Ray that every time he'd had a touch he'd go out and blow all the money in a couple of weeks, then he'd be skint. Whenever he did a job the police would have him in one cell and me in the other, and because I was so young they'd say things like, 'Well, if your husband's innocent, how come he's been throwing money all round Hastings?' or 'How come you've got so much jewellery on? Where's the money coming from to pay for it?'

So now that I had this little parcel hidden away, I knew I mustn't touch it for a while. And even if I did sell the stuff I mustn't be seen to be spending the money, because that's like rubbing the police's face in it – and why give the Old Bill the hump for no reason? So I told myself I wasn't going near this stuff until I was sure I was safe.

Not so thick now, am I?

• • •

I went back to work as usual and still nothing had been said about any stones missing. In fact the owners of the company were very nice to me and really were beginning to trust me to put things in and out of the safe every day. I told them I wanted to learn about jewellery, not just as a sales assistant. I mean, anyone can sell something if it's got a price on it. But I wanted to know all about how to grade diamonds or at least the descriptive terms to use; for instance:

River R	Rarest White
Top Wesselton	TW Rare White
Top Crystal TCR	Slightly tinted white
Cape CA	Slightly yellow
Light Yellow LY	Yellowish

It was so hard to learn, but I had to learn. Most people think that the bigger the diamond the more it's worth, but that's not the case. It's all about the colour, and without giving too many trade secrets away what I'll say is, 'Girls— if your bloke brings you a diamond and it's looking a bit yellow, get rid of him and the diamond because he's a fucking cheapskate and the rock's crap!'

I was doing OK and I was learning a bit about diamonds, but I was nothing like a professional and I was beginning to get bored with the job. Within about three weeks I wanted to leave and start selling my stones. I told my bosses that unfortunately my right eye was troubling me and I needed some time off, but they said I hadn't been there long enough. Well, that was it. I told them to keep their job and I left. Nothing happened after that. I was never asked about anything and the police never came to the door, so I reckon I'd gotten away with it. I mean, who in their right mind could accuse a twenty-two-year-old girl of such a crime? I'd been just the thick cunt with the dodgy right eye, keeping her mouth shut at work and doing her job.

I guess I was happy with myself, because even though I'd got no money I'd got these stones hidden away. Maybe four weeks after I'd left the jewellers I moved to a new address, a two-bedroom council flat in Tufnell Park. I was sure I would soon have my Debbie back. I hadn't missed a visit; I'd done all the things they said I had to do, like get a flat, get a job . . . (Well, I'd *done* a job.)

I went and took a few stones out of the tin. I remember I went to a couple of dealers down Shepherd's Bush. I'd been to them before, with my old friend David, so even though they didn't know me I just mentioned David's name and I was in.

It was so funny. I was still young and wet behind the

ears, and I showed this bloke a couple of stones and he goes, 'No, no, darling, they're not real.'

Yeah, in your dreams, you cunt.

So I told him OK, I'd throw them away, and I opened the door of the shop and made out like I was throwing them out.

Then he jumped up and grabbed my hand. 'Hang on, love,' he says, 'let me have a proper look. I'll just go out the back and put them on the machine.'

Well, I didn't know about any machine, and I'd never seen any machine in the shop I'd worked in. But I did know not to let the bloke take my stones out the back. So I told him to fuck off, said I'd sell my gear elsewhere.

The bloke got the right hump with me. Then he tried to pull the oldest trick in the book. 'I think I'd better hang on to these and phone the police. I bet they're on the missing list.'

I knew he was trying to frighten me into selling the stones to him, but I wasn't having any of it. 'You phone the police on me, mate, I'll come back and burn your fucking shop down.'

It didn't occur to me that this bloke was a well-known criminal; but fuck it, he wasn't going to bully me. If the police had found out I'd nicked the diamonds, I'd have suffered the consequences – even if it meant going to jail. But I didn't get caught, did I? So where does this fence think he's coming from, trying a move like that on me? I might have only been twenty-two, and I'd only ever known violence since the day I was born, but all of a sudden I was being bullied by someone I didn't even know. Well, I wasn't having it. I never set out to cheat the fence, so why should he try and cheat me?

'No way, mate—give me back my stones. I'll take a clump off you if I have to, but *I'm coming back!*'

I never got a clump and he never got to buy my stones from me and his shop never got burned down. But I learned never trust a fence, because they are the worst kind of people to deal with. (I should know. During the eighties I became one of the biggest fences in the country and the police didn't have a clue.)

Let's face it: a fence is like a bookie. You hate him because you need him, and what you get on any deal will always depend on how much the fence is holding in his petty cash. The more money he's holding, the more he'll put a squeeze on the seller; and because the seller is usually skint he sells the gear at silly, silly prices and walks away promising himself he'll never go to that particular fence again. But they do, and so did I, and so do many other people, week in, week out, each one trying to bluff the other one.

Then I met Boisie Hannington – the best fence, the best thief, the best jeweller, antiques dealer – and in eleven years of being with him, nine of them married years, he virtually pulled all his brains out and gave them to me.

CHAPTER EIGHTEEN

King Richard

I can't remember exactly how I found out my dad was ill. I think I must have phoned my mum. She told me my dad had come over all funny and looked like he had yellow jaundice and had gone over to Hammersmith Hospital for a test. I wasn't that worried. As we used to say in our house, 'He's been dying for twenty years and he still ain't dead.' (I used to say he was too wicked to die.)

When my mum and dad got married, my dad was six foot three and built like a brick shithouse. After he had TB and one of his lungs out, he went from fifteen stone to about nine stone and stayed like that for the rest of his life. (As well as the nickname Creeping Jesus, we used to call him Gandhi because he was so skinny.) A nurse would come from the clinic to see him. Her name was Sister Jones and she spoke perfect Queen's English. I remember her telling my mum that my dad had never recovered from that operation, and that it was because he'd had such a rotten childhood with his own mum that he couldn't show any love. (My answer to that was always that he shouldn't have fucking had us then.) And the reason he hated

Christmas was because his father died on Christmas Eve and his mother used to kick the shit out of him at Christmas time.

Anyway, I told my mum I didn't want to go and see him in the hospital – if the truth be known, it was because of that habit of mine to start laughing when I'm nervous and not be able to stop. I knew that if I saw my dad all yellow I'd start laughing and he might get out of the hospital bed and kick the shit out of me.

Make no mistake, even though I was over twenty and had been away from home for nearly seven years, was married to an armed robber out of Plaistow, had already embarked on a life of crime (albeit fairly small-time at that stage) and was afraid of no man or woman, I can honestly say I never ever answered him back. It wasn't out of love or respect; it was pure cold-blooded fear.

However, I did go. I waited until I knew my mum or my family weren't there and I went up to Du Cane Road Hospital and found my dad down the end of the ward, lying in one of the old-fashioned beds that hospitals used then . . . And I got such a shock I don't think I'll ever forget it. He looked so ill and so small: all you could see was this thick mop of black curly hair – not a grey hair on his head – and a bony face. It was horrible. He was waiting to go down to the theatre and he looked so pathetic I just stood there frozen to the spot.

He never said a word, just stared at me, and then little tears came out of the corner of his eyes and he moved his hands (still huge) to wave me to sit down. I sat on the edge of his bed and he put his hand over mine and said, 'I'm not coming out of here, Joan. I'm not coming out. Don't tell your mother, but I'm not coming out.'

Then he squeezed my hand and fell asleep. Silly bollocks here thought he was brown bread and called the nurse over, but it turned out his pre-med had worked and he was only asleep. Here was I, tough as you like, confronted with this weak old man (only at fifty-eight, he wasn't really that old) and I didn't know what to do. I went and asked the doctors what was wrong with him, but you know what doctors are like – they tell you sod all. They're going on about tumours and this and that, but they don't come straight out and say the big 'C' – cancer.

We'd never known death in our family, or cancer. Other people got that kind of illness, but not us. We're O'Learys, and we're tough, especially my dad.

So the next day I phoned my mum and she said she'd been to see him and he was still sleeping, and maybe it was best if I didn't go and see him. So I said, 'OK, I'll go tomorrow.'

But when I put the phone down I just knew that if I didn't go and see him, I'd never see him again. And I guess somewhere inside me I thought that if I went to see him he just might say something nice to me; I didn't care what it was. Maybe he might even tell me he loved me (yes, and pigs might fucking fly).

I went to see my dad and I deliberately didn't wear make-up. I better tell you, my dad never allowed us to wear make-up and, as with most things in my life, tell me I can't do it and I'll do it, tell me I can't have it and I'll get it – no matter what, no matter how. I was always ready to pay the price, even if it meant going in the boob (jail). I've never been frightened to suffer the consequences of my actions and never will, even if it costs me my life. But on this occasion I didn't wear make-up.

Anyway, I went to see him expecting the worst. I didn't have much money, so I stopped off at a greengrocer's shop in Old Oak Common Lane and nicked him some oranges and grapes and bananas. Then I went over to Elmses sweetshop and bought him some ciggies and a paper. While the treacle (tart: girl) behind the counter turned round to get the fags, I nicked a load of Crunchies and other chocolate bars and off I went. It wasn't far to walk down Du Cane Road from Old Oak Common Lane to the hospital; the hospital was right next door to the Scrubs prison, which I've since visited a few times.

All the way to the hospital I was just reflecting on my childhood and what a bastard my dad had been to us, and I was thinking: *I can't believe I've just nicked all this gear for him. If he knew, he'd break my neck.*

When I got to the ward my dad's bed had been moved nearer to the door. I never gave it much thought. My dad was sitting up. All the yellow was gone from him and he looked the best he'd looked in twenty years. He didn't have his glasses on and his hair was all brushed back. He looked really handsome, and I could see by the expression on his face he was really pleased to see me. God, I felt good. I didn't have two bob in my pocket, I was separated from my husband, had just come out of the nick, and I didn't give a fuck. My dad smiled a real genuine smile at me. It was so natural I just went and sat on his bed and held his hand, and for the first time in my whole life his hands didn't frighten me.

He looked at me and said, 'You shouldn't be spending your money on me, Joan; you've got better things to do with it.'

'That's all right, Dad,' I said. 'I don't mind.' *If only you knew . . .*

We had a bit of small talk and my dad says, 'You know I told you yesterday I won't be coming out . . . Well, I mean it, I'm finished.'

I told him not to worry, and how good he looks, and he just fobbed me off. He said, 'I'm worried about your mother,' and I told him to stop his nonsense (I can't believe I spoke out to my dad) and then he just looked at me and squeezed my hand and said he was sorry. I didn't know what he was referring to, and I asked him what he meant; and he just said it again: 'Sorry.' I think it was then that I knew my dad was going to die, and he knew I knew, and I think the 'sorry' was for our childhood. Then he fell asleep. He didn't die then, he died early the next morning. He had cancer of the pancreas, whatever that is, but on the death certificate it says he died of pneumonia.

My mum phoned the next morning and told me he was dead, and I told her I knew and she said, 'How do you know? The hospital have only just rang.'

I told her, 'Mum, don't worry, I just know, OK?'

How did I know? Well, I was fast asleep in bed, I don't know exactly what time it was, and all of a sudden I felt a cold chill run through my body. I woke up quick and I knew that Gandhi was dead. It was about twenty minutes after that that my mum phoned and told me.

• • •

I'd never been to a funeral before, so I didn't know what to expect. I had nothing to do with the preparation or the cost. (And let me make it clear, even if I was a millionaire I wouldn't have paid a penny towards it. I owed my dad nothing, nor do I owe any member of my family anything.)

One thing I was asked to do by my sister, Trish, was to

go down Churchfield Road, Acton, with her and take my mum to see my dad's body laid out. I really was scared. I told Trisha I didn't want to go, but there was no way my mum could go on her own so I finally agreed. So that was that and off we go, Mum looking like the perfect widow, all black with her veil, and Trish and me with our veils. I had a black cashmere lady's Crombie coat on, black leather gloves and patent brogues.

I'd never been to one of those places before, and I thought you went into a room and they gave you tea and biscuits or something. No such luck. We rang the bell, and before we got through to the main room we were all huddled in a little box of a hallway where you couldn't have even farted or you'd have knocked the next person over.

I said out loud something like, 'My prison cell was bigger than this poxy little space,' at which my mum threw me a look with her one good eye that could kill a weaker person.

Then the door opened and before I could even blink there he was – King Richard – laid out in his coffin in a white number. What happened next was the funniest thing that'd happened to me at that stage in my life. There's King Richard, looking like an angel, and I took one look at my sister Trish, hoping not to make eye contact, because I knew what she was thinking. And I knew if we looked at each other we'd start laughing, because we were both thinking the same thing.

I have to go back to my childhood to explain what was in our heads.

When we were little and my dad lost his temper or was doing something that held his concentration, he'd kind of grit his teeth and tuck his top and bottom lips in and he'd look really mean. You'd be so scared because you knew a right-hander was coming. It was a horrible face and it used to haunt me, just like his big hands did. Well, that's how he was laying there – teeth gritted and lips tucked under, and for a split second I thought, *Yeah, now get up and hit me, you old bastard.*

I look at Trisha and we both burst out laughing, and what with my mum giving it the Mother Teresa bit and us laughing it's like something out of a *Carry On* film.

Then my mum starts screaming and crying and kissing him, and somehow she's managed to grab me up near her (I nearly fell into the coffin) and is telling me to kiss him – 'Go on, go on, he's your father!' My face was right up close to him but I couldn't kiss him. Her voice and that Irish accent were really going through me. All I wanted to do was get out of there, and I never did kiss him; but I did touch him and all the fear went out of me, and I've never been scared of dead bodies since.

• • •

There was only one person I would have liked to see at my dad's funeral and that was my oldest brother, Michael. In my heart I knew he wouldn't show, but it didn't stop me wishing. I hadn't seen him then for about eight years. In fact none of us had seen him since the night he left home.

It was when I was about twelve and Michael was twenty-one. My dad had been well on the drink for years by then.

Michael was a toolmaker by trade. He'd done a seven-year apprenticeship and had bought his first car, a right big old beast – I think it was a Consulate, but he looked after it like it was a Roller. He used to pay my brother Barry and me half-a-crown to clean it at the weekend. He was a right good-looking bloke, with thick, black, curly hair – though I preferred it when he had it cut real short. He was so particular about his clothes. He used to do a bit of boxing and by all accounts he was quite good at it, but no one ever gave him much encouragement.

Out of all of us, I think Michael was lucky really. He had his own bedroom, his own stereo and he always got a good dinner. Not because he was the favourite or anything, just that he was the oldest and from a young age he went out to work. At one time he had a job in a fish shop down South Acton and he used to stink of fish when he came home. God, it was horrible. Even though he'd get straight in the bath you could smell the fish all over the house. It didn't get much better when he started his apprenticeship – the smell of fish was just replaced with the smell of grease.

Still, the good side was he'd always give you money to go down the launderette and wash his jeans for him. When he bought a new pair of Levi's he'd lay in the bath with them on until they shrank down to his size. As a little girl I used to think he was off his head, but obviously as I got older I realised that's how everyone shrank their jeans in those days.

I guess being nine years younger than him all I could ever be was a little sister, handy for sending down the shops or round the laundry. But I can never remember him being horrible to me. He never hit me or anything like that.

Michael was just different from us. He would answer my dad back and never showed any fear. He'd come home and stay in his room like he wasn't one of us. (Mind you, who'd want to sit in a room with my poxy dad?)

I noticed, as Michael got older, that my dad never used to hit us when he was around. There was one time, however – it was a Sunday morning – and my dad was in bed; we were all downstairs with my mum and there was a right nice atmosphere (there always was when my dad wasn't around). My brother Barry, who was very tall and about thirteen at the time, was sitting on a dining-room chair. He had a right skinhead haircut and was so hand-some you could take a bite out of him. The door opened and in walked my dad with a face as long as Blackwall Tunnel. He walked straight over to Barry and gave him one almighty punch, right in the face, without warning and without reason. Barry must have seen stars as he went flying across the room.

I held my breath because I knew something was going to go off. Michael said to my dad something like, 'If you ever hit those kids again I'll fucking open you up' – so then my dad goes to hit Michael.

I've never seen Michael move so quick. He went to grab my dad and he was crying with temper, and then he ran out to the kitchen to get a knife. My mum was scream-ing, Denise was screaming, Barry was crying, and my dad, whose bottle had well and truly gone by then, was trying to get out of the house. It took all the strength my mum and big sister had between them to get Michael off my dad, and if they hadn't he'd have been surely dead.

Then my dad made out he was having a heart attack – falling on to the chair, puffing and panting – and I can remember thinking, *Die, you bastard, die and give us all a break.* But as usual he made a miraculous recovery once Michael was out of the room.

Soon after that, Michael left home for good, and we never saw him again.

• • •

I don't remember too much about the funeral. Loads of his family turned up, people we'd never met telling us what a wonderful brother/uncle/nephew he was, blah-blah. I thought to myself, *If he was that fucking wonderful, how come you've never been to see him in twenty years?* I can't stand hypocrites. It's terrible now, looking back, to think two of my dad's brothers were talking to me and I didn't even know who they were.

When we all got back from the crematorium we had the party of all parties – plenty of food and drink, plenty of good music – and even though I didn't know half the people there we all chatted as if we'd known each other for years. And when it was time to go we all exchanged phone numbers and addresses. The one I gave was moody (false), though – well, what's the point, when you know you won't really phone or write, let alone see each other again? Even at that young age I used to think, *Tell them what they want to hear, it's easier.*

CHAPTER NINETEEN

My Kind of Guy

Like I said, I'd been given a two-bedroom council flat in Tufnell Park Road. I couldn't believe it – at last I had a flat where I could bring my Debbie home to. I'd left London just a couple of months after my seventeenth birthday and this was my first permanent home there for years, my own flat. I also had £800,000 worth of stolen diamonds buried in a tin outside the walls at the back of Wormwood Scrubs Prison.

Even though I didn't know then what my rocks were worth, I didn't care. They were money in the bank – and my bank was in the ground outside the prison. The way I saw it, all the creamy criminals thought they were clever having floor safes in their houses or deed boxes in Harrods or Selfridges. I always thought that was silly, 'cause if the police searched your house they'd find your safe or the place where you hid the gear – then not only are you nicked but you also get bird (time) and lose the gear. By burying the gear away from the house I knew I'd always be safe and that no copper would ever get my stones. More importantly, I still didn't tell anyone. The way I saw it, the less people I told the less people could grass me to the police and get me nicked or rob the stones from my hiding place. No way, mate. I don't like the 'hole in the wall', which is what London criminals of the seventies and eighties called a bank; I like the hole in the ground.

I'd been in the flat for about a week when I met my future husband and mentor. His name was Donald Thomas Hannington, or 'Benny' or 'Boisie'. The only people who called him Boisie were his family or people he'd gone to school with or been in prison with. The first time I met him he asked me to call him Boisie.

I'd gone over to a pub I liked to drink in, a pub I knew as a child. It was still full of gangsters – plastic and real – and ex-cons and prison officers from the Scrubs. To me it was home. On this particular day I went alone to the pub to meet a girlfriend who sold stuff on the cheap. I was to give her a shopping list of things I wanted for my flat. I had no furniture in the house but I had about £750 cash in my sky (sky rocket: pocket). I was wearing Levi's jeans, very high black sandals and a white Levi's top, carrying a small leather pouch with a strap you wrapped round your hand. My hair was pure white and cut short. I couldn't really walk in the shoes but I'd told myself I'd only got to get from the cab to the pub; as soon as I got inside I could sit down and take the shoes off under the table and no one would notice – at least that was the plan. But as with most things in my life, it never went to plan.

As soon as I stepped inside I could smell a bad atmosphere. For a start there were about eight blokes all along the bar pretending they don't know each other, all wearing identical cheap Burton leather jackets, trying to look cool. At the end of the bar was a public telephone and one

of them was pretending to be talking on it. I just knew
something wasn't right but I had no idea that they were
there for me.

As I went up to the bar, telling myself I was going to
fall arse over tit in those shoes, I heard someone say, 'What
you drinking, Joan?' It was a couple of girls I'd gone to
school with, and we hugged one another and were just
kind of chatting, like you do when you haven't seen someone for years: *How's so-and-so? Have you seen that one? How
many kids have you got?* But I kept looking round to see what
these blokes were doing, still lounging about drinking half-
pints of lager.

After ten minutes or so the girl I had to meet came in
and I got up to buy her a drink. As I got to the bar the pub
door just flew open and in rushed this bloke, who I'll call
Tommy. I'm not prepared to say what the argument was
about, but I'd had a row with him a few weeks earlier and
he'd threatened me. He was a police informer, I knew that,
and an alcoholic, and he had a reputation for hitting
women. He came straight over to me (the smell of cheap
aftershave and beer on his breath was making me sick) and
told me he was going to blow my legs off. I told him try not
to get my shoes 'cause they're new, and I start laughing.
Then I noticed that the men in cheap leather jackets all
seemed to be looking at me. And I said to myself, *These are
Old Bill, but why are they looking at me?*

My thoughts then go to the list in my pocket and the
girl I'm buying the drink for. I pull her to one side and tell
her all the men round the bar are policemen. I still don't
know why they're there, but I'm not going to give her the
list now, I decide, because she's known to the police as a
shoplifter and a kiter (a credit-card fraud), and if I hand

Boisie rocking the *Miami Vice* look in the early eighties.

Boisie and me, staying at the Fontainebleau in Miami, where they filmed *Scarface*.

My wedding reception at the Greek restaurant near Acton Town station, which also featured in many episodes of *Minder*.

In Miami in 1984 on a very important 'business trip'.

Glammed up ready to go to the Jockey Club in Coconut Grove, Miami.

At home in Hornsey Road. You can see those dreaded ornaments in the cabinet behind me!

Having a Sue Ellen moment, sitting on my throne in my ex-council house. This was before David and Victoria Beckham did it!

Fernando Pruna visiting us in London for Christmas. Happy times. RIP.

Me and Boisie at home during the early stages of pregnancy. After a 12-year wait, I never thought I'd have another child, so I was over the moon.

About to pop – this was the start of going into labour and Benny was born the next day.

Baby Benny at two days old and Mummy Joan looking very trim!

Getting ready for our first night out after baby Benny was born.

The day of Benny's christening – we hired a massive hall and 200 people came. It was a beautiful occasion and Benny was a happy, smiley baby who never cried once.

On the beach in Mar del Plata, Argentina, having visited Fernando in prison.

Me and Boisie in Cyprus in 1990 – this was our last family holiday together.

In my shop in Tottenham Lane, Hornsey, when flock wallpaper was still in fashion!

After a difficult time, I took myself away to Estepona for a break from everything.

Getting ready for our first night out after baby Benny was born.

The day of Benny's christening – we hired a massive hall and 200 people came. It was a beautiful occasion and Benny was a happy, smiley baby who never cried once.

On the beach in Mar del Plata, Argentina, having visited Fernando in prison.

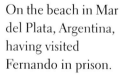

Me and Boisie in Cyprus in 1990 – this was our last family holiday together.

In my shop in Tottenham Lane, Hornsey, when flock wallpaper was still in fashion!

After a difficult time, I took myself away to Estepona for a break from everything.

Age 33 in Estepona. The pictures say it all.

In my antiques shop, rocking the Patrick Cox loafers.

At home in Hornsey Road with my OCD in full swing – note the ruched curtains which match the shell suit and earrings.

Benny saw this photo recently and told me that he knew when he saw me dressed like this when collecting him from school, either he or the teacher was in trouble!

Promoting the book in New York in 2002, including appearing on *The Montel Williams Show* and making a documentary about stealing diamonds.

In a coffee shop in Crouch End with my beautiful granddaughter, Olivia Hannington.

over the list I could get done for conspiracy. I tell the girl I'll give her £50 and to get a cab home and I'll phone her later. (Tommy is still at the bar and getting even drunker.) I walk round the other side of the bar to phone for a taxi for the girl, and I happen to see a woman who went to school with my sister Denise. She's with a man of about thirty or more who I think looks Italian: short black straight hair, very dark skin, and his arms look muscly. But most of all I notice he's got part of his nose missing. So I look away because I think he might get embarrassed if he catches me staring at him – not to mention that he might give me a smack in the gob.

I finish making my phone call and I'm just about to walk out the pub door when I hear Tommy call out my name. 'Oi, O'Leary! Come here, you Irish slag, I want a word with you.'

Well, that's enough for me. I've spent the first twenty-two years of my life getting hidings from men and if this fucking small-time police grass thinks he's going to embarrass me in my own area, then he doesn't know me too well.

I just turn round, take off the new shoes, put them on a chair with my bag, and by this time he's running at me . . . Well, I just lose it. I mean, this is out of order. The girls I was talking to earlier start screaming, and in the meantime I'm having a bare-knuckle fight with the grass. I can see the guys in the cheap leather coats making a run at me, and at one stage I'm fighting about seven blokes, all coppers, all big bastards. Here I am, having the fight of my life, and I don't really know what it's all about. Obviously I'd had a row with the grass – but why are all these police here in plainclothes?

I knocked Tommy spark out. I'd like to say it was with

a fist but it wasn't; I hit him with a bar stool and he fell like a sack of potatoes.

For the next ten minutes all hell broke loose. Women were screaming at the police and blokes were shouting to leave her alone, she's a woman. I must have broken every glass ashtray, bottle and table in the pub but these coppers couldn't hold me down, I was so angry with them for running at me. The grass had hit me first, so I didn't understand why they hadn't nicked *him*. At some stage the police finally managed to catch hold of me and pin me down. Blood was pouring from my nose and my feet were cut to pieces because I'd taken the shoes off (let's be honest, it's not easy having a tear-up in a pair of five-inch heels).

I was on the floor, face down, my hands behind my back, when all of a sudden I heard a voice saying, 'Let her up, she's only a kid. Let her up.' I couldn't see who was talking, but the voice was so nice. It was a man and he was saying, 'This is out of order; why don't you try and hit me? Let the girl up, you lousy bastards. Let her up or I'll bury the lot of you.'

The police then got me up on my feet, but told me I had to sit on a chair until a police van arrived; my hands were still behind my back, in cuffs. I then got a look at the bloke who was talking to the police, and realised it was the bloke with the dodgy nose. He was standing up by now and waving his hands at the police, who were telling him to mind his own business or he'd also be arrested and taken to the station.

All of a sudden, that was *it*. These four coppers just dropped like flies. *Bang, bang, bang, bang* – one after another they hit the floor. I never really saw what happened after that because a police van pulled up outside and there was a commotion all over the pub as I was frogmarched bare-foot out to the van and thrown in the back. I've always been able to wriggle my hands free from cuffs, and as we pulled away I did just that, and threw them at the coppers with me, saying they might as well have them back. I promptly got a smack in the mouth from a big fat northern copper. It really hurt, but I wouldn't cry.

After about four hours in the police station I was released on bail. As I was being brought out I saw Tommy sitting in a side room with two plainclothes officers. He was talking away and they were writing stuff down, and I shouted out, right loud, 'Don't forget to sign your statement, you fucking grass.'

I was nearly put back in the cells but so what? He was a grass and he put people away that he grew up with – I mean, you just don't do that.

I got a cab straight back to the pub and went looking for my shoes and my bag with the money in it – lucky for me, everything was behind the bar. Then I asked the bar staff who the bloke was and they told me his name was Benny Hannington, and that he'd just gone in a cab to a pub in Shepherd's Bush called the Queen Victoria, on the Uxbridge Road. I went straight down there. I wanted to thank the bloke for trying to help me out; and I wondered how come he never got nicked, 'cause he really did knock four coppers out earlier on.

I walked in and there he was, at the bar, this geezer Benny Hannington. I went straight over and put my hand out. He looked at me and then shook my hand. 'You know, mate, I really appreciate you helping me,' I said. 'I right appreciate it.' I was a right cockney little thing.

'That's all right, love,' he said. 'What are you having?'

I said no, that I wanted to buy him a drink to say thanks, and asked him what he wanted. When the drinks came, I was just about to pay for them when Benny said to me, 'Are you sure, or what?' Sort of getting angry. 'What kind of people do you mix with?' I didn't know what I'd done to offend him, and then he said, 'When you're in my company, darlin', I pay for the drinks.' You know, like, 'I pay, I'm a man'.

I went to him, 'Yeah, but you're an old man, mate, and this is the eighties, and where I come from women pay their way, mate.'

He just couldn't believe it. 'You've got some fucking gob on you, ain't yer.'

And that was it. We just clicked.

He was only a small man, about five feet eight, and there was part of his nose missing, gone. I thought to myself, *Don't fuck about with him* – I just knew not to. I found out later that it was a freak accident. He was on a bank robbery and it came on top, the car crashed and he went into the windscreen. He didn't go through it, but it took part of his nose. He was a right funny bloke, and everyone was supposed to be scared of him, because rumour was he'd killed someone, but I liked him instantly. I remember him saying to me, 'So what do you do, darling?'

'I'm a thief,' I said.

Well, this bloke looked at me and was so shocked that I came straight out and said it. I mean, I've never pretended to be a hairdresser or a doctor or anything I wasn't. I was a thief, so why tell lies? Even when the Old Bill used to nick me and ask what I did for a living, I'd say, 'I'm a thief, but you ain't clever enough to nail me. And if you do, then I'll go to prison and carry on thieving when I come out.'

Anyway, we arranged a date and I stood him up. The reason being he was a lot older than me, about seventeen years difference in our ages. I was young, and I wasn't very clever with the sex thing. I was frightened of him because he was an older man and I thought he'd definitely be wanting to get his leg over. *But if he thinks he's getting me for a meal and a bottle of champagne, he can fuck off. Like, he can have me for nothing if I want him, but I don't want him yet; I don't know him that well.*

So we played that game for a few weeks, and then eventually he found me in the street in East Acton, going up to my friend's house, and he said, 'Are you taking the piss or what? Do you want to know or not? Because you're driving me fucking mad.'

I said, 'Yeah, all right then, come over to my house tonight and we'll have a drink.'

'Now if I come over there, you're going to be there, ain't yer?'

I said, 'Yeah,' and that's how it happened. That quick.

He didn't know much about me; you don't chat all your business straight off. He did know I'd been married and was now separated, and that's about it. I told him about Debbie, how I was fighting to get custody of my girl, and he said, 'Do you want your girl?' I told him of course I did, and he said, 'Well, you'll get your girl.' But still I didn't know him well enough to trust him or to tell him too much about that side of my business.

• • •

Benny moved in with me. I had a bed, a cooker, some net curtains and that's all. Then I came home one night, walked in, and there's all this cream gear: paintings in gilt frames, ornaments set out all over the place, secretaire

141

roll-top bookcase. It was a very small flat and it was full of furniture and stuff that looked like it was from *Upstairs Downstairs*. That's all I knew about antiques.

I couldn't get my head around it – I thought he was a painter and decorator. He used to get up in the morning, put on clean overalls and go to work. He'd come home at night and there'd be green and blue and red paint on them. I knew he'd been in prison, but as far as I was concerned he was now a painter and decorator – and I quite liked that. I'd had villains before; now I had one who'd had a past and moved on. *I don't know he's spent twenty-eight years in the nick; I don't know any of that, and you don't ask.*

My friend Jean knew him very well, so of course I went round her house and asked her stuff about him. She told me he wasn't known to be a woman-beater. 'He's right staunch, he's old score, you know, nice geezer. He's not into women; he's into antiques. He can have a terrible fight but he don't go looking for it . . .' *My kind of guy,* I thought.

I said to him, 'I know you're not a painter and decor-ator,' but he wouldn't say what he did. For months we were living together and he'd go to work at the same time every day and come home covered in paint. Yet he was bringing antiques back with him, or paintings, and he'd say, 'Oh, I bought that in an auction on the way home.' Coming home with paint on him, I found out later, was because he had all these warehouses and lock-ups and he was decorat-ing them at that time, so in that respect he wasn't lying.

He just forgot to mention that there were £2 million worth of antiques in there.

• • •

I'd been with Benny a few weeks when one night we were at my flat and there was a knock at the door. It's Ray Pavey, who's just come out of prison, and he's like, kicking it. He's got a new Jag and he's looking good, like a million dollars – a silver-grey cashmere coat and a pinstriped suit with the half-inch stripe down the side like in an American gangster movie. (It sounds awful now, but in those days it was the bollocks.) Ray said he wanted to see me, have a private word. At that stage I hadn't really told Benny my business and he was a bit iffy, asked me if I wanted to go. I did, and I said so, and then off I went with Ray.

We drove up to Highgate. Ray had received a form or a letter from the Social Services in Hastings that basically said he agreed to give up all his rights to Debbie. He'd signed it. It also said that I was to give up all my rights to Debbie, too, so she could be adopted. I wouldn't sign it. In the end Ray made it clear that I had to. I can't and won't go into the details. Let's just say I felt tricked into it.

Ray Pavey dropped me off down the road from my home. As soon as I got in I collapsed in a chair and broke down in front of Benny. I told him the whole story. I'd only known him a little while, a few weeks. At this point I don't think we were even properly living together, but he was obviously staying there that night. I told him what had happened and he just flipped – he couldn't comprehend it. Neither could I. But then, after that, there was nothing more I could do. Nothing except a couple of grief-fuelled attempts at revenge by me and by Benny, who was determined to kill Ray for me. In the end Ray just disappeared off the scene, and Debbie was beyond my reach. For a while I felt hysterical, but ultimately I spent the next few years kind of resigning myself to the fact that I had lost her.

CHAPTER TWENTY

Learning the Trade

Benny came in one night with a Pierre Cardin leather case. He put it on the table and said to me, 'I think you're a right staunch bird, Joan.'

This was right out of the blue, so I said, 'What do you mean, Benny?'

'Well, I don't know a lot about you. I've only known you a few months. You ain't asked me for money and you seem to like – I don't know how – an old fart like me. Open the case and you can have anything you like out of it.'

I opened the case up and it was like Pandora's fucking box. I had never seen anything like it. It was crammed with antique jewellery, rings and bracelets, fob chains, watches, silver seals. There must have been more than 300 gold sovereigns in there. Out of everything I saw, I picked a marcasite ring made in the 1920s – in value about fifty quid, which would be worth £300 today. And Benny couldn't believe that from all this stuff – diamond necklaces, Cartier watches – I'd picked out a two-bob ring. But to his mind it must have seemed like, *She's all right. She's obviously not a grabber; she's not greedy.*

In fact I chose the marcasite ring because I happened to like it. He told me I was the first woman he had ever met in his life who, when he'd offered her something, just took what she wanted and not any more. I wasn't that material. I liked a nice home and nice clothes. The antique jewels didn't really hit my head until I knew what they were worth.

Then he said, 'Tomorrow I'm going to show you something.'

The next day he took me to all these different warehouses and lock-ups. We went into one, and I remember thinking at the time, *What is this load of old crap?* They were antiques, but in these gloomy surroundings they just looked like piles and piles of junk, covered in dust. I didn't know they were worth bundles.

'You know, Joan, I trust you. I think me and you are going to be together a long time. You seem to know what you're at. But you must never tell anybody about these places. If you do, I'll kill you.' He said it quite matter-of-fact – but you'd better believe it.

'I won't tell anyone, Benny. I won't tell anyone.'

Looking back, I know that I was the perfect candidate for him. If I'd been a boy he was teaching it would have been fine, but it was great that I was a woman: not only could he teach me, he could fuck me as well. We could live together and we could become a team. He was a professional criminal, self-educated, prison-educated, from the nick and the street. And I was the dogsbody, the apprentice, the joey, the runner – but I was learning. I used to keep my mouth shut, never used to question anything, just take it all in. Benny could charm anyone – he wasn't a womaniser, and that's probably what made him charming, because he was an ugly cunt; he was very quiet, but he was interesting, and he was loyal. It wasn't until years later that I realised how manipulative he was.

He showed me the warehouses and the lock-ups, and obviously I was inquisitive, so I said something like, 'Well, what are you exactly?' because I still didn't get it.

'I'm a thief, you stupid cow, what do you think I am? But I'm an antiques dealer – no one knows what I do, but I thieve it.'

I could tell it was great for him to unload on me about himself, because I was like *Wow* and wide-eyed and everything. He came from a 'totting'-type horsey family. He was adopted by the Hanningtons and never knew who his real dad was. He had a bad upbringing and at a young age he started going to jail. He couldn't read or write properly and while he was in prison he taught himself how to do both, and at fifteen he started picking up antiques books. Like I'm interested in diamonds and gold, he was into antiques. When I first started dealing in that world I didn't have a clue; I mean, what did I know about fine art or antique furniture? The only furniture I knew about in those days was the stuff you bought on the high street for your own home. But Benny knew more about antiques right across the board than anyone I ever met. If you showed him something, no matter what it was, he could tell who made it, what wood it was made of, how many were made, etc. Whether it was furniture or glass or China, it didn't matter: Benny could tell you how much you could get for it, straight or stolen. Show him something, anything – a table – and he'd be able to say, 'It's good quality, old but not genuine antique, it's been dipped, probably made by such-and-such . . .' without even touching it.

Benny used to take me to auctions all over the country, educating me on what was crap and what was cream and how to spot fakes from the real stuff. I had to learn from someone – and he was the best, no doubts. We'd spend hours looking at glass and China and I'd have to try and register all the hallmarks in my head. In the van on the way home I'd have to repeat all the right markings back to him. Sometimes I'd just get all confused and I'd say, 'Boisie, I can't stand doing this! Why have I got to learn all this stuff?'

'Knowledge, darlin',' he'd say, 'knowledge.'

'But why have I got to have this knowledge? I hate antiques . . .'

Then he'd get the hump and say, 'What's the point in nicking fucking gear if you don't know what it's worth? Just shut up and I'll educate you.'

Other dealers, people in the trade who knew him – everybody said the same thing: he was a walking encyclopaedia. He just knew everything about everything.

• • •

I was at home watching Spurs playing Arsenal on the telly and the phone went. It was about nine o'clock and I'd been expecting Benny back by this time. Now he was phoning me, and it sounded as if he was in a bit of trouble. He told me to come over to this address in west London. I didn't ask questions; I got ready to go.

Benny told me to wear pumps (his name for trainers) and a polo-neck, something dark, and to cover my hair, which was very long, bleached blonde. I said I'd be there in twenty minutes. I'd be using the back streets; he'd taught me the burglars' route to get from one part of London to the other without using main roads.

The house was this lovely big detached place off the A40, up near Hanger Lane, probably worth 400 grand. It turned out he'd been given a piece of work: the house was crammed with antique furniture but he'd only gone in there for one particular article, apparently. I parked up behind his white Bedford van and we went over the back gates. I was shaking, very scared, and what made it worse was him saying, 'If it comes on top and somebody comes, you've got to hit them. You've got to fight.'

I said to him, 'But I can't, I'm scared, Benny. Supposing it's a big man?'

'You—fucking—fight.'

He wasn't physical; he didn't get hold of me by the neck – you just knew, from the way he said it, you just knew you had to do it. And he's your bloke, you want to please him, you want him to love you and think you're clever. That's what it's all about . . . And you'll do what you've got to do. I'd have done anything he asked except sold my body.

Benny had already been inside. I followed him up the stairs and he showed me what he'd come for: a secretaire-cum-bookcase with inlaid marquetry, and when you opened up the top it was a leather-pad writing desk. It was a real trumpy piece of furniture, massive, worth about £30,000 in 1980. And he couldn't lift it. He said, 'You've got to help me with this.' It nearly killed me. You know your own strength – and I was strong – but it's just about impossible to actually pick up something that's bigger than your own body weight. I did it, though.

We carried it downstairs and just as we got it outside I start laughing. My nerves were shattered, that's what did it. There we were in the back garden on a freezing winter's night, and it was more than my life was worth to drop it. One scratch and it would've gone from thirty grand to ten or whatever. I still don't know how but we carried it out to the van and I was shaking with nerves in case I lost my strength.

I always relate crime and danger to sex; to me it all comes under one roof. That night when we came home from our very first robbery together I couldn't help but notice something. It happened later as well, but that night more than any night in the whole of our life together. Benny sat down in his chair, kicked his shoes off, rolled a joint, had a couple of drinks – and now he was buzzing like a fucking bee. Then we went to bed and he made love to me like I was Madonna. I realised the pattern of our relationship was that every time we had a touch (made some money) – every time I did something good for him, or what he would consider good – it would come out in our sex.

So I knew then that if you want the sex and the love and the attention you crave, do what you've got to do and you'll get it. So I did what I had to do.

We put the secretaire-bookcase straight into our bedroom and it was sold three or four days later. When the business was done I wasn't there, and Benny never told me what it was actually worth and what he got for it. He got the money, whatever it was, say thirty grand, but he didn't come in and say, 'There's fifteen.' The way I book it now (but not the way I booked it in the early days) is that if I get caught with you, I'm going away for the same amount of time. And don't think they're going to be lenient because I'm a bird. They'll know I'm a professional because I'm with you – I'm part of it and I'm going down.

I have to admit, I made a lot of cock-ups along the way that cost Benny thousands of pounds. In that council flat in Tufnell Park you couldn't move for antiques. He literally had every room decorated in paintings, China, glass, Georgian tea sets, French clock sets – even our bed was Victorian – and he was always having a go at me for breaking something. I hated antiques and I hated having chairs that I couldn't sit on in case they got dirty. It was like living in a fucking museum. *Why can't I have furniture that normal people have and aren't afraid to dust or polish?* I mean, it was all bollocks to me. I never really got attached to possessions; I preferred people to possessions.

One time Benny brought some paintings home, early Victorian. They were in big gilt frames, about five foot by five foot. One was a painting of a landscape, and they were all dirty and dusty. So Benny's plonked them down and gone off, and because I was so clean and tidy, always cleaning the flat, I thought I'd give them a dust. I set to but the dirt wasn't coming off. It was the natural patina, but I didn't know that.

Anyway, I went to get a wet dishcloth and washed all the frames. They looked lovely and clean.

So I rolled a joint – and at the time I used to smoke very big joints with too much weed in them – and I'd had about four toots and my head was buzzing, and I thought, *I'll please Benny – I'll clean these murky pictures.* I kept wiping the landscape but it wouldn't come clean, so I went into the kitchen and got the Jif out, squeezed it all over the painting and then got a green pot-scourer and started to scrub. I was really scrubbing it when I noticed the colours looking different and starting to fade; still, I wasn't too bothered. And common sense told me that if I left the Jif on a bit longer it'd lift the dirt out. Fucking right it lifted the dirt out.

The phone went and I answered it. I'd now sat down with the joint, not a care in the world, forgot all about the paintings. I was on the phone gossiping when Benny came in. He went, 'All right, babe?' and went into the living room, and the next thing I heard was something like, 'Oh shit! Oh my God, you cunt. You're on drugs.'

I was nervous and I said to my friend, 'I'd better go. I think he's got the hump because I'm smoking weed in the day.'

I remember him standing there with his hands on his hips, this little fella, saying, 'Are you fucking mad? You need a doctor, there's something deranged about you.'

And I still didn't know what he was talking about. I was just standing there, feeling like a schoolgirl, like an idiot. I said, 'But I cleaned it, Benny—don't it look better?' It really looked like he was going to have a heart attack. I kept saying, 'Yes babe, but what do you think of the frame? I've cleaned it up good, ain't I?'

'The frame, the fucking frame, never mind the frame. What about my painting? That's a £38,000 George Niemann landscape . . . !' (George Niemann was a Victorian landscape painter from Germany.)

He wiped all the Jif away and the colours came off with it, smeary, like a watercolour, and the painting was fucked. I'd thought I was doing a good deed by cleaning his shitty painting, and now I was upset. 'I don't know it's an antique. If it's an antique, then tell me not to touch it, surely that's common sense.'

He screamed and shouted at me so much I thought I was going to get a clump. I started laughing – nerves again;

I certainly didn't find it funny. I was laughing and crying at the same time and then I ran out the house. I stayed in a hotel for two or three days, I don't really remember. Benny was panicking and worrying, and I think he was worried about losing a good catch like me. Eventually I went back home and we started laughing about it. And he said, 'It's only money, babe.'

Till the next time I made a cock-up.

CHAPTER TWENTY-ONE

Robbery Incorporated

I knew I was a failure (or at least I felt like I was) because I'd lost my Debbie. I was so young and yet already I was divorced from my husband; I couldn't read or write properly, so couldn't get a normal job – at least that's what I believed at the time. After losing her I accepted that I'd never have any more children, so from then on I became a jewel thief. I told myself that if I couldn't have Debbie then I'd have everything else in the world that money could buy – and fuck society and fuck the system.

For someone like me, coming from the family I came from and then being with Ray for seven years, to be with Benny Hannington was a different life. For the next eleven years I could never say I was happy, but I was content; it was a peaceful life. Meaning I wasn't being abused. But I believe in my heart he really did manipulate me because I was putty in his hands. I'd do anything he asked. As for Benny – there he was, he's got this bird, he can go to work with her, she does what she's got to do. She doesn't ask questions, she pulls her weight, she doesn't ask for money – and guess what, he's fucking her . . .

The way I booked it was I'd be doing stuff at night for Benny or with Benny, and during the day I'd be an independent kiter, doing my own thing. So Benny was in the shop, doing his business; I'd be out with him at night, doing our business. But for eight hours during the day I'd be out kiting, working the dodgy cheques and credit cards. And that's how I was for nine years non-stop. Three hundred and sixty-four days a year, and sometimes on a Christmas Day just for the hell of it. I just didn't know any other way.

Basically, during those years we were like Robbery Incorporated.

The kiting had actually started for me when I came back to London after finishing with Ray. I didn't have much money; I didn't have a lot of brains. I had looks but I wasn't too aware of them. I didn't like women much and I didn't trust men at all. I remember waking up in the flat in Mildmay Grove and I couldn't think how I was going to pay the rent.

Then some post came to the flat that was obviously for people who used to live there. I opened these envelopes and inside one of them was a chequebook. I'd never had a bank account and didn't know a lot about banks and cheques. And I thought, *Well, you've got a chequebook, you can write a cheque.* In the early eighties you could still write a cheque without a banker's card, up to £50. Basically if you bluffed it and could forge the signature, you could write a cheque.

I got all dolled up and went down to Highbury Corner. The shop's not there any more, a small fashion shop that sold lovely clothes, and I remember going in there thinking, *Let me just try this little shop*. I didn't particularly want the clothes; I wanted to test if I could do it. In my mind I'd already clocked the quick way out and what road I'd run to, so if it came on top I knew there was an outers (escape route) because I knew the area like the back of my hand.

Anyway, I was clever enough to buy something about thirty-five or forty pounds. While I was doing this, the assistant was trying to sell me something more expensive, over a hundred. I told her that I couldn't write a cheque for that much (I'd made some fanny about why I hadn't got my banker's card – said it was out of date or something), and I'll always remember her saying, 'What you do is, write three cheques but date them different.'

It was a like a lightbulb going on.

So now I knew that if you didn't want to use a card and you didn't want them to phone up the bank, you wrote separate cheques with different dates . . . It was as if this saleswoman was educating me without knowing it, because I really hadn't known about these things. I did it and got away with it, and I got the bug for kiting. There were fifty-two cheques in the book and in two days I done all of them and had a ball. I thought, *I like this. I'll have some more of this.*

Later, when I was with Benny, he'd bring me the chequebooks and credit cards home of a night, saying he'd bought them from Fred up the road, or that he knew a man who knew a man who knew a man, etc. Though he taught me loads of things, there were lots of things he didn't tell me. For one, he didn't tell me it was him that got the books. But he always seemed to know the history of them. Of course he knew the fucking history – he'd nicked them from the houses he robbed!

Most of the time I never questioned what Benny said, though. He was older and wiser than me, obviously much more mature and he'd seen more of life . . . Say we went out to dinner with another bloke and his wife; I was always the youngest, and they'd all be talking about the war – 'Do you remember the doodlebugs?' 'Do you remember Al Martino?' Every now and again I'd say something like, 'I'm into Bob Marley,' and Benny would pull a face. 'Oh, grow up, act your age! You're a woman now.'

And I'd be thinking, *Hang on a minute, I'm only twenty-two, I'm only young, mate.* But I didn't have the guts to answer him back.

When it came to clothes, though, I wore what I wanted, where I wanted, when I wanted. For instance, I knew that to be a good thief and to avoid getting caught I had to keep changing my appearance. I'd go back to the same shops when I was working the dodgy cards or chequebooks, day after day, never looking the same. Always with a different coloured wig. One day I'd have short blonde hair, the next long red hair, the next brunette.

I used to be like a whippet when I was out grafting. I could be in at least fifty different shops in a day and I'd get something from every shop. I'd make the staff carry all my bags to the car. Always giving them a nice fat tip, it never failed. I learned to speak with all these different accents. Let's say I was speaking all day with an American accent; sometimes, even after I'd finished a day's work, I'd have got into it so much I'd forget to switch back to my usual cockney accent. And I wouldn't realise, not until I phoned one of my mates to tell them I'd a nice bit of gear to sell them and halfway through the conversation she'd say, 'Joan, why are you talking like that?'

'Like what?' I'd say, with an American accent (or Scottish, or Irish, or whatever – I could do any of them). Then I'd realise and switch off. My mates used to say, 'Are you smoking that weed again?'

They all knew I smoked weed – but only in my own house or in a hotel suite. Thank God I never got hooked on drugs. I've tried most of them at some stage of my life, but usually at home on my own or with Benny. One night Benny bought some charlie home – everybody used to go on about how you could fuck all night on it. It didn't trouble me to take it, because I knew I was safe with Benny. I wouldn't take it up my nose, so I mixed it with weed and we smoked it, got right off our heads. But as for sex, it was a joke. We were glued to the chair, buzzing like bees, but neither one of us could get up. I remember Benny saying, 'You roll a mean joint, Joan, but next time, after I've laid out £300, could we at least have the fuck first so I feel like I got something for my money?'

'*How* much did you pay?' I said. 'Do you know it's dearer than fucking gold?'

We didn't do it again after that. Really I believe that if you're a thief then you shouldn't take any drugs, because you should always have a clear head.

• • •

That I'd mentioned the price of gold to Benny Hannington was ironic, because it wasn't until I met him that I learned how to tell if a diamond was diamond or to test gold – I didn't know the value of gold or diamonds, I was just good at nicking them. Before I met Benny I'd take stuff I'd nicked to the receiver, who'd put it all on the scales, weigh up the gold, tell me the stones were snide (like the uneducated mug I was, I'd believe him) and I'd be happy for the price I got for the gold alone. I have to laugh now, because the receivers were all twice my age, knew the game inside out and used to rip me off every other day – but I never knew it until Benny educated me. Then all of a sudden I'd be going back to the dealers, telling them what I had and how much it weighed or what carat the diamonds were, etc. I was like a walking dictionary. And when the dealers tried to underpay me, I'd pull them and let them know I was educated now and that they couldn't rip me off any more: *I test my own gear, I know what I've got, so you either treat me fair or I'll go somewhere else.*

I don't blame the dealers. After all, if I walk into a jewellery shop or a pawnbroker's to sell some jewellery and don't really know the weight or the carat of the gear, that's my problem, not the dealer's. If he offers me a price and I accept it, it's me who's the mug – not the dealer. But you only learn that by experience. I was just lucky and got educated very young; I couldn't go wrong.

By working in shops I then started stealing diamonds. But Benny didn't know that. For a long time I never even told him about the first lot of sparklers I'd nicked when I was working as an assistant in that jeweller's. So I came home one day and was in the toilet for ages, and he went, 'Joan, what you up to?'

I came out the toilet, having cleaned it all up, and I showed him. 'Here, look. That's what I was doing in the toilet.'

He looked and he couldn't believe it. All these diamonds – full rings and loose stones. Benny just could not believe it.

He soon cottoned on. 'Fuck me, Joan,' he said, 'I thought I knew all the tricks but I never heard of this before.' That's how he booked it: *Not only can this bird do the business with me, she can do something I can't do. I'm going through windows at night nicking furniture and selling it for thirty grand and I risk getting caught – and she can walk in the jeweller's and swallow something! No one sees it go and we still get thirty grand.* (Later I had an operation to have half my stomach removed, and was in a lot of pain. The doctors said I had duodenal ulcers, caused by stress, but maybe it was years of swallowing diamonds, I don't know.)

This particular little lot, I remember, had a shop value of £350,000. Something else Benny taught me was to always take the stones out of the shanks (the gold bands) and sell them loose. The shanks have markings on them, so without them the stones can't be identified. Through a dealer we might get seventy grand, but because Benny had his own shops – in Camden Passage, Tottenham Lane and later on in Old Mill Street, Stamford Hill – sometimes he'd reset the stones in new shanks and put them on display in the window.

I didn't always swallow them and shit them out. Benny put me wise to the chewing-gum trick, one of the oldest in the book.

This was the way it worked. I'd hire a bloke to work for me for the day and together we'd go to some posh jeweller's; I'd pretend to be the brass – a high-class prostitute – and the bloke would be the fat businessman in the suit, the sugar daddy. I'd be wearing a mink coat and Cartier diamonds, and there's a limo parked outside – the whole bit. I'd have already been there the week before and spotted the prize in the window (the prize being the piece of jewellery I wanted) and would have had the same ring made up by a jobber in Hatton Garden. Only it would be a fake diamond, in a real shank with proper markings.

These rings could be anything from £25,000 up to £300,000 or £400,000. And of course, when you're talking that kind of money and the people in the shop believe you to be genuine, you really are getting star treatment. They're not looking over their shoulder, watching you. To them this is business: they can see something like five, ten grand commission for them in this.

So the sugar daddy would be choosing the ring for me, and I'd be putting on a high-class accent – *OK, yaah, darling* – speaking oh-so very nicely: 'Could I possibly see, do you think, that particular one over there, with the heart-shaped diamond?'

What you had to do was play the game. If you had to be in this place for two hours, well, you'd just sit there as if you had all the time in the world. I'd be playing up to the bloke who was with me, going, 'Oh plee-ease, darling,' and letting him have a couple of grunts and groans: 'Oh I don't know, I'm not sure, it's very expensive . . .' I'd be kissing him, all over him like a rash, and the assistants would be watching us, thinking, *Yeah she'll get it.* After a while we'd get our target assistant going – he'd be flapping around, knowing he's got to get this sale.

Still, you take your time, let another half-hour go by, no rush, no panic.

At some point during all this, while the assistant had his back turned, I'd have already stuck a bit of chewing gum under the table or the counter. When the time was right, I'd get the real ring in my hand and wet my palm – just lick it – then just stick the ring into the chewing gum. The staff wouldn't see any of this, even if the shop had CCTV. When I'd got the real ring under the table, I'd bring out the fake ring. Then I'd give it to the assistant – they'd have what they thought was the real ring back in their hands. And they wouldn't suss it out, because the actual shanks were always gold. They wouldn't even check it closely, they'd be so busy thinking about their commission.

Eventually I'd say, 'Yah, I'll put a deposit on that. My friend here will pay. Is American Express all right?'

'Yes, madam, American Express. No problem.'

Ten thousand pounds on the card, which was dodgy anyway. Then I'd leave the shop with my hired bloke and send someone else there ten minutes later, pretending to browse around or buy something. I would've told them the exact spot where the ring was stuck, so they just had to pull it off the gum and pocket it.

And that's what Benny taught me how to do. It was foolproof; I did it for about ten years.

CHAPTER TWENTY-TWO

Marks & Sparks

An acquaintance of Benny's, a bloke called Martin Black-burn, was recently out of prison. (I say acquaintance, but at the time Benny would have called him one of his best friends – they'd spent several years in the same jail together.) He didn't have any money; he didn't have anything. So Benny said we should go out, the three of us, and get him some clothes and this and that for his flat – on dodgy cheques. I didn't say no to Benny very often, but I didn't like this Martin Blackburn guy. I'd first met him when Benny asked me if I'd go and visit somebody in Parkhurst. It was the way he shook my hand; he didn't have a firm handshake – it was weak and just horrible – and his vibes were awful.

Anyway, he was now out of prison. The clothes he had on were what he'd had before he went into prison, these awful Elvis Presley-type clothes that had been the fashion then but weren't now.

At first I said I wouldn't do it. I said he was too ner-vous, that he wasn't a kiter. I said he'd bring it on top for me. But after a bit of gentle persuasion from Benny I agreed to do it – but only if Martin Blackburn signed the chequebooks himself. I wasn't going to commit myself because I was already on bail for fraud, and if I got arrested, for committing any sort of crime, I'd have been breaking my bail conditions and would have been sent straight to Holloway. I didn't want to go out with this Martin Blackburn, but I end up doing it; and off we went to Ealing for a day kiting.

The idea was that if we were in a shop and for whatever reason it came on top – if the shop assistant got suspicious and called the police – then if I got caught in the store I mustn't run. The story was that I was very young and that I'd met this older guy (Martin, who was close to fifty) in the pub and he'd promised to take me shopping and give me a good day out – *I'm just a tart, I met this old geezer, and he said he'd take me out* . . . And even if the police didn't believe it, let them prove it. I had a lot of difficulty with that from the off; as much as I disliked the police, I still didn't want to sit in front of them and let them think I was a brass – 'cause I wasn't.

We got clothes and household stuff – kettle, stereo, television, things like that. We'd hired a suite at the Hilton and we literally just went back and forth with the goodies (though obviously the big stuff, like the television, we dropped off at one of Benny's warehouses). So we had a pretty good day. Martin had seen these big round rugs in Marks & Spencer for £49.99, and he said, 'Oh, I'll have one of them'; I told him they were rubbish, not to bother – fifty quid was a lot of money then, and they were shit. Later, in another M&S in another part of Ealing, he saw the same rugs and decided he was going to get one. He wanted it, and so – fair enough – he was going to sign the book.

So Martin Blackburn's about to buy the rug, and I'd already explained to him that when you're in a shop and you think no one can see you, they *can* see you because there's a camera up there. And if you're giving it all that out the side of your mouth, or twitching, looking round, those cameras are picking it up; there's someone in a room watching this. I told him before we went to work that if it got iffy he shouldn't talk out the side of his mouth, he should just talk naturally at the counter. He was a burglar – that's what he did – and I was a fraudster, so I knew about these things and I thought it was fair enough to tell him. But I reckon because I was so young he thought I was just being cocky; he couldn't accept someone my age – especially a woman (he didn't like women very much) – telling him what to do, and he didn't like it that I knew the game. But for me it was *my* game and I was very good at it – and I didn't want to go to jail.

Anyway, we're at the counter, Martin and myself, buying the rug, and the girl's rolled it up, no problem, no suspicion. (Benny's hovering in the background so that if it comes on top he can cause a diversion, but he won't get arrested in any way, shape or form – it's nothing to do with Benny.) Martin asks the assistant if he can pay by cheque – yeah, no problem – and he's just writing the cheque when she points out the price; and for some reason these rugs are three quid dearer in this M&S than they were in the other one. And of course we can't write a cheque for more than £50 without a cheque-guarantee card or a quick phone call to the bank. Now, realistically you wouldn't give two hoots how much dearer it was if you weren't paying for it anyway, but Martin goes, 'No, no, in the Marks & Spencer down the road they're only £49.99.' The assistant goes away to make an enquiry and I'm sort of saying to him, 'Look, Martin, does it fucking matter? Why are you making such a disturbance in the shop – we're getting away with it anyway. Let's get out of here.'

'It's not the cost,' he says, 'it's a matter of fucking principle . . .'

And I'm thinking, *Is this geezer on the same planet as me? We're out thieving. He's just finished doing ten years.* So we start arguing, and all of a sudden he's throwing a wobbler in the shop.

This was summertime; it was warm, and I had wedge-heeled sandals on – the kind where one toe pokes through, not exactly shoes for running or fighting. And I remember saying to him, 'Martin, I think you're going to bring it on top for us.' I could see Benny in the background, and he was like, *What's going on?* but of course I couldn't be seen on the cameras looking at him.

Martin Blackburn was throwing such a wobbler at the counter that even the staff clocked how ridiculous it looked. The assistant obviously got suspicious and must have contacted whoever upstairs, and you could just sense they were coming towards us – security staff or whatever. I can remember Martin pushing me on to the girl at the counter and running off, and Benny running in another direction. I'm thinking, *Yeah, very nice. So basically neither Benny nor Martin Blackburn have done anything to get me out of this situation.* Admittedly I wasn't signing the books – but I was on bail so who was going to buy this story that I met this old guy in the pub? It would have been some silly jury that didn't suss I was involved in this little lot.

The long and short of it was that I got away. There was a terrible struggle in the shop; I jumped out of my shoes and lost my top. Next thing I knew I was running down Uxbridge Road towards Ealing Broadway in my bra and trousers. I knew the area like the back of my hand, so I knew where I was running to. Then all of a sudden I realised I'd overtaken Martin Blackburn (I can't see Benny), and I turned round to find the Old Bill chasing us. Then Martin overtook *me*. Then I'm running through traffic, jumping over cars trying to get away from the Old Bill. I mean, I don't want to get caught; I really do not want to get caught.

I got away from the police, for the moment at least, and for some unknown reason Martin was running in the same direction as me – but it was every man for himself. I ran past Martin again, but as I did so he turned round and pushed me into the police. At this stage I didn't struggle: I was nicked and I didn't need to be nicked for violent conduct. Really, I couldn't get my head round what had just happened. But in my heart I was thinking, *This guy just pushed me. I'm working with this guy and he just pushed me!*

I wondered how I was going to go home and tell Benny this. I reckoned he just wouldn't believe it, 'cause he thought Martin Blackburn was like, staunch and everything – after all, Benny had known me for only about eighteen months; he'd been in the same prison as Blackburn for several years.

Anyway, both of us were arrested and taken to Ealing Police Station. I didn't know it at the time but Martin Blackburn was on licence. Round about then, in the early eighties, the IRA were at their peak and there'd been some big decision made (it was announced on television) that if you had any sheds or garages or warehouses you were renting out you should check them out – you know, it could be the IRA renting them from you. And Martin Blackburn basically said to the police that if they let him out of this little lot he'd tell them where there was a warehouse full of stolen antiques. From the police's point of view, whoever owned the antiques was a much bigger fish than us doing our kiting. So Blackburn struck up a deal for himself with the police.

• • •

Benny was always so calm. I don't think I ever saw him cause trouble with anyone in all the years I was with him. He was shrewd and funny and was under no illusions that he would ever win a Mr World contest, but he was as slippery as an eel. If you met him you wouldn't have thought he'd spent one day behind bars. He hated talking about crime, and he wasn't interested in people's lives or their business – as long as they didn't nonce their kids or beat their wives. He'd rather look at an antiques book or a bit of gold than a porno movie or a naked bird. And he was loyal to his own. He would go to the other side of the world to help out a friend if they were in trouble. But if he was crossed, he was as dangerous as bad can be.

When Martin Blackburn crossed him, Benny actually cried before he went to look for him. I'd never seen a man cry before. My dad had had the occasional crocodile tear in his eyes when he was pissed and mumbling about Ireland, but with him it was only drink talk, all part of the act. With my Benny it was real. He'd looked out for Blackburn all those years in prison, so obviously they'd become good mates. Then we'd taken care of him when he got out, and how did the slag repay us?

He screwed me on a bit of work and then he grassed me and Benny to the Old Bill – that's how. They might've wanted their big fish, but they still carted me straight off to prison with no bail. I never made a statement, I never spoke; I refused to say anything. I was charged with fraud, deception and conspiracy. Benny wasn't charged – not for that job, anyway.

The warehouse full of allegedly stolen gear was worth about £1 million at the time. Of course Benny was angry about losing it. But I think he was angrier that we'd helped this bloke and he'd gone and done a right bad deed to us. Yes: Martin Blackburn had to pay; he knew the rules, he'd done enough bird. But Benny couldn't find him anywhere. Well, he wouldn't, would he – the Old Bill had put him on a one-way plane out of the country. And Benny copped four years; luckily for him, he only did ten months in the end, after winning his appeal.

CHAPTER TWENTY-THREE

The Muppet Wing

I was on remand in Holloway for eleven months. I don't know if it's changed since, but in those days the law said you had to go before the court within a year and a day of being charged. Obviously I was getting a bit pissed off. I couldn't believe I was on remand for so long – it wasn't the crime of the century, like I'd done a murder; it was only money, really, only fraud, not messing with people's lives. Benny made some enquiries and eventually I got word from the solicitor that my court appearance would be coming up within a few weeks.

I was in the cell with this young girl – she was a prostitute and a druggy – called Jane. And me and her, we've got our cell quite sorted – we're clean and tidy, we've got our Nescafé, we've got this, we've got that. She used to puff weed every night. She was so young and I felt sorry for her; and because I hadn't mixed with drug addicts on the outside I wasn't aware of how sleazy they can be, how they can lie and you'll believe them – I didn't know about that. I just knew she was on drugs, and to me it was like, *So what?*

I'd listened to this girl's story and taken her under my

wing. I was very good to her, gave her clothes and just generally looked after her. I had everything I wanted in prison, and I shared it with the right people; she wasn't doing me any favours, she wasn't cleaning my cell or anything, I was just looking out for her.

So anyway, when we heard that my hearing was coming up, Benny said, 'Right, what do you want to wear going to court?' He brought me various rig-outs and told me I had to choose how I wanted to look for the court, because I wasn't sure which way to play the judge – whether to go looking like a dollybird or a secretary. In the end I decided that I'd go formal: white blouse, black suit, flat shoes. I had a pair of Churchill brogues – you had to get your foot measured for them, but these shoes would last you twenty years. And then I had a pair of Gucci shoes, and I don't mean to be flash but the girls in Holloway didn't have Gucci shoes. I remember this little bird, Jane, making comments: 'Oh, aren't they lovely! Oh fuckin' hell, I wish I had a pair like them,' and I said to her, 'Look, when I go to court I'll leave them for ya,' and I meant it. My idea was when I went up there I'd leave all my clothes behind, because it's what you do. You don't want to wear those clothes again once you've worn them in the nick. This is what I thought was right: whatever you've got – your radio, clothes, whatever – you leave for other prisoners and you go out with a clean slate.

The next Sunday afternoon we were all down in the exercise yard for a bit of fresh air. In Holloway it's a big square with gravel paths and grass verges. I used to stand there and think, *How am I going to get up that wall?*, because it looked so easy to break out. I'm not saying I would have broken out; it was just silly thoughts on the spur of the moment. I wasn't doing long enough to warrant breaking out, for a start – I just fancied a bunk-up round the corner, then I'd get caught and brought back.

Anyway, my eyes were very bad and I didn't have my glasses on, but I could see this little one – the drug addict – way over there, sitting on a bench. She had this little posse around her, and she was giving it all that with her legs. I couldn't see what was happening, and I remember I started walking slowly over there to have a nosey. It didn't look like there was any problem. As I got nearer I wasn't looking at her, I was looking down at what was on her feet. I knew she could see me coming. I was looking down and getting closer and closer, and the girl had my shoes on. I didn't have to ask anybody – they were *my* shoes. They were from Gucci and they were mine and I knew they were mine because nobody else had a pair. They were brand new – they hadn't even been worn – and there was this dirty fucking slag wearing them.

That was bad enough, but probably wasn't all that bad. What was bad was that I had trusted her and I'd been good to her. Did this little punk think she was going to get the better of me? Even though I wasn't much older than her, compared to her I felt about fifty; and I'd already been in jail, so I knew the score. *Nah, I ain't having that, no way.* I was getting up a bit closer, but with her she had this butch who used to protect her, called John, or that was her prison name at any rate. She was a hermaphrodite, so was built a lot bigger than any of us, and she was very close with the druggy.

John was in for murder – had killed someone at King's Cross – a sleazy murder, for fags or whatever, I don't really know. She fancied this little one, Jane, and this little one now saw me coming towards her, and I could see she was telling the butch I was getting near. So I started going into a pace to go and kick this Jane straight in the head – there were no questions to be asked; she nicked my shoes, she knew what I was like, so she had to pay the price, simple as that. I was running like, a hundred miles an hour, and as I went up to kick her, this fucking butch came from nowhere and did me in the back. And she had Doc Martens on!

There was this other woman standing there who I got on well with. When we'd first come across each other we'd nearly had a fight – and thank God we didn't, because she was one of the hardest women in the nick. But I'd stood up to her and she'd realised I wasn't frightened of her because if she hurt me she'd have got done from the outside anyway. I'd told her that if she ever came near me her family would get killed, so end of – fuck off! So then we became great friends, which was handy, and she watched my back.

So John winded me and I went down. As fast as I went down, my pride wouldn't allow me to stay down, so when I saw her boot coming right at me, over my face, I grabbed her leg and twisted it over. Then the other woman was on her and it just went off. It was just off, off, off!

The girl who had my shoes, Jane, she had long hair, and she was screaming and crying because I had her by the hair and was smashing her head on the bench. I wanted to break her nose. I kept smashing her head; smashing it . . . I'll admit, a lot of the problem was tension – we hadn't been out, cooped up all day – but that's not really why I was doing it. It was because I was good to her: she'd robbed me, and you just don't do it, you don't rob from your own. *If I get six months for this, I'll do the six months . . .*

Now there's this all-for-all going on, and because I was so popular in the nick it was like everyone was sticking up for me, wanting me to win. And I was winning. But the next thing I knew, the screws had me down and they were really hurting me. Then I was in such a situation, fighting with the screws, that I had my mouth on a screw's tit – right on her breast, over her clothes – and I remember saying, 'If you don't let me up I'm going to take your fuckin' nipple off. Let me up!' We're all covered in blood, claret everywhere. One minute, this Jane bird's on the floor, unconscious, the next, I've bit the screw. You don't think of the consequences at the time; you're just in there, you're on your own, you've got to stick up for yourself – because if you don't do something, someone else is going to do it to you.

I remember it tasted all salty in my mouth, and then I saw the blood so I knew I'd done her damage. She'd passed out – the screw passed out.

By this stage they'd called in the men. (If they can't control the women prisoners they'll call in men, with truncheons and this and that.) There was a hard core of about six of us left in the yard. All the other prisoners had gone or been taken inside now. But my mate – she was so strong, Jesus she was strong – the screws couldn't control her, they couldn't get her up, they couldn't get her down. They didn't take any prisoners that day, they gave as good as they got. I was covered in blood, head to toe; wherever I had a hole there was blood coming out of it.

The next thing I knew, I was lying on the floor and they'd got my hands pulled one way and my legs pulled another, and they'd got me in a head-lock. Everybody was inside now; the last prisoner in the yard was me. I don't know how (I think I was semi-conscious) but I got away – I was up and running, just running all over the fucking yard. I didn't know what I was doing, what I was trying to do. They couldn't catch me at first, it was cat-and-mouse, and my adrenaline was pumping; for a while I just thought it was very funny, and then they got me. And when they got me, oh God.

All the other prisoners were at their windows, going berserk, screaming and shouting: '*They're killing a prisoner in 'ere, they're killing a prisoner in 'ere!*'

All I remember after that is this door opening and a pain in one of my legs. I don't even remember what leg it was, but the pain was awful.

That's how I ended up on the Muppet Wing. C5, it was called in the prison, the wing where psychiatric cases were taken. They would say they put me there because I was insane. But I wasn't insane, I was very aware of what was going on around me. I just had a bad temper.

• • •

When I woke up I was in a straitjacket. My legs were free but the top half of my body wasn't. And I remember just sitting there, off my nut on some gear that they must have given me to calm me down.

Although I was injured a lot, and I knew I'd have some bruises and some marks, there were no broken bones, nothing like that. But when I woke up, in that straitjacket, oh my God, my head was out to here like a football.

Strangely enough, I didn't feel the pain. Not because I was gone on their medication. It's like I've got this great ability to switch off – somebody can be kicking the shit out of me, and I'm feeling the blows but I'm not *really* feeling them. It's happening but I'm not feeling it. I'm somewhere else.

So I knew that I was injured, but I also knew that something else was wrong, and I remember thinking, *How big is my face?* I couldn't move, I couldn't feel anything yet, but my face was huge.

I'd just had a visit, three days before, so I wasn't due a visit for another eight or nine days. You didn't make outside phone calls, so no one was going to know what'd happened to me until Benny next showed up. I don't remember how many days I was kept there in isolation – two or three, maybe. I was in and out of consciousness, and I remember them coming in and saying that the officer I'd assaulted was in hospital. They told me she was in a serious way and that if anything happened to her I'd be charged. In other words, I wasn't getting out of there.

Eventually they came in and undressed me. I was really weak and floppy. And all of a sudden the whole atmosphere had changed. 'Are you OK?' they were asking. 'Do you want anything? Do you want a bath? No, we won't come in; we'll fill the bath up, we'll shut the door . . .' But I had to have help to get into the tub. They actually did bath me in the end, and one of the screws said to me, 'Where on earth did you learn to fight like that? Nobody's ever fought like that. What did you take?'

I didn't take anything; it was just in my mind to go that way.

I was still in punishment but in a different part of punishment now. I had a chair and a table and a bed (all screwed down), but no inside toilet. I had a pot. It was six days after the incident when they came in and said to me I had a visit. They asked if I wanted to go on the hospital wing – meaning, to be in bed – for it. I said, 'I think you know the answer to that – I want to go on the fucking visit. End of.'

They told me I was Category A now. I'd be on a closed visit, behind the glass.

I didn't care and I was taken down. There was a lot of activity, screws everywhere, and because Benny had spent twenty-eight years in the nick he knew there was something wrong. He didn't know what had happened to me, and he was shitting himself. I still hadn't seen what I looked like, because I hadn't seen a mirror or anything, but I was aware that my head and my jaw were just huge. I remember Benny sitting there on the visit. He was sat there . . . and he just looked. And I remember him putting his hands on the glass. I was more worried that I was going to get told off, that he'd have a go at me for whatever, and I wouldn't give him eye contact. Also I was very dopey – he could tell straight away I was off my nut on some medication – and basically he went fucking berserk.

He didn't even stay for the visit. He got straight up and said, 'I'm dealing with this.'

He thought I'd been unnecessarily over-medicated. He didn't even speak to the prison authorities, he just phoned his solicitor and got through to the Home Office. That was a Saturday. He then sent in an outside doctor (the authorities can't stop you doing that) so they now knew my injuries were terrible. They *were* bad injuries, but then you recover – it was only a clump. But by the Monday, they'd called me up and the deal was this: the officer was in hospital with a serious injury to her breast. She was hurt but she'd recover. The prison authorities wouldn't charge me for it and I wouldn't charge the prison for what they did to me – the unauthorised medication.

Obviously Benny was a lot older than me, a lot wiser and he had a lot more contacts, knew what to do. By Tuesday I was out. Up in court, got bail, out. I'd served eleven months and three weeks. Shame he couldn't have done it a bit earlier.

CHAPTER TWENTY-FOUR

Second Time Around

I'd just come out of prison when I got married for the second time, on 8 June 1982. Two weeks later I was given thirty months, less the eleven or twelve months I'd served on remand.

We were married at Acton Register Office, and had a reception afterwards in a Greek restaurant. Benny was loaded, only I didn't know what he was worth – and to be honest, I didn't care. I had my own money, my own car, a wardrobe of clothes any other girl would kill for, and I was very proud I never had to ask a man for money.

I'd already decided that I wasn't going to use any dodgy credit cards when I was buying my clothes for the wedding. I'm very superstitious and didn't want to wear anything that was knocked off – not by me or anyone else. I went out, two or three days before my wedding, and I had about five and a half grand in my pocket. The trouble was, I'd put on nearly two stone. Benny used to bring me roast dinners and puddings during the time I was on remand, and because I'd damaged a bone in my back I couldn't do any exercise, so basically I sat on my bed all day getting bloated. By the time I got out, I'd gone from a size 10 to a 14–16 and I was really paranoid about my weight.

My hair was long, a sort of brown colour with no blonde at all, and I hated it. It'd not been its natural colour for at least ten years and I'd actually forgotten it was so dark.

I ended up with a navy-blue dress with a grey pinstripe, a little white Peter Pan collar and a white petticoat that was meant to hang two inches below the dress, down to my shins. The dress was fitted at the waist and flared out; I don't know why I bought it – I guess I was just panicking – because anyone who knows about fashion knows that if you're overweight you don't wear flared dresses. Needless to say I looked and felt like a right cunt. I hated face make-up such as foundation – I was twenty-five with a good complexion and only ever wore stuff on my eyes and lips – but it was my wedding day, so I decided to give it a go. I ended up looking like a right wally and felt like one of the Waltons going to Sunday church.

The weather was so hot – I think London was having a heatwave at the time – and when I got to the register office all this shit on my face started to run down my cheeks, and I really did look a state. When I get to the reception, every-one kept saying how lovely and beautiful I looked, and I thought, *You lying bastards.*

I've ripped up most of my wedding pictures because I hated how I looked.

• • •

Even before I met Benny, instead of going clubbing most nights, like some women I knew, I used to thieve every night and save up my money. I wanted to buy a house and furnish it so the authorities would give Debbie back to me. They never did, but it still didn't stop me thieving. On the odd occasion I did go for a drink with my mates, I could never relax. I never saw the sense of getting all dollied up, going out with the girls, because at that age it seems obvious that you're out on the pull. But I wasn't. I just used to keep slipping away to do a bit of work and then I'd come back to the pub again, by which time everyone would be pissed and would've pulled their bit of cock for the night, then they'd go home and think they'd had a great night. It never ceases to amaze me how women, young or old, married or single, just go out with a bloke because he's got money. As long as they get their drinks paid for and a meal at the end of it they'll open their legs.

I'd go home alone and sit up all night with the gear I'd nicked. Yet no one ever really knew what I was up to and they knew better than to ask. The way I looked at it was I didn't ask people their business so they didn't need to be asking me mine.

People have this idea that criminals only mix with criminals and straight people only mix with straight people. That's such a lot of shit. There's no such thing as an underworld or a criminal's world. We're just people. Some of us choose to go one way; some choose another. Some of us become armed robbers or tie-up merchants or drug dealers or diamond thieves . . . The list of what you can be is endless. But ultimately we're only people and we're all going to die sooner or later – it could be cancer, it could be murder, it could be a crack overdose, it doesn't matter. The only thing that's true is that we all die.

For people like me, who want to be a villain or a gangster or a thief, we know for a start that there are no written rules. But once you choose that way of life, you do live by a certain standard whereby words like loyalty, respect and honour mean something. Partly you learn to look out for each other. If you're on a bit of work and it comes on top, you don't run away and leave your mates behind. You try to help them. If it comes to a fight, you've got to be prepared to stand and fight. At least you'll have tried to help your mate.

I've been rich and I've been poor. I've had £60,000 Cartier watches and then I've had nothing. But I've never sold out. In this entire country there's not a policeman who can say they've ever given me money for information. Fuck that. Whatever holes I've dug myself into I've dug myself out of again. I've known a few OK policemen; and if I saw them in a pub and I wanted to talk to them, I did. But not about grassing other criminals – I'd talk to them about me, and my business and a bit of trouble I might be in. And if the copper could stop me going to jail, then I'd give him a nice diamond or some money to go on holiday. Fucking right. They use us and we use them; that's what makes the world go round. Those people who think that all policemen are straight are very silly.

There's only one world; we're just all living our lives in different ways. Some criminals get caught, some don't. But whatever your chosen path, you accept it: the good times and the bad times. You just learn as you go along. By making plenty of mistakes, you learn – and I will always accept responsibility for my fuck-ups.

I remember when I went back into Holloway to serve my sentence, loads of the women would be crying or trying other ways to get attention. They'd set light to their cells, they'd mutilate their bodies with knitting needles, they'd cut their wrists – they'd do anything to get someone to come and unlock their cell door, just so they might get taken to an outside hospital and have a chance of running away. I could never understand all this, because if you want to act all tough and hard out on the street, and if you want to be all dolled up in designer gear and you decide that the only way to get what you want is to commit crime, you know what you're doing. When I committed crimes, when I was using stolen credit cards to lead a lavish lifestyle, I didn't give a fuck. I knew if I got caught and went to jail, I'd accept it without tears or regrets. I also knew I'd probably come straight out of jail and carry on committing crimes. Jail can't change you. Only you can change you – and I didn't want to change. I enjoyed the lifestyle I had, and as long as I wasn't hurting anybody I wasn't going to stop. But if I ever found myself crying because I was in jail or in a police cell, I think I'd have had to go straight.

Women become fucking strange when they're in the nick. They arse-lick the screws – like that's going to get them out any quicker! They like to start fights, but when it kicks off they start screaming. I saw so much sexual abuse going on in prison between women, the ones who had the most power would dominate the others. And most of them don't stop talking about sex. I'd much rather have served my sentence in a men's prison. At least I could have talked about football and boxing with blokes, and they wouldn't be screaming and crying like most women do.

CHAPTER TWENTY-FIVE

The High Life

My marriage to Benny Hannington was supposedly what the eighties were all about. Fast cars, fast living, Michael Jackson at the top of the charts, *Dallas* and *Dynasty* on the TV – I loved the glamour of that period. We didn't need outsiders. Benny was always in control of everything. He controlled me right through those years, though I didn't know it at the time. It wasn't in a violent manner – Benny didn't have to be violent; he could be controlling with his mind.

We had a home that was like a palace to whoever came there. Boisie had every room expertly decorated with Victorian and Edwardian gear, art deco, art nouveau. I used to think it was funny that our flat in Hornsey Road only cost £27,110 from the council, yet we had about one million pounds' worth of gear in there. We never had a floor safe or an alarm or even a panic button – just grilles on all the doors, window locks and an army of weapons hidden around the flat. Had anyone got in, they sure as hell wouldn't have got out in one piece.

I'd have lavish dinner parties for my friends and I'd

182

spend hours cooking roast dinners. We had a wide circle of friends. They weren't all criminals. They weren't all straight. Some of them were very rich but many of them were poor. It didn't matter to me; I just liked people and the fact that I was living this fast life, full of wealth, cars and money, flying around the world. I was still the same person inside. I never thought I was better than anyone else. I was just scatty Joan who only talked about football and boxing.

I don't even know how much money Benny and I had. Probably we had millions – several millions – going through our hands. That's not a lot of money in this day and age, nothing on the drug deal. But in the eighties we were among those early criminals to be in the millionaire league without getting it over the pavement (i.e., doing an armed robbery of a bank, or hijacking a security van).

I remember I used to walk round looking like a Christmas tree, with diamonds on every finger, head to toe in gold, wearing designer clothes and fur coats. Not just for vanity or 'cause I loved it (which I did); there was another reason. Say six months later Benny got nicked and the police got all our money – having mink coats and diamonds was always handy because you could sell them and keep going till you sorted yourself out. It never troubled me to do this. These things can always be got hold of again. I mean, it doesn't make sense to me to have mink coats but no food in the cupboards. Often women get given something and don't ever want to part with it. But as far as I'm concerned, you should be loyal to the man; and when he's in trouble and needs the ring off your finger, or tells you the BMW's gotta go, then that's the way it is. If you respect your husband then that's the way it is. I guess I've lost a lot in my time by sticking by my husband, but I liked him more than anything he could ever give me.

I was totally wrapped up in my world of crime and the high life. Every day was different. We never booked holidays, we just got up some days and Benny would say, 'What do you want to do today?' and I'd tell him I wanted to go to Miami, or New York or Spain. It didn't matter where – he'd just send me down the road to buy the tickets and by lunchtime we'd be all packed and on our way to the airport with £20,000 in cash in our pockets and not a care in the world. And we wouldn't come home till we'd spent all the money (which never took me long).

I remember one time in the early eighties we went to Spain because it was the eighteenth birthday of one of Benny's friends' daughters and we'd been invited to the party. We were only going for one week and I took seven suitcases of clothes. Benny went off his nut when I came down the stairs with all these cases: 'I'm not fucking carrying seven fucking cases. We're going out to the sun. You don't need lots of clothes, you stupid cunt!'

Funny, I'm not a stupid cunt when I'm running over rooftops or swallowing diamonds or helping him carry big lumps of furniture through back gardens after midnight. No, I'm 22-carat then . . .

I used to go to the hairdressers every day to get my hair and nails done. Once again I had long blonde hair – peroxide blonde. And I recall I once fancied a change of image. (I kept a certain image for myself; for work purposes I would change my image as often as most people change their socks.) Walking down King's Road in Chelsea I saw these punk rockers, and one of them had pink hair. For me this was not unusual – I'd had pink hair myself in the seventies – but it seemed more generally acceptable in the eighties. So off I went to Toni and Guy in Sloane Square, and I told this bloke there to dye my hair pink on one side and emerald green on the other. Then I got him to cut it short and spike it up. I came out of this shop thinking I looked the bollocks (God, I must have looked a right pillock), went over to Harvey Nicks in Knightsbridge and bought a pair of leather jeans and Jean Paul Gaultier T-shirt. I paid about £1,400 for the trousers and £250 for the T-shirt. Back home I got a razor and slashed the trousers until they were hanging off me. I had a pair of Doc Martens, silver, and I stuck gold sovereign coins all over these boots with superglue. In the trade at the time sovereigns were about £50 each and I had eight on each boot, which would have come to £800 – and the boots only cost a pony (£25). I wasn't so much in the fashion of the times as I was creating my own fashion, because I hated looking like everyone else. I wanted to be different. Well, I was definitely fucking different that day.

But, as with most of my five-minute fashion wonders, Mr Hannington was *not* amused. I was supposed to pick him up from his shop at Old Mill Street in Stamford Hill. Benny was standing outside talking to a couple of punters. He saw me pulling up in the BMW and began to walk towards the car, smiling (Benny always looked like he was pleased to see you even if he only saw you the day before). I got out and he looked me up and down. I think he went into shock. He stood there, as stiff as you like, with his gob open and just stared at me. Of course, I always giggle when I'm nervous and this time I could feel the giggles coming on bad – the fact that he wasn't saying anything was making me very nervous – when all of a sudden he just exploded. I'd never seen him lose his temper before then, not towards me at any rate. He started raving at me: 'You on fucking drugs or what? You are definitely on drugs. Now get home, wash that shit off your face and take that stupid fucking candyfloss off your head!'

I told him it wasn't a wig, it was my hair, and he just didn't believe me. He reached out his hand and grabbed my hair, pulling it really hard. I don't think he wanted to hurt me, I think he just wanted to prove himself right. By now I'd broken into hysterical laughter. When he realised it really *wasn't* a wig, he just backed off, stood there staring at me again. 'If you think you're working in the shop like that,' he said quietly, 'you can dream on. I'm a business-man; I can't have my punters looking at you. You're a fucking nutcase.'

• • •

We were people who didn't keep a lot of money in the bank. Benny was registered, he was in business, but he always said there was no point in having money in the bank, especially for the likes of us who couldn't prove where it came from. Instead we had deed boxes at Barclays and in Mayfair; in those days you could have a deed box for £28 a year. Say you've got a hundred thousand pounds. You don't want the cash, that's no good to you, because you can't put it in the bank and get interest. You've got to go out and buy something that's going to be worth a lot more in a year or two. So we'd buy big – a big diamond. I had rocks hidden away for a rainy day. I'd buy good watches, Rolex and Omega, items you knew in years to come would be worth bundles as long as they were in mint condition.

Also you had to have something on the walls, some-thing that you could take off the wall and sell at any time – that's what it's there for: to sell. In the house we had some good paintings, including a Joshua Reynolds and a Matisse, a couple of pieces of Chippendale, tapestries, signed bronzes. We were living with all this stuff but the beauty of it was that it was worth money. To be honest it was like living in a museum and I hated it, hated antiques, but at the end of the day it didn't matter because I was brought up not to believe in banks and insurance and all that.

It didn't ever please me to see lots of money in the bank.

Looking back I can make a joke about ironing the money because obviously it seems funny – only it wasn't; it was Benny's obsessive nature. Say he'd gone and sold something and we'd got a lump of cash – it could be five grand, it could be twenty, a hundred – he'd bring it home, tip it all out from a bag on to the floor. 'Just iron that, babe,' he'd say.

Oh here we go, I'd think, but I'd know what I'd got to do. Sounds like a joke but it's not so funny when it's you standing there fucking ironing it.

I'd have to sort it all out then – separate the tens and the twenties and the fifties – and Benny always said to make sure there was steam in the iron so I'd get the creases out. It had to be crisp; he loved crisp money. What a wanker. I like money too – but money's money, mate. Ironed, wrinkled, dirty, money's still money. And our money was always dirty. Still, I'd do as I was told and he'd put it in shoeboxes and 'file' it under our bed. We had an antique bed, it was very high up, like the old beds used to be, and underneath it we must have had about fifty shoeboxes, some of them with twenties in, some with tens, fifties. And when we needed money we just went to what I called the filing cabinet, under the bed.

I never argued back. Except the time when we had a big lump in cash and he wanted me to iron every single note and file it in order, by serial number. That's where I drew the line.

• • •

My husband came home from work one day and told me to get ready, we were going to meet a German man in the St James's Hotel in Mayfair. I got the hump about this. When I was growing up, there was still a lot of resentment towards German people because of the war and as children, we were taught to dislike them. So I was apprehensive to meet this man, but as it turned out we got on really well. Benny said I had to put on my best English accent because this was right important business and we'd earn a fortune. He wouldn't go into detail; he just said I'd to listen to everything that was said at this meeting and mustn't interrupt.

I knew the St James's Hotel – Benny and I used to go to dinner there quite often. So I got myself ready and off we went. On the way, Benny told me that these two men were in England on behalf of a prominent German family who wanted to sell some jewellery. It belonged to one of the wives, and the family didn't want it to be public knowledge that they were having money worries. Also they didn't want the German or British press to get hold of this information.

We got to the hotel and met a man, his name was Heinz, said he was the wife's personal secretary. We were all at the bar, just engaged in idle gossip until our table was ready. My first impression of Heinz was that he was a raving homosexual, but he was a nice bloke.

I remember that as we all went into the restaurant and sat down at the table Heinz asked Benny if he could please sit next to me because he thought I was very funny. I didn't mind – he was quite a laugh too. I think he knew that I'd sussed out he was a queen and he realised it didn't trouble me. I must admit I was a bit shocked at what we were being told about the family and their financial situation. Benny and I thought it was some kind of wind-up or fit-up to do with the police. This bloke Heinz, although very nice, was also a bag of nerves and kept looking round the restaurant to see if anyone was watching us, but no one was.

Then he pulled this brown envelope out of his brief-case and handed it to Benny, and asked him if he could give him some idea of the value of the jewellery shown in the photos inside. Benny said that would be impossible, he'd need to have it in his hand in order to value it. Then the bloke said it would be impossible to bring it through Heathrow airport without customs seeing it, and that it could cause a right scandal if anyone discovered who the stuff actually belonged to. Benny then asked Heinz why he hadn't tried to sell it in Germany. At this Heinz got very angry and told Benny, 'I came to you because I heard you could help me.' Benny went white. He stood up and called a waiter over and asked for the bill, then leaned over and said to Heinz, 'You're in my fucking country now and you'd better learn to be a bit more polite if you want some-one's help.'

Benny threw about £300 on the table to pay for the meal, even though none of us had eaten anything much – I think we'd only had the starters. However, I could see that my husband was really angry so I thought I'd better not open my mouth. As we got up to leave, Heinz held his hand out to shake Benny's hand. He told Benny that he was sorry if he upset him, he just had to be very careful who he dealt with. Benny quietly told him that *we* had to be careful who *we* did business with. I knew that Benny at this stage felt that this Heinz bloke wasn't telling him the truth, and that he thought maybe the jewellery was stolen.

Anyway, things calmed down a bit. Benny and Heinz made peace again and we all sat back down at the table and carried on with our meal.

During the meal and a few glasses of red wine later, Heinz was a bit pissed. We were also drinking but we weren't drunk. Afterwards we all went up to Heinz's room and ordered some more drinks. Heinz told Benny that if we bought the jewellery and there were no problems over it, the family might also consider doing a deal for a castle and some land they had to sell. I remember thinking, *Is this bloke for real? One minute we're talking about jewellery, now all of a sudden he's talking about castles and land in Germany. What do we want with a fucking castle?*

But my Benny, who by this stage was also well on the way to being pissed, was getting deeper and deeper into conversation about jewellery and land and castles, and all I wanted to do was go home and have a joint. Six hours of listening to a German accent was sending me off my nut. I think we eventually left Heinz in the early hours of the morning, him promising that he'd phone us at home first thing the next day. He did. He wanted us to meet him later that evening, but Benny told him he had prior engage-ments for the next two days. He didn't really; he just wanted this bloke to sweat a bit. From Benny's point of view, this guy needed us, we didn't need him, and the longer Benny held out, the cheaper he'd get the jewellery for. I never usually questioned Benny's business dealings, but I did ask him if he was really interested in the castle or the land in Germany. He said no – but pointed out that Heinz didn't have to know that; if Heinz thought we were interested in the land or castle, he'd bend over backwards to do a deal with the jewellery.

Not long after our first meeting with Heinz, I went with Benny and a couple of other people to Germany to look at and buy this jewellery. We went to Munich, a right cold place where everyone looked miserable. It wasn't a very friendly country and I found the people a bit standoff-ish. Heinz took us to some restaurant and all through the meal he kept saying that Hitler had dined in the same restaurant, and its claim to fame was that Hitler had walked out without paying the bill. I think this story just about summed up the Germans to me at the time, though of course my mind has been changed since. All I wanted was to do our business and go home.

We got our deal on the jewellery. We bought diamonds, tiaras, brooches, rings – loads of stuff. I had to wear a load of it on the way home on the plane, like it was my own personal property. That way I wouldn't have to pay tax on it. I kept thinking, *If I do get stopped, how will I explain why I'm wearing £2 million worth of jewellery that's not insured?* But I guess when I was younger I was without fear, so I put a lot of it on anyway.

It did cross my mind that this Heinz bloke might try to pull a stroke, so we came to an agreement whereby I wore some of the jewellery home, another guy who'd put part of the money up drove to Munich and took some of it back to Italy, and a lot of it was to finally end up with a third buyer from America. But the money was not going to be handed over until I was back in London. That way it wouldn't have been to the Germans' advantage to pull a stroke at the last minute. Heinz wasn't too happy about this, but as far as I was concerned it was the only way I would go through the airport wearing jewellery worth £2 million. Also, Benny made Heinz sign receipts that described the details of every article we'd bought, and – without telling Heinz – posted these receipts back to London before we even left Munich, so that if I did get nicked at the airport we at least had proof of purchase.

Everything went very smoothly. I had all this jewellery on, but because the weather was so cold I also kept my mink coat on. I had a pair of mink gloves on, too, so no one saw the rings on my fingers. The only problem was that I had to put rings on my toes as well. These were 6-carat, 8-carat and 12-carat diamonds. They were all set in 18-carat gold or platinum, and when I finally got home to London my feet were killing me, those rings just dug into my toes. At home, Benny tried using olive oil to get the rings off, because by this time my toes had swollen up over the rings, but they wouldn't come off. I was in so much pain. Finally he got a small metal-cutter and got them off that way, which wasn't so bad because it was the diamonds that were worth the money. Gold is gold and it's no big deal. I didn't mind anyway: Benny bought me a couple of nice pieces and that put a smile on my face.

Plus I got a share of the profits once Benny and the other two men had sorted out the final figures, so I guess everyone was happy, especially Heinz. I think his job – whatever that was – was on the line if anything went wrong.

CHAPTER TWENTY-SIX

A Bit of Work

I'd worked in Benny's shops on and off over the years, but I was beginning to hate antiques. Everywhere I went I saw antique furniture, paintings, China. Even our house looked like a gallery. Benny developed this obsession with decorating the upstairs toilet. Every night he'd come in from work, have his dinner, roll a joint, pour a drink, take a bath, then lock himself in the toilet. He'd spend hours in there, sticking foreign postage stamps on the walls. He'd be all crouched up on a ledge, sticking them one by one, side by side, and I was convinced he'd lost his marbles.

Then, when he got bored with that, he'd come downstairs and start cleaning the China. He'd lift bits down, one by one, dust them, put them back. I'd be sitting there in total silence until I could bear it no longer and I'd jump up and say, 'Why don't you have a wank over them? I hate all this crap. Men don't dust things and stick stamps on the wall. It ain't normal. It's *boring.* I'm in my twenties and you're in your forties. I'm not ready to lock myself in the house with all this crap.'

'*Crap?*' he'd say. 'Your fucking mates would kill to have a home like yours, and all you do is moan.'

He was never physically aggressive (he was usually too stoned) but then he'd start lecturing me and pointing to a bit of China. 'Now this—this bit of *crap,* as you call it, Joan—is an early Victorian figure' (or statue of such-and-such a person made in such-and-such a year by such-and-such a company) 'and is worth about £500. This is *class.* We've got three thousand bits of China in our cabinets and they're all worth that much and more. And if you add up everything in all these cabinets you'll find a nice few grand . . .'

Like anyone else, I like to have a nice home, but you've got to be able to live in it and put your feet up without worrying whether you get a bit of dust on the Chippendale.

Bollocks, I'd think. *Get rid of the Chippendale. Get proper fucking chairs you can actually sit on.* Sometimes I'd win the argument and we'd sell the chairs, say, and I'd go up to Harrods and buy two big five-grand sofas or whatever. I'd hand over ten grand, feeling like this was the furniture normal people had. But when I'd got something new, Benny would come in from work and the first thing he'd say would be, 'How much this modern shit cost you?'

'Nothing,' I'd say, 'I swallowed them. And I'm going back next week for the coffee table,' and we'd both start laughing.

It was on one of these occasions when we'd been rowing about the furniture that I decided that I couldn't stand the boredom of my life and that if I didn't make a change, I'd crack up. We had shops and cars and everything we wanted but I was cracking up. There was nothing to tie me to the house (Benny junior wasn't born yet) and I had nothing to occupy this brain of mine; I just had to be *doing* something.

This was late July and I was working in one of my husband's shops in Camden Passage. I was on my own there, changing it around for the hundredth time; I guess that was the perfectionist in me, always putting things in order, always cleaning and dusting the China and crystal, the jewellery and paintings. Only I didn't use Jif any more! I'd been with Benny long enough by now to know only too well how to handle precious things, how not to clean paintings with Jif and not to use a scouring pad to clean fine China.

I had my reggae music on and didn't have a care in the world, but I wasn't happy. I wanted to be out on the street, sniffing about, seeing what was happening, seeing who was about, what the girls were wearing, what colours were in fashion. I'd think I was missing something if I didn't go on the streets or drive from one part of London to the other to see one of my mates. 'No particular reason, just popped in,' I'd say. Then off I'd go again until I'd find myself outside some posh jewellery shop, looking in the window to see what rings I fancied; I'd go in, do a number and in twenty-four hours I'd be a nice few grand in front. More ironing, though – because after all those years with Benny some of his bad habits were beginning to rub off on me, and ironing money was one of them. I'd already started storing it in shoeboxes under the bed, but to me it was just paper: if it ran out I'd go and nick some diamonds and get some more, no big thing.

Anyway, all these thoughts were going through my head on this day when the buzzer went and I got up to see what the customer looked like. There was a man outside in a pair of jeans with creases down the front and a white Fred Perry polo shirt. He was about six feet two inches tall with cropped blond hair: in a nutshell, a right nice bit of meat and two veg. As I got up to press the buzzer to let him in I got my foot caught on a nail sticking out of the bottom of the counter, and fell arse over tit. The bloke witnessed the whole thing and when I'd composed myself and let him in he had a right grin on his face. *That's all right,* I'm thinking, *you pretty mug, 'cause if you buy something I'll charge you over the top and when you walk out I'll be laughing at you.*

However, I smiled back at him and asked him if he was looking for anything in particular, and as cool as you like he said, 'I think I've just found what I'm looking for,' fixing his eyes on me. I didn't blush or anything, I just asked him again how I could help him. He could see I wasn't inter-ested whether he bought anything or not, and he'd sussed that his lovely body, muscly arms and pretty face weren't getting my attention. He then asked if I had any Rolex watches for men.

I say, 'No, mate, I'm not a jewellery shop. I sell antiques and China and some antique jewellery, but not Rolex watches.'

(I could have said, 'No, but my husband's got about a hundred Rolex and Cartier watches at home, buried all over the house—come back tomorrow and we'll have a trade.' I could have said that but I just couldn't be bothered.)

I was a bit on my guard. This bloke just didn't fit the picture of someone who would walk into an antiques shop in Camden Passage on a hot sunny day wearing jeans with a crease down the front. People in London didn't have a crease in their jeans any more; it was considered naff in the eighties. No, this bloke didn't fit the script, I'm afraid.

However, I let him carry on looking round. I didn't pick up any bad vibes from him, didn't feel I was in any danger. To me he was what we call a FTW (Fucking Time Waster), probably waiting to meet his girlfriend. Blokes who look like this one did usually have a million girlfriends, and I thought, *Good luck to him* . . . But then I thought, *Or maybe he's a kiter and he's taking his time before he asks if I take Amex or Visa, etc.?*

And of course this occurred to me because it was what I'd been doing a few years earlier, and I knew all the patter, all the chat-up lines, all the old bollocks. Usually I'd know when someone was going to come out with it even before they'd opened their mouths, 'cause I'd said it all before, heard it all before. But I'd moved on now and I swallowed diamonds and didn't have time to chat to people. I'd always be thinking about my next jewellery theft – even if it wasn't going to happen, I'd be thinking about it. So I was saying to myself, *This FTW is interrupting my quiet time, my thinking time, with his dodgy fucking jeans on* . . .

He then got my attention again by asking me the price of a silver knife in one of the cabinets. I told him it wasn't a knife as such, that it was for opening letters. It was about eighty quid or something so I told him it was one-and-a-half (£150). He took it in his hands, looked it up and down and asked me if it came with its original box. And when I told him yes, it did (liar), he pulled a wad of cash out of his back pocket and counted out the £150 on to the glass counter – all new money. I must admit I felt a bit guilty then, and as I was wrapping it up I said to myself, *You can't cheat him just 'cause he laughed at you when you fell over.* So I made out I was looking for the price ticket and then told him I'd made a mistake, it was only such-and-such, and of course he was well pleased.

One thing led to another and we struck up a proper conversation. As I handed him his package I laughed and told him that the article I'd just sold him had a proper name, if only I could remember it; I was like, 'I've only been in the game about ten years so forgive me for being thick.' He picked up that I was taking the piss out of myself and we both laughed, and it was a good half-hour or more before he finally left the shop, promising to return soon to buy something else.

I was well happy I'd made a sale because I knew it would shut Benny up at night when I got home. He was a born salesman, but me, I couldn't give a monkey's. I didn't need to sell Benny's antiques to get my money; I just had to pop out and do a bit of work. Benny was getting older and was content to sit at home or in one of his shops, chatting to the old girls about China and pottery or their aches and pains or their cat who's got to go to the vet's. But me, not yet thirty and with a brain that never went to sleep, I wanted to be out on the street; I still liked the buzz I got when I found a good shop where I could switch a stone or two; I was still hungry, still ambitious.

In fact, the more diamonds I stole, the more hungry I got. They were like drugs to me. I had to have them. I had to see if I could still do it. It wasn't even the money any more; it was the buzz of being able to do something other women didn't or couldn't do. I didn't even meet men who did what I did, yet to me it was easy. And the day that bloke came into the shop, I decided it was time I went back to work properly.

So I went home and told Benny I wanted to leave the shop for a while, and asked if he could get some staff in to cover me. He hated hiring staff: firstly because he had to pay them; and secondly because we were both thieves and he didn't trust anyone else. But he agreed, said that somehow he'd manage – leaving me free to drive all over the place looking for a bit of work.

It was three or four weeks later that I found the right bit of work – or rather, the right bit of work found me.

I read an ad in a jewellery-trade paper, for a manager in a right top-class jeweller's. I hadn't worked in anybody else's shop for years and I decided to go for the interview, so I phoned up and made an appointment in my own name. At the interview I'd tell them I was married to a jeweller and antiques dealer and would give them one of Benny's cards, should they wish to phone him. I'd tell them that the reason I wanted the job was because I was bored with the antiques side of the business and wanted to work just with jewellery.

People always bought that story. But I knew the reason I got jobs wasn't that I was married to Boisie Hannington or because I was oh-so clever. I got them because when I went to interviews I'd be wearing a nice designer suit and I'd have the matching shoes and bag; my glasses case matched my handbag, which was Louis Vuitton. I had long blonde hair and red lips. It was usually men, aged about sixty, who owned the shops I robbed – too much money and not enough sense. They were never interested in me being the manager of their shops or whatever; all they wanted was to fuck me from the minute I walked through the door. I oozed class and confidence. (I thought I was on the set of *Dallas* and was Sue Ellen playing up to someone to help J.R. get his next deal!) I flirted with these people, right in their faces, and they could look but they couldn't touch. Yeah, I knew what they were thinking, but I always thought it was OK: *You can think and you can fantasise all you like, but you're the one who's gonna get fucked in the end . . . So you just keep dreaming, my friend.* We'd be playing mind games but they could never win because they'd never know what I was thinking.

I was always totally focused while giving my CV at the interview, and I'd always get the jobs right there and then – no references, no phone calls – purely on how I looked. *Oh you stupid dirty old men . . .*

So there I was in front of the two partners of this particular shop. They asked me if I could stay and start work straight away. I told them it would be at least one week before I could start (I'd never appear too eager). So we agreed a starting date and they told me about my wages, and said that as the shop's manager I'd have to be a keyholder. Meaning that I'd be taking the keys home at night and that I'd have to give my address and phone number to the police station nearest the shop in case the alarm went off out of opening hours. (Because if it did, the police would call me and I'd have to come and switch it off.) So not only was I to be the manager of this high-class shop, I'd also be taking the keys home every night!

I shook their sweaty little hands and was out the door buzzing like a bee.

I was walking down Covent Garden towards the underground car park where I'd parked my car, deep in thought. I was thinking about the interview and how stupid these two men were for employing me without even taking up a reference. *My God,* I laughed to myself, *I bet they're waging bets right now as to which one of them's going to have me once I start work.*

I was crossing the street to enter the car park when these two blokes in an XJS Jag pulled out and nearly knocked me over. It was so quick – one minute I was deep in thought, the next I was diving out the way of this car with its windows open and music blaring out.

I was just about to give its occupants a load of lip when I recognised the driver. He was opening the door as if he was going to get out and help me, but he couldn't for laughing. Then he said, 'Every time I see you, darling, you're on your arse with your legs in the air.' It was the bloke who'd been in Benny's shop a few weeks earlier. Still laughing, he pulled me up. 'You must be on a death wish,' he said, 'you're always falling over.'

'I suppose you think you're clever, you stupid prick,' I told him as I brushed myself down. I thought I was going to explode. 'I'll outlive you, you mug—now fuck off out of me way, I wanna get to me car.' And with that I walked past him down into the car park. I was so angry, especially as neither him nor his passenger had said sorry. I was in a right mood by the time I'd got my car and drove to the ticket office, and the attendant taking my money got a load of mouth for charging me more for a couple of hours' parking than a few grams of gold would have cost. When I got to the car-park exit and was waiting to pull out onto the main road, I saw the guy who'd nearly knocked me over standing there on his own. I couldn't see his friend or the Jag. He came over, said he was really sorry; he'd told his mate he'll see him later and wondered if I'd like a spot of lunch in the West End on him. It was obvious he fancied me – I'd sussed that out the first time he came in Benny's shop – but I was married, so I never got on the cheating level; I couldn't be bothered with it.

However, I hadn't had any lunch and I thought this bloke was genuine, so I decided to accept his offer. I told him yes, he could buy me lunch, but I made it clear that there wasn't going to be any funny business afterwards. This made him laugh, and I opened the passenger door and let him in the car. I still didn't know his name and he didn't know mine – but still he didn't ask and neither did I.

We were driving down the road when he asked what I wanted to eat and suggested we could go for a pub lunch? I blurted out, 'I thought you invited me for lunch—what am I going to get in the pub, a bag of fucking crisps?'

Again the bloke burst out laughing, and banged the dashboard, telling me I was a funny little bird. I laughed with him, but I said nothing because my mind had wandered back to the jewellery shop and the interview . . . *What a result – I get to be a key-holder as well.*

I suppose by this time I was getting bored with just swallowing or switching diamonds; I wanted to move up, see if I was clever enough to knock off a jeweller's shop from the inside without getting caught. The problem was doing it on my own, which I knew would be hard. After all, it's one thing to swallow 200 grands' worth of rocks, but this shop had £7 million in stock on the premises. It was a gift. I was bursting with excitement to go home and tell Benny my good news. *Yes, and I'll definitely give Benny a shag tonight . . .*

'Did you hear what I said?' the bloke next to me asked. 'You don't want to go to a pub, so where do you want to go?'

I told him the Dorchester and he asked me if I was sure. 'I always eat at the Dorchester,' I said, 'and if you can't afford it, then I'll pay for you, mate, not a problem.'

So the Dorchester it was. I gave the jockey outside a £20 note to park the car and in we went. I loved this hotel, splendour and class written all over it – not to mention the money in there. Women with big fat diamonds would be sitting in the reception area, then the small fat husbands or sugar daddies would appear and they'd walk off. And I'd tell myself, *Thank God I don't have to sleep with men who look like that to get me diamonds or me furs or pay for me to eat in good places. No, not me, mate. The things I can get myself.*

When we were finally seated in the restaurant, I ordered a dry white wine and he ordered vodka and tonic. He was sitting opposite me and he didn't take his eyes off me, asking all these questions: 'What's your name? How old are you? Is that a wedding ring on your finger? You got any children?'

'What are you, a fucking policeman?' I said.

'No,' he said, half-mocking, half-angry, 'no, I'm not. I'm a businessman.'

'Is that right?'

'That's right. I'm a businessman and that's all you need to know.'

I thought, *I don't want to know your business. You're probably a drug-runner, with your suntan and fucking muscles. But I don't care as long as you ain't a nonce, I don't care.*

Our drinks came and the waiter asked if we were ready to order. I ordered smoked salmon, and as the waiter walked away the bloke tapped my glass and said, 'Here's to you, whatever your name is. May all your dreams come true,' and in one mouthful he knocked his whole drink back, then straight away looked to call the waiter back again.

Some three courses and coffee and liqueurs later, having talked about everything from football to boxing to bare-knuckle fighting, I found out he lived in Islington. I said, 'I lived in Islington but I don't know you.'

'Well you know me now,' he said, 'and every time I see you now I'll shout out to you.'

I never told him why I was in the West End that day and he never asked. I told him I was married and that sometimes I worked in my husband's shops and sometimes I didn't. I could see he couldn't quite figure me out, especially as I told him my husband was eighteen years older than me. I knew he was thinking I was some Poor Little Miss Rich Housewife needing a younger man to sort her out, and reckoning if he played his cards right it could be him. *Yeah, dream on, mate. Dream on.*

All I needed was to rob that fucking jewellery shop, that's all *I* needed. But I also knew I'd need help, and I thought maybe I'd enlist this guy – but I had to find out more about him. I told myself I'd ask Benny when I got home. He'd know; he knew everyone – and if he didn't, he knew a man that did.

I found out over lunch that this bloke was still looking for a Rolex, or a Cartier, and would pay good money for one. So when it was time to go, I gave him my home phone number. I told him that we never answered it, we always let it go on to the answer machine, but that I always answered any messages. I told him I could get him his watch, but I didn't tell him Benny had them at home.

'Won't your husband get the hump for you giving me your number?'

'No, mate. I want to do business with you, not fuck you. Why should my husband mind?'

The bloke told me I was hard work, at which we both laughed. We came out of the hotel and he saw me into my car. He told me he'd get a cab, and we shook hands, then he kissed me on the cheek and off I drove. 'Be lucky,' I shouted.

'I will,' he said and put his hand up and saluted like he was a fucking soldier.

• • •

I went home and found Benny already there, smoking a joint, drinking neat brandy and listening to Supertramp on the stereo. I walked in, kicked off my shoes and fell right into his lap and kissed him full on the lips. I felt him rise straight away but I had some things to say first.

'Make that go down,' I said, 'I've got something to tell you. I've had a right good touch today, babe. I got the job I went after and then that bloke who bought the silver knife a few weeks ago nearly knocked me over in the car park and we ended up having lunch in the Dorchester.'

'What you doing in the Dorchester?' he says.

'I told you, babe, this face nearly knocks me over and he feels guilty so he takes me for lunch, end of. Oh yes, I nearly forgot – he wants to buy a watch off you. He wants to spend ten grand. But I don't know, it could be all bollocks, babe, you know what men are like.'

And we both started laughing. I took a swig of Benny's brandy and nearly choked; give me a diamond any day.

I told him all about the jewellery shop and that the owners reckoned it had £7 million worth of stock. I said how I'd clocked that it had four big time-locking safes and that there was only one CCTV camera out the back in the office, but it was ancient and I thought it was a dummy. I'd find out for sure when I started working there next week.

Then Benny said, 'Joan . . . Will you finish what you started?'

'What you talking about, babe?'

He stood up and I saw the biggest hard-on I'd seen in months. We flew up the stairs, taking the brandy and weed with us, and a good night was had by all.

The Shag that Saved My Life

The bloke (let's call him Jerry) did phone the house and eventually bought a watch from my husband. In fact they kind of struck up a friendship; he'd go in Benny's shop for a chat and he always bought something, which pleased Benny no end.

I started working in the shop a week after my lunch with Jerry. For the first few weeks, I worked as normal: from nine in the morning until six o'clock, and going home every night. (For the record, Benny was still sticking stamps on our toilet wall and was now talking about putting a fucking fish tank in there, which he wanted to sink into the wall. Oh my God, I seriously thought he was losing it.)

I had to sell, mostly, and do the window displays. I was good at doing the displays, plus it allowed me to move freely with the stock from the safes to the window. If I took something from the window and changed it for something in the safe it could always be found. I knew that the two owners were testing me every day but I never gave them an inch. I worked hard, was good with the customers, and nothing went missing.

Everyone was happy, except me.

I was in the stockroom one day, looking for a pair of earrings for a customer waiting in the shop. We didn't have them so I had to take a pair out of the window display, which you got to from the stockroom itself. I was leaning over a tray of gold rings to get to the tray with the earrings when I got the sleeve of my blouse caught on a hook. The tray tipped over and all the rings fell over the floor. I left them there and went back to serving the customer. Once I'd finished, I went back to pick up the rings and put them back on the pad. I was sitting there on the floor putting the rings back one by one – I think there must have been about twenty on the pad. I had no intention of stealing them, but I was curious about just how many I could get in my gob without swallowing them. I had a mouth full of rings when the door opened and one of the female assistants came in. She didn't see me. She sat on the floor, lifted her skirt right up around her hips and pushed her knickers to the side, then proceeded to shove jewellery up her fanny. I could not believe it.

Then, as quick as a flash, she pulled her skirt down, but as she was about to turn back to the door she looks my way. I don't know whether it was me or her who got the bigger shock, but I do know that what she didn't know was I was choking on about four diamond rings. I'd been so busy watching her that I'd forgotten I had the rings in my gob. So now, in order to make sure she didn't notice this, I put my hand over my mouth as if I was in shock, and straight away jumped up as though I was about to say something

and pointed to the door. She understood my meaning and went back into the shop. As soon as she'd gone, I spat three rings out of my mouth – but there was one still in there, stuck in my throat. I couldn't swallow it and I couldn't bring it up. I knew I was choking and could die right there and then in the stockroom of the jewellery shop.

All I could do was laugh at my situation. I mean, I'd done this a hundred times in the past but this time was different; I'd planned the other ones and this time I hadn't even had any intention of stealing the rings! I'd just wanted to see how many I could get in my gob. I hadn't asked the shop assistant to come in and start shoving gold up her fanny, had I? (And what a stupid cow. I mean, all that trouble to nick a bit of gold and she'd only get scrap money for it anyway! Fancy getting nicked for a bit of scrap. *She'll learn*, I thought.)

But my mind was back on the fact that I was choking. My ears were beginning to pop. *You mustn't panic. Slow your breathing down. Now put one finger down your throat and try and get it hooked in the band of the ring and pull it up . . . Oh fuck, the little finger I'm using is too short . . .* Finally I got the third finger of my right hand down and pulled the ring out of my throat. I got sick all over the floor but it didn't matter – I wasn't dead! I walked straight out of the stockroom, brushing myself down, and went through the shop and on into the toilets. I washed my hands and swilled my mouth out, fixed my hair and then went into my office. I felt really sick. I looked up at the ceiling and I told God what I thought: 'You ain't very clever, pulling a fucking stroke like that on me. Especially as I wasn't even nicking anything.'

However, I had to deal with the girl. After all, I was the manageress – so I had to say something, didn't I? But I'm no bully and I didn't know what to say. 'Oh excuse me, can you tell me why you're shoving gold up your fanny?' Well of course I'm not going to say that. I knew what she was doing: she was nicking stuff, wasn't she? But I still had to say something. I got up from my chair, made the sign of the cross on my chest and went to the door and called her in. She had a hanky in her hand and her eyes were red from crying. I felt right sorry for her. I told her not to cry, that I didn't even want to know why she'd done what she'd done but that she had to put the stuff back – because I was in charge and I wasn't going to get into trouble or get nicked when I hadn't done anything. I told her not to do it again and that I wouldn't tell anyone this time.

(Well, who was I going to tell, for fuck's sake? I was a thief myself; hadn't I just nearly choked practising my art? I laughed to myself, thinking that I'd still rather swallow diamonds than do what she'd done with that gold.)

When she went back out on to the shop floor I looked up again and told God: 'I know you was testing me today: first you try and choke me, then I have to deal with the bird. But I never tried to corrupt her, I never said it was OK for her to steal, that's her business.'

But I never grassed her to the owners; I just said no more about it – which was just as well, because she never turned up for work the next day, or ever again after that.

• • •

After about three weeks one of the partners all but told me that his marriage was over and that what he needed was someone like me in his life. He knew I was married, and I made it clear to him that I wasn't interested and had no reason to cheat on my husband. But it didn't stop him trying, and I soon got fed up of being there with this bloke always following me around. So one night after work, instead of going straight home to Holloway, I got off the train at the Angel Islington and went to a pub called the Red Lion, just over the lights from the Tube. I'd bought a drink and sat down in a corner on my own, when the door opened and Jerry came in. I saw him before he saw me; he was with two other blokes who I knew very, very well. They were friends of my husband's. One of them saw me and straight away came over with outstretched arms.

'Hello, my darling, how are ya? Where's that old man of yours, at home counting his money?' He asked if I wanted a drink and I said no thanks, I'd just got one, and when I'd finished it I'd be calling a cab and going home. 'Mind if we join you, can't have you sitting there on your Jack Jones, can we?'

By this time Jerry and the other bloke were walking towards us, smiling. 'Hello, mate,' said Benny's friend.

'Hello, sexy,' Jerry said as they all sat down. My husband's two friends were surprised I knew Jerry, until he informed them how we'd met in Benny's shop.

'So why you on your own, Joan?' one of them asked.

'I'm thinking.'

'What you thinking about?'

'Do you really want to know?' I said. 'Well, I'll tell you. I'm thinking how I can knock off a jewellery shop of seven million quid's worth of stock on my own without getting caught.' Now, these two friends of Benny's knew I was a thief, but they didn't know I swallowed diamonds. Jerry didn't even know I was a thief, and he seemed really shocked when I said what I said. But he said, 'What do you mean? What shop?' He was staring at me. 'Let us in on the action.'

'What do you know about knocking off jewellery shops?' I said.

'It's easy,' he says. 'Go in there masked up, put the gun over the counter, tell them what you want. If they don't want to play ball then you just put one in them, get the gear and out you go, jump in your car and away you go, no problem, darling.'

'What—you'd shoot them,' I said, 'just like that?'

'Of course you shoot them, you silly cow. If they want to play heroes then you shoot them—'

'Oh no,' I said, 'I'm not into the shooting lark. There's got to be a way where it can be done without anyone getting hurt. I'm not going to jail for shooting no one. I'm not that kind of thief.' I tell them I can earn money without shooting people; Benny would kill me if I did something like that. You only shoot people who've hurt you or your family, I said, you don't shoot anyone for money.

'Not for money; there's got to be a better way,' I told these blokes, sitting opposite me with their tongues hanging out. 'Anyway,' I said, 'let's change the subject. Who wants a drink? I'll buy a round before I go.' And that's exactly what I did. I bought a round of drinks, said my goodbyes, walked out onto John Street and got a cab home to Hornsey Road and Benny.

I fell asleep that night promising myself there had to be a way that I could rob this shop without anyone getting hurt. There was a way, and I was going to find it . . . And I did.

This was the routine at the shop. I had to be there at quarter to nine, no later, as that gave me fifteen minutes to open the shutters. They were electronic and you moved them up or down by inserting a key. Once inside the shutters, you'd turn them down again and leave the door open to let some fresh air into the shop. You were perfectly safe because the shutters were down and no one could get to you.

The alarm then had to be turned off within a certain number of seconds. You punched the code in, which stopped the alarm straight away, then you could walk through to the back office where all the safes were side by side, all with a time-locking device so they would all open at the same time: nine o'clock on the dot. Then you'd have one hour to tidy the shop, Hoover the carpet, have a cup of tea and a fag before putting the jewellery in the window ready for opening to the public at ten o'clock.

I would be on my own most of this time: the owners never came in until about eleven or twelve-thirty. We had a part-time male assistant who came in at nine-thirty until two, which was the busy period. There were three windows to dress. One was for diamond rings, one was for diamond pendants, bracelets and bangles, and one was for 18- and 22-carat gold objects. It was the assistant's job to take the stuff from the safe and bring it to me to dress the window. First I'd do the rings, then the bracelets, then the gold. I'd convinced the owners it was a good idea to move the things in the window around daily. That way, if a customer saw a ring in the window today and not in the same place tomorrow, they'd think it was sold – so the people who walk past regularly think it must be a good and busy shop. Well, that was the psychology of my thinking; and it usually worked and my bosses agreed, so they let me carry on doing what I wanted as long as the money was coming in the till, which it was.

So now I knew the layout of the shop. There were four

big freestanding safes at the back of the shop and another two in a downstairs room, which I'd only just learned about. I knew that loose stones and money were kept in those safes and they only ever got opened when the owners were having what's called 'a private sale'. This is where one jeweller sells to another jeweller without paying the VAT. At this shop it was usually stolen property they were dealing in and the business was done downstairs behind closed doors; all men, no women.

I used to make out I didn't know what was going on, but I did. I never missed a trick but I said nothing. *Play stupid, play the good shop manager, do what you got to do, just learn the way of the shop. Learn the way of the owners. Learn everything you can about the inside of the shop. Where are the cameras? Are there cameras on the street outside? How long will it take the police to get to the shop if the alarm goes off? God, so many things to find out . . .*

For the next few weeks, I went to work as usual and paid attention to everything, finding out what I needed to know. I used to tell these things to my husband at night when I got home and he'd say, 'Why don't you just swallow a few stones, Joan? Just stay in the job – milk it. Take a few each day, bring them home and I'll make you some dud ones up so you can put them back and no one will notice?'

But I didn't want to milk it. I wanted to see if I could rob it in one go, without drama, guns or violence. I just wanted to see if I could do it 'cause I knew I could.

During this period Benny asked around and found out that our new-found friend Jerry was an ex-armed robber and that when we first met him he'd not been long out after serving eighteen years for an armed robbery. He had a good reputation as a thief and wasn't thought to be a grass or on drugs, and he could hold his own. He wasn't short of a few quid but a few more would go down very well, thank you. He was hungry for a bit of work. Jerry wasn't married – I think his wife left him when he was in prison – and he didn't have a regular girlfriend. He was older than me but younger by about seven or eight years than Benny. He seemed just the right person to help me rob the shop.

We were talking to him one day about this, and I explained how because I was working in the shop there was no need for guns or violence to be used. With me on the inside, being the manager and having a set of keys, it was all going to be so easy: we'd walk away with £7 million in jewellery and cash. All we had to do was decide when and how we were going to do it.

After a few more meetings it was decided that on a particular day I would go to work as usual and do all the things I'd normally do until the assistant turned up. Then, when he knocked on the window for me to let him in, I'd open the shutter just enough to let him inside and would leave it to him to lock the door behind him. But when he walked through to the back of the shop to take his coat off, I'd open the front door again – without him noticing – and pull the shutter up a bit more. Then I'd walk through to the back of the shop too and start chatting to the assistant and having my tea. By this time three men in suits would be under the shutter into the shop and out the back before we knew it and would tell us to shut up. I'd act all scared as they tied us up then robbed the shop. No one gets hurt and we're seven mill-plus in front.

Not bad for a silly Paddy girl, I thought. *Not bad at all.*

Then I'll stop, I told myself. *They say it's a man's world and women are stupid, but I don't think so, mate.*

• • •

The morning of the robbery, I got up at about six o'clock. I had a cab coming at eight o'clock, giving me plenty of time to do what I had to do.

I wasn't nervous. I was totally focused on what I had to do. But there was a nagging feeling in the back of my head; something was bothering me, about a conversation I'd had with Jerry and the other two guys in the pub the night before. We'd all been talking about what each one of us had to do and where we would all meet up in a few days to split the gear, etc. We already knew that I'd get a pull from the police because I was the manager. I knew that once the police realised I had a criminal record and was married to Benny Hannington they'd try to blame Benny, but that didn't matter. Benny would be found to be working in his own shop that day, and it wasn't the sort of robbery they'd have him down for.

So as long as I kept my cool, and didn't grass on anyone if the police turned the pressure up, I could handle it. I'd had plenty of experience of being interviewed by the police, and the older I got the wiser I got. *Let them nick me*, I thought. *I'll only tell them what they need to know. It don't matter if they think I'm guilty; they can't prove it.*

With this in mind in the pub, having discussed it over and over, we settled down to have a drink and tell a few jokes before we went our separate ways. During the chat, one of the guys said, 'Have you seen that film with Robert De Niro in? The one where they all wear masks of Ronald Reagan and other famous people on this robbery.' He went on to describe a certain scene in the film: the guys have got inside the place they're robbing; and there's a girl there who one of the blokes starts slapping about. 'Then she tells him she's the one who set up the job in the first place,' this bloke in the pub continued, 'thinking he'd be nice to her. How she's a friend of so-and-so. "I don't give a fuck who you are," he says, then smacks her in the mouth, turns her face down on the table and fucks her up the arse.'

They all started laughing. Not me, though. My mind started doing overtime.

'Try that with me,' I said, 'and I'll cut your dick off and shove it in your mouth. And if you kill me my husband or my friends will kill *you*.'

I went right on and on, and kept asking why he'd said that while we're talking about a bit of business: 'What's your problem?' He assured me he was only joking, said not to worry, so in the end I just said OK and made my excuses and left, arranging to see everyone tomorrow.

So now, on the morning of the job, I felt more and more uneasy as I was making my breakfast. I just didn't like what the guy had said. I took some tea and toast in to Benny and we sat in bed together talking about the job. But I was very edgy. The buzz was gone. I was thinking, *Shall I tell Benny? Will he get the hump with me if I pull out, all because of what that guy said? Will he think my bottle has gone?*

All these things going through my mind as the clock ticked away.

I got in the bath and lay there thinking about what had been said. *Surely they wouldn't do a thing like that; the money's more important than fucking my arse, if that's what he's got in his mind.* But the thought nagged away at me and I wasn't happy. I remember thinking I'd shove a blade up my sleeve so that if anyone did try anything funny I could slice their hands off – but it would still be three against one.

I told myself I was being ridiculous. We were supposed

to be going out to earn £7 million today and all I could think about was why that bloke had said such a thing.

I got out the bath, went back into our bedroom and started getting ready. The clock was still ticking away – 7:30, then 7:45. Benny got up and took a bath while I was getting ready. I wore a black two-piece suit, skirt and jacket, white blouse, my hair in a bun, black stockings and suspenders. Benny came back in the room and saw me fiddling with the suspenders – and picked this moment to get a hard-on. I was pretending not to notice but he just dropped his towel, got back into bed and asked me if I fancied a quick one. I told him I couldn't; I'd just had a bath and I'd have to re-do my make-up.

'Fuck your make-up,' he said, and pulled me back into bed.

I kept telling him I was going to be late for the job, but he didn't seem to care and was all over me like a rash, ripping my stockings in the process. Not that I minded. We were both laughing and fucking at the same time; the whole thing was absurd – I was supposed to be taking part in a £7-mill robbery and Benny was supposed to be on his way to his shop, and there we were having a bunk-up!

We eventually composed ourselves – then started running round the house like nutcases trying to get ready before my cab came. But although I managed to get together in time, the cab was late and I eventually got to work forty minutes late.

The assistant was waiting outside, but there was no sign of the robbers. I guess they must have realised I wasn't coming and had scarpered. I apologised to the assistant and let us both in under the shutter, locking it and the door behind me (making sure I double-locked it before I went down the back). Ten minutes later there were firemen all over the place; there was a fire three shops down and we had to evacuate the premises in case of a gas explosion.

We went out into the street, where there were loads of people about, and in the crowd I saw one of the blokes. I looked him straight in the eye and he realised it wasn't going to happen. Even if I had got to work on time it would have come on top anyway because they'd have been in the shop when the fire brigade came and it could have got very nasty.

• • •

I carried on working at the shop a bit longer, about six weeks I think. And during that time I swallowed about twenty diamond rings and switched a load of diamond bangles worth about £400,000. (Well, I know I've got a big gob but even I don't swallow bangles.)

CHAPTER TWENTY-EIGHT

The Best in the Business

Some time in about 1986 (I think it was then because I still didn't have a child), I was at home one morning and got a phone call from my friend TH. I'd taken up my husband's obsession with cleaning the ornaments in our cabinets one by one and putting them back, and was feeling bored shit-less. I was wondering what to do next, and thought maybe I'd start sticking stamps on the kitchen wall. After all, Boisie had now finished the toilet wall and had his fish tank sunk into it . . . But before I could think this through any further I was disturbed by the phone ringing. 'Is that you, hen?' said the strong Scottish voice at the end of the line.

I recognised the voice immediately. 'Hello darlin',' I said. 'How are you, you old sweaty sock?' ('Sweaty sock', of course, meaning Jock. Though you don't call a Scotsman a sweaty sock to his face unless you want a smack in the mouth, it's fine if he's your mate!)

'I'm all right, hen. Will you pick me up from the

airport? I'm coming to see ye later on and I want to be back in Scotland by tonight.'

'All right,' I say, 'what time is your plane, mate?'

'I'll be getting the ten o'clock and should arrive at Heathrow just after eleven—'

'What, this morning? It's after seven, you haven't left much fucking time.'

'Sorry, hen, you know how it is.'

So after I'd had a quick shower and got dressed, I got the trademark red lipstick on and did my hair (I don't know why – I always ended up tying it back and putting a cap on), then off I went. I only lived about fifty minutes away from the airport, so I didn't have to rush too much.

I was wondering what TH wanted, whether he was in trouble. *Maybe he's killed someone or he's done a bit of bad business and it's coming on top.* It would be fair to say that TH was built like a brick shithouse. He was short but with shoulders like two buses side by side, tough enough at that time to run the streets of his town. No one, and I mean no one, fucked with this man. He had more soldiers under him than the British Army and they'd kill you on a phone call. However, I'd never seen that side of him. To me he was a mate – or, I should say, he was me husband's mate. We'd all met in Portugal a few years earlier. I wouldn't say we were great friends but there was a lot of mutual respect insomuch as a criminal from Scotland can give a criminal from London married to a Paddy. At the time TH was divorced and dating some bird but I didn't think it would last.

It was usually business that brought us all together. Maybe he had something for Benny or Benny had something for him. We'd meet up and go for dinner or to a club and mix business with pleasure. I'd feel safe in his company. He wasn't a bully or flash. I guess he'd be like the Tony Soprano of the eighties: you get one of his, he'll get ten of yours.

I knew as I pulled into the airport car park that I'd soon find out what he wanted, but I had to wait about twenty minutes before I saw him coming towards me. We shook hands and I gave him a hug and told him he'd picked a moment to call.

'Why, what was ye doing, hen?'

I told him I was dusting the China and he thought I was taking the piss: 'I thought ye had a cleaner!'

'I have,' I said, 'but I can't help it. I got nothing else to do, TH. Boisie's at work all day. I can't stand going in to the shops 'cause it's all antiques and jewellery and I get them at home, so I keep dusting and cleaning. I think I've got that illness where a person can't stop cleaning.'

'Oh, Joan, you've been watching some shite from America!'

We both started laughing and got in the car. Forty minutes later as we pulled up outside my flat, TH pointed out that I'd been doing ninety down the motorway.

'I wanted a piss, TH,' I said. 'And I ain't using the motorway toilets because you don't know who's sat on them before you.'

'Oh, hen, you really *are* fucking losing it.'

And we both started laughing again.

There was more laughing later, when Benny came home after I'd called to tell him TH was in town for the day. I made them a big fry-up for lunch and they both sat down at the table to tuck into steak, eggs, tomatoes, chips and baked beans. There was coffee and a bottle of brandy on the table. I then handed out these big wedges of bread, cut really badly, which always got Benny annoyed. 'Where's the electric knife I bought you off the oyster? Why don't you use it?'

'In the cupboard, because every time I use it I cut me poxy fingers, so you'll have to eat doorsteps and like it!' And we all look at this bread and start laughing.

We left the table with our bellies full and went into the front room. The men sat down and drank a glass of brandy, and then Benny started rolling a joint.

'Are ye still smoking that shit, Benny?'

'Well, I'm a bit too old now to stop, mate. I'm over forty-five. I'm still out grafting day and night and I still run ten miles every day, so the weed ain't hurting me.'

Now we're sitting comfortably, TH pulls out a platinum credit card and hands it to Benny. 'Ye see that, Ben. That's got £300,000 worth of credit on it, and it hasn't been reported lost or missing yet. The people are oot of the country and won't be back for a month.'

'How come you know?'

''Cause I know the chauffeur,' TH grinned. 'He's having it off with the bloke's wife and she told him she hates her husband but won't leave him 'cause the money's all in his name and if she leaves him she won't get a penny. Her husband don't suspect a thing. It's all arranged. They went away yesterday but my mate's got a set of keys to the house and the bird has given him all her husband's details. We've even got the bloke's driving licence and he's the same age as me.' It turned out they had some other bird staying in the rich bloke's house, too. So that if some shop assistant made herself busy checking the Amex card – because they got £50 for every stolen card as a reward, £100 for a gold or platinum one – and wanted to report it, there wouldn't be a problem; if anyone phoned the house the bird at the other end would pretend to be his wife. 'She can answer any question Amex throw at her,' said TH. 'It's a piece of piss, Benny. A piece of piss.'

'I don't mean to be funny, mate,' Boisie says, 'but what you telling me for if you've got it all sewn up? What can I do to help you? You don't need me to be in on this.'

'No, I don't,' TH said. 'I want Joan to come to work with me. Everybody knows she's the best in the business.'

'But I don't want to do that no more,' I blurted out. 'It's not my game – I moved on from that game, TH. I thought you knew that.'

'Yeah, I know, but this ain't silly money, Joan. You've got three hundred grand credit. It's a brand-new card. Look, it ain't even been signed, babe.'

My husband's eyes were gleaming. But I hadn't yet said I'd do it. I didn't fancy kiting any more. I was out of practice, and anyway I wanted to know what items I'd be expected to get and what my whack was going to be.

To this, TH answered, 'Fifty-fifty. Fifty for me and fifty for you, Joan, straight down the middle.'

'Who's signing the card?'

'You are.'

'But I thought you said it's a man's card . . .'

'No, it's got Mr and Mrs on it. It's just that the account is in his name. Both him and her can use it without the other one being there.'

I really wasn't sure. And then TH said they wanted me to start today.

'Today? It's nearly two o'clock now. I need an hour to get ready, that makes it three o'clock, and the shops close at five or six, even the West End, so where would we go? What sort of stuff do you want me to get?'

He said I didn't have to get the bulky stuff; I could get jewellery, a couple of good Cartier watches – 'Ye know, hen, His 'n' Hers; the ones all covered in diamonds' – and maybe a few diamond rings and bracelets. 'You get what you want, hen, and we'll split it fifty-fifty.'

'Who's watching me back?' I ask.

'Ye've got me, hen, I'll be with you.'

I looked at Benny, who just said, 'It's up to you, babe. It's up to her, TH. I don't force her.'

'Oh come on, hen, we'll have a laugh, and I promise if it comes on top I'll get you out. You won't get nicked. It's easy money, Joan, a piece of piss.'

Yeah, I'm thinking, *a piece of piss.* But I still wasn't sure. I'd given up kiting. 'I'm going to the toilet,' I said, which was an excuse to leave the room and I hoped that Benny would follow me out a couple of minutes later, which is exactly what he did. I was in the bathroom washing my hands when he came in and shut the door.

'Well, what do you think, Joan? Yes or no.'

'I don't know. I haven't done that for ages. If I get nicked I'll get seven years, babe, and we don't need the money, do we? We can't fucking spend what we got. And if I get nicked and go to jail I'm never gonna get a chance to get pregnant.'

'Yes you will,' he said. 'You're only young still—'

'I know, but you're not, you old bastard. You won't have no lead left in your pencil by the time I come out of jail.'

'Well, I'll buy you a fucking dog then,' Benny said. 'I'll buy you two fucking dogs. Come on, Joan, the clock's ticking and it's got to be done in one day, that's the deal. Yes or no.'

'You ain't coming,' I say. 'Someone's got to stay in the house, and if I go to jail I ain't having you and me in jail at the same time.'

'No, all right. I ain't going. Anyway, you've got TH watching your back.'

'OK. OK, go and tell TH.' Benny gave me a hug and went downstairs, shouting up, 'Shall I roll you a joint, babe, to steady your nerves?'

'No, I don't want one,' I snapped back. 'I got to keep a clear head.'

I stripped off and got in the shower. I didn't want to do this: we really didn't need the money and I kept thinking about something going wrong and me getting nicked. But then I just figured it was too late to worry about it now: I'd said I'd do it. So I spent the next hour getting myself transformed.

First I gelled my long blonde hair back, then I put a pair of tights with the legs cut off on my head and over that a long red wig, 100 per cent real hair. I used a brown eye pencil to draw over my blonde eyebrows, put brown eye-shadow on my lids and then black eye-liner, and finally a pair of black eyelashes. I used a spot of orange blusher followed by bronze lipstick and brown lip-liner. *Not bad*, I thought. I then got a light-brown pencil and gave myself a few freckles, just for effect.

Slowly but surely I started to get in the mood. *So now, Miss Redhead from Scotland, what you gonna wear? You're supposed to be rich, so I better dress you rich and classy.* I started talking to myself in a Scottish accent as I put on a cream YSL blouse with a brown two-piece skirt suit, the skirt being pencil-line and tight. I wore flesh-coloured stockings and brown Italian leather stiletto shoes. I put a heavy gold chain round my neck and a 4-carat diamond on my finger with a wedding band in front. *Just add a full-length red fox-fur coat and a Louis Vuitton clutch bag, and hey baby, here we go . . . and I ain't gotta swallow nothing.*

I was getting excited now. I wasn't Joan any more, I'm some redhead from Scotland, and I reckoned most men would want me! As a final touch I put a dab of Chanel No.19 on, then I checked myself over in the mirror and down the stairs I went. TH couldn't believe it.

'Fuck me, hen, you're gorgeous! Who taught you to change your appearance like that?'

'Nobody, TH. I just know how to do it.'

'You look lovely, darlin',' Benny said, kissing me on the cheek; then he whispered in my ear, 'When you get home tonight keep that gear on, I wanna fuck you in it . . .'

I knew it. It was the same every time I dressed up like someone else to go and do a bit of business; he'd want me like that. I pushed him away and called him a pervert, and TH said, 'Are ye being dirty to your old woman, Benny, 'cause I'll have you arrested,' and we all started laughing.

It was now three in the afternoon. We decided that the only place we could go to work was Brent Cross shopping centre, which would be open till eight o'clock and which had at least six good-class jewellery shops in it where I could do my thing. In the taxi on the way there I told TH I didn't want him to come into the shops with me – 'I want you to stay outside and not take your eyes off me. Make out you're looking at something in the window and if you see me drop me bag on the floor then you'll know I'm in trouble. If not, don't come near me. When I come out, see if anyone is following me.'

With this agreed, we strolled through the shopping centre and headed for the first jewellery store. Brent Cross is a huge indoor mall of hundreds of shops selling pretty much anything you might want – designer goods, shoes, leather clothes, TVs and videos, etc. – as well as a branch of Fenwick's, a John Lewis and loads of places to eat. You could have a good day out there, with all classes of people shopping, but in the late afternoon it was fairly quiet.

I entered the jewellery shop and spotted a young male assistant, a tall, thin kid of mixed race, about eighteen years old, wearing a white shirt and black trousers and a tie with the shop's logo on it (which for obvious reasons I won't go into details about). I go over to this lolly on a stick and in my best Scottish accent I ask to see a particular ring in the window. 'It's the 3-carat emerald-cut diamond,' I say, pointing to the display. The price was £24,000. I spent a good ten to fifteen minutes trying the ring on, during which time I took my coat off and sat down. I couldn't help but notice how the assistant didn't seem bothered whether I bought the ring or not; he was just going through the motions. *That's not how it used to be,* I thought; *when I was doing this in my early twenties the shop assistant would be all over you for a sale like that.* Still, I reckoned maybe this guy was on a good wage and didn't have to graft or kiss arse to get his commission.

Eventually I said yes, I'd have the ring, and took my Louis Vuitton wallet from my bag. I had about £3,000 in there, which of course he noticed, plus several credit cards. I handed him TH's platinum card and he informed me that he had to get a clearance from Amex because the shop-floor limit was only £10,000. 'That's OK,' I said, 'I think I'll need to sit here and relax anyway before I spend this amount of money,' and gave a nervous little giggle.

It was going to take at least five minutes, and I knew there were cameras in the ceiling and someone could be watching me, so I had to act natural – not bite my nails, not move about too much, make out I was putting lipstick on and use the little mirror to look around a bit. I was keeping nice and calm and had reassured myself there was nothing going on behind me . . . Except there was – Jesus, of all the times to want to fart! But even if I had it wouldn't have gone anywhere because I was sitting down in a skirt tighter than a duck's arse. Anyway, just then the assistant came back; I thought he was going to ask me to go to the phone for a security check, but he said, 'No problems, Mrs S—, just sign here and I'll wrap your ring.'

I started to get up out of the chair, forgetting I had wind, and as I reached my feet the fart came out. Although the bloke didn't hear it (or pretended not to), I nearly died of shame. Ladies don't fart in front of men, not even criminal ladies. *Never mind,* I thought as I signed the bit of paper and then casually put my coat back on. I took the receipt and popped the little ring box into my bag and out the door I walked – with a £24,000 ring. I could see TH by the window and I looked him in the eye so he knew everything was OK, then he watched me walk along the mall and into a café.

By the time he came in I was finishing my coffee. He sat down and I handed him the box with the ring in it. He put it in his pocket and I told him what shop I was going to next.

'OK, hen, I'll be there once I pay for the coffee.' He shook his head. 'Jesus, Joan, you're a cool customer. You should be on the stage, hen.'

'Yeah, I know, TH, I know—more like the dock at the Old Fucking Bailey.'

'Ah, get out of that,' he says, grinning. 'Only another £276,000 to go . . .'

'Fuck me, I better go for those His 'n' Hers Cartier watches!'

I got up to walk out, and looked at my mate. 'Hey, TH.'

'What?'

'This has got to be better than cleaning China.'

• • •

It was now well after six o'clock in the evening and so far I'd spent more than £120,000. (I don't want to give exact details; let's just say there were a couple of watches, three rings and some bracelets.) I must admit I'd never had it so easy on a bit of work. No one questioned the amount of money I was spending on the card. No one followed me out of the shops. It was all too easy, and I was buzzing again, enjoying every minute. The same routine as in the first shop: walk in, do my thing, go to a restaurant, hand the gear over to TH and then on to the next shop. (The reason, I should say, why I handed the jewellery over to TH was if I got nicked in a shop, they wouldn't find any of the other jewellery. Obviously, if they found all the other stuff on me they'd use it as evidence. But by handing it over to TH, whether I got nicked and went to jail or not, I'd still have my share when I came out.)

Like I say, I'd spent over £120,000 on the card, and although I was enjoying myself I was beginning to feel very hot with the heavy fur coat on, especially as we were in an indoor shopping mall, what with the lights being so bright.

I'd just handed TH a £12,000 tennis bracelet, which is a thin bracelet covered in diamonds usually set on 18-carat gold. They were very popular in Miami (a sign of wealth or a sign that your old man's a drug dealer) and I already had one of these bracelets that I was given as a present by one of my husband's Cuban friends a couple of years before. As I handed over the package, I was just about to tell TH that I was too hot, I needed to go outside for ten minutes, and ask how much longer we needed to go on for, when TH said to me under his breath, 'Count to three, babe. I think it's on top. There's four security guards closing in on us.'

'Are you sure it's us they're walking towards?'

'Yes,' he said quietly. 'OK, Joan. You start to run. I'll keep them away from you.' As he was saying this, I bent down and took my shoes off. 'Which way?'

He nodded behind him to an exit and that was that: with a shoe in each hand I ran out of the restaurant. The problem with Brent Cross was that the immediate area is surrounded by dual carriageways, and there was no other place for me to run to. I was running and running, couldn't see a fucking thing now that it was getting dark, and I had this full-length fur coat on and it was weighing me down.

All of a sudden I hear TH's voice: 'Hen, keep going, I'm right behind you. Just keep running.'

Then he overtook me, but grabbed me by my hand and told me we've got to run on to the dual carriageway, there was nowhere else to go.

I quickly looked over my shoulder and I could make out the shape of someone about twenty feet away. It was a Black security guard. *Oh fuck it, we've got to have a fight.* Through deep breaths I said to TH, 'I think he wants to be a hero.'

'Well, if he gets hit by a lorry on the motorway,' TH said, 'he'll be a dead fucking hero.'

With TH gripping my hand we're over the barrier

and running through and around cars and lorries, beeping and flashing, but we got to pass over four lanes of moving traffic going opposite ways to get to a grass verge on the far side. Somewhere in the midst of all this I've managed to pull the seam of my skirt apart and can move my legs more easily. I've got my shoes in my pocket and my bag in my waistband. I can hardly run any more, the coat is weighing me down, but I can't take it off and throw it away because it could be used as evidence at a later date.

Then we're across the central reservation, TH pulling me so hard he's nearly tearing my arm out of its socket. We dodge past a car, flashing its lights and beeping, and coming straight at us there's this big lorry with no chance to stop. *It's gonna hit us for sure.* I yell or scream something at TH, crapping myself, and he shouts, 'Jump, hen! Jump!' I feel this sudden wind as the lorry misses us by a whisker and then we're off the road at last, jumping down. *Oh my God. It's not just a grass verge. It's a fucking river. I can't swim. I can't swim!* TH's let go of my hand. The water is cold and black, I lose my breath and I can't see a thing. I know I'm gonna drown for sure. All of a sudden, when I think it's all over, I feel this big firm arm round me throat. He puts his hand over my mouth. '*Shh . . . Shh.* Don't worry, hen, I've got ye, I've got ye. Keep your head up but don't make a sound, there's six coppers and two security guards up on the motorway. I don't think they realised we jumped.'

'How do you know?' I whisper with my teeth chattering. 'I only saw the one guy.'

'Trust me, Joan, there's coppers all over the place.'

Just as he says this we see a flashlight sweeping round in our direction. I feel TH's arm holding me tight. 'Hang on, Joan—go under the water, go under. I won't let you go. Just till the light passes us,' and he pulls me under.

I can't say I was frightened. After all, when I was a child my dad used to hold me under the bathwater and I'd learned to hold my breath and not panic. So that's what we did, the two of us under the water, fully clothed, for what seemed hours but was probably just a few minutes. The light had disappeared when we came up, both of us desperate to cough out some of the water and shit that we'd swallowed.

For some strange reason I saw the funny side of it. I could see the headlines: 'Couple Die in River (having just nicked £120,000 worth of jewellery)'.

'Joan, they've gone,' TH said. 'Can you climb up, babe? Are you all right to climb up?'

'Are you taking the piss, TH? I can hardly move in this coat, it's too heavy. Help me get it off.'

Somehow we got my coat off and TH got his off (a big full-length, single-breasted job) and he pushed me up on to the grass bank, and *snap*! There was a flashlight in my face. There he was, crouching down, the big Black security guard who was chasing us in the mall. He must have known we were in the water but had said nothing to the police.

'Get back in,' he grunted at me, 'they're coming back this way.'

'Who?'

'The coppers.'

'Why you telling me this?'

'Shut up and get back in the water, you pussy clot, I'm trying to help you!'

Of course TH could hear what was going on and pulled me back into the river.

'*Shh*, quiet, hen . . .'

We waited a couple of minutes and I heard voices above us. I couldn't see anything in the dark but I could hear the Black security guy telling someone he'd seen us jumping into a car that had slowed down and had 'gone that way'.

'Fuck it,' I heard a voice say, 'we nearly had them.'

'We'll get some roadblocks set up on the North Circular,' someone else said. 'They won't get far, it's a straight run.'

Then one of the coppers said to the security guard, 'Well done, mate, well done. You tried your best. Can we contact you later for a statement?'

'OK, officer.' He coughed and spat out. 'Do you mind if I take a breather for a minute, only I'm all out of breath.'

'No problem, mate. You just sit there. We'll see you later.'

It went quiet then, apart from the cars and lorries above us. TH had got his hands firmly round my waist and was holding me so tight I can't breathe. I couldn't even talk. So I slid my hand behind my back and grabbed hold of my mate's bollocks, gave them a right good squeeze. Immediately his grip loosened and he whispered in my ear, 'What you do that for, you Irish cunt?'

'You're squeezing me too hard, TH, I couldn't breathe—'

'Squeeze me bollocks like that again and I'll fucking drown ye.'

'Sorry, TH.'

Then, from above us: 'You can come out now.' The security guy bent down to help us out of the river, the two of us like drowned rats – and I still had the wig on. TH asked him how come he never grassed.

''Cause I ain't no informer. I ain't no hero for the white man.'

'But we're white,' I say. 'We're white, mate!'

'No bother with that, sister, we're on the same side.'

I looked at TH and then at the guy. 'Well,' I said, 'there really is a God after all,' and all three of us burst out laughing.

The bloke told us we could get a black taxi over the other side of the dual carriageway. So once again we played Russian roulette with the traffic and once again I nearly got hit – by a van this time – but we made it and walked a fair distance until eventually we saw a black taxi heading towards us. The guard put his hand up to stop it for us and then opened the door. TH jumped straight in and I then remembered I'd got three grand in my purse. I told the security guard, 'Here, this is for you.'

He couldn't believe it as I took the wet money out of my bag and started shoving it in his pocket. I kissed him on the cheek and he just held up his hand to his face and clenched his fist, and then off he went.

As we drove in the taxi to Shepherd's Bush I said to TH, 'Oh, yes, you owe me fifteen hundred quid, mate.'

'What for?'

'I've just given that bloke three grand. If we're fifty-fifty on the profit, we're fifty-fifty on the expenses.'

TH looked at me and said, 'If that's the case, hen, you owe me a new pair of bollocks 'cause you squeezed the fucking life out of mine!'

• • •

When we got home, still dripping wet, and told Boisie the story, the only thing he was upset about was that the wig got ruined and he couldn't fuck me in it. (Men, I ask you. All they think about is their dicks.)

Did I learn any lessons from that job? Definitely: that my mate was a stand-up geezer.

TH missed his plane in the end. We still had all the jewellery, which we split fifty-fifty. We cut up the card, burned all the receipts – and the wig. Not bad, I guess, for a few hours' work, even if it did nearly cost me my life.

CHAPTER TWENTY-NINE

Fernando

It's no secret that my son's godfather was one of the biggest drug barons in Miami. When they finally got him they took six of his planes and boats. He really was the governor. So it's not as if Benny and I never had the chance to make it big in the drug world; but from our point of view we were jewellers and antiques dealers, and we just didn't want to be involved. (Besides, we were worth about £7.5 million in cash, diamonds, antiques and other things that I choose not to mention.)

The man's name was Fernando Pruna. When we met him he was in London on holiday, and his wife, Eudelia, was still at home in the States. He was a big man in every way. He was tall, well-built, expensively dressed and just had a way about him that made you know this was no mug. I think he was about fifty years old but he had the build of a man much younger. He came in our shop to buy antiques and we just struck up a conversation. One thing led to another and he asked Benny and myself to join him that night for dinner at the Hilton. We didn't like the food at the Hilton, though, so we told Fernando we'd take him to a good restaurant a few minutes from the Park Lane Hilton, Le Gavroche on Upper Brook Street. The food was second to none.

After dinner we went to the Embassy Club and sat there drinking Irish coffee. Fernando and Benny were smoking those big cigars. The more I listened to this man, the more I liked him. He was originally from Havana in Cuba. He told us he'd not been out of prison long. He'd been sentenced to thirty-five years, commuted from the death sentence, for what he called 'alleged counter-revolutionary activities'. When he was let out of prison, he said, a free man at last, 'It is like ginger ale—it bubbles all over.' What we didn't know, and what appeared in a Miami newspaper in 1989, was that his bubbles would burst big-time five years later.

He told us with such pride that he was born to the family of a prominent Havana lawyer. He'd been edu-cated in the USA and then became an executive of three different Canadian mineral firms. He'd returned to Cuba in 1957 (the year I was born) and a year later was elected to Cuba's House of Representatives; all was flourishing until a man called Fidel Castro came along and Fernando quickly became a counter-revolutionary. Castro arrested Fernando in April 1959. After one botched attempt to escape, Fernando eventually got away and set up a resist-ance movement, but he was recaptured in the mountains of Pinar del Río, where he was engaged in guerrilla war-fare. At the age of twenty-four he'd been sentenced to death by firing squad. For whatever reason, the death sen-tence was not carried out and he spent the next twenty-odd years in the Combinado del Este prison.

Fernando was freed in 1980 and, like most Cubans

who'd been freed, went to live in America. He was stripped of all his wealth – his homes, his company's assets – and sent to Miami with nothing except a suit he borrowed from his lawyer and shoes that were too small for him. Yet this was no ordinary man. He could speak seven languages fluently, knew just about everything about anything, and was, at the time we met him, an investment broker. (At least, that's what he said he was.) I can't remember everything he said that night. What with all the Irish coffees going down my throat, not to mention the poxy smoke from Fernando and Benny's cigars, my head was so dizzy. But I remember I noticed that he had such class, the way he carried himself, the way he spoke; he loved life, he loved people and most of all he loved his wife and family. When he spoke about his beloved Cuba his eyes would fill with tears, he missed his country and its people so much. I felt so humble in his presence.

Before Fernando went back to America we struck up a friendship that I just knew only the death of one of us would end. I certainly know that when Benny died all the other couples we'd been friendly with throughout our marriage soon deserted me, but Fernando and his wife Eudelia never did.

Fernando made another visit a year later, for Christmas, this time with Eudelia. The four of us – me, Benny, Fernando and Eudelia – were going to Amsterdam and then on to Germany. The reason for our trip was that Fernando was having a boat built and wasn't happy that the agreed price of £7 million had gone up and not for the first time; I think he wanted to take a look for himself and kick arse.

We'd all been out for dinner, and afterwards Fernando

and Eudelia had gone back to their hotel. Benny and I had just settled down at home to a nice joint when the phone rang. It was Fernando, telling us he wanted to change hotels; maybe he would try the Ritz after all, which was where we had recommended to him in the first place. So we ended up going to Park Lane, picking up Fernando and Eudelia and taking them there. It was late at night, but Fernando was buzzing – and it wasn't drugs. (He'd made it clear to us he didn't take drugs or even smoke weed.) I think he fell in love with the Ritz that night. He made the staff show him loads of rooms and finally chose one of their best suites, which was about £4,000 a night. We said our goodnights and came home.

We went to Amsterdam first and stayed in the Hilton, which was far superior to the Park Lane one. We went to our suites and I began to feel unwell. I used to drink and smoke a lot of weed in those days. But I only ever smoked in the privacy of my own home, and as I could drink anyone under the table without getting drunk I knew it wasn't that. Besides, I hadn't had a drink on the plane. But I knew I was ill. I had pains in my stomach and head, and all I wanted to do was to get in bed and sleep. But we'd already booked a table in some restaurant, so I put the pain out of my head, had a bath, put on the slap, put on the uniform – full-length mink coat and five-inch stiletto heels – and went down to the bar to meet Benny and the others. We all got in the limo and went to a restaurant where I ate smoked salmon and caviar, which unbeknown to me would be my downfall later on that night.

Afterwards we all went to the red-light district. In my mind I didn't really believe that women stood in shop windows with their bits hanging out all over the place; I thought that was only in the films. However, I soon learned the reality of it all. Benny and Fernando walked in front of Eudelia and I, and we were just chatting together, not taking much notice. One minute our husbands were in front of us, the next I got a glimpse of the biggest, fattest, ugliest woman I'd ever seen in my life, sitting in a shop window. She had no bra on and her tits looked like footballs. Her belly was resting on her kneecaps and there were all these people – Benny and Fernando being no exception – standing outside looking at her. This bird was behind her little window (or maybe the window wasn't that little; she was just a big bird), and all of a sudden she got out this big white thing, which for some reason reminded me of the cigars Benny and Fernando smoked. With one hand she lifted up her belly, opened her legs so wide even the worst striker at Man United couldn't have missed getting one in her net, and with her other hand shoved this thing right up inside her. She was working it in and out while she then tried to get her left nipple in her mouth. I was rooted to the spot. I myself was no virgin and I'd been married twice in fifteen years, but I'd never done things like that.

She then shut the curtains and we walked away from the window. As we did so some pimp on the door, a big hat on and snide-gold medallions round his neck, said in broken English, 'Come on, you lovely people, who's going to be the lucky one and pay me to let you have the lovely voluptuous Candy all to yourself?'

'Candy?' I said. 'The only candy my old man's getting tonight is from me, you fucking pervert.'

We carried on walking up the street. There were a lot of people around, laughing and joking, and there were also a lot of junkies and pimps around, looking for someone to rob or hustle. Out of nowhere this bloke, who was built like a brick shithouse, came up and said something to Fernando. I didn't hear what it was, but Fernando told him to fuck off to which the bloke promptly replied, 'You never said that last night when I was fucking your arse. You don't want to know me now you're with your wife.' Fernando and Benny were not amused but they decided not to make a big thing out of it. After all, as hard as these two men were, they were in a right dodgy area in a foreign country and really didn't need the aggravation. I remember hoping we weren't going to have a fight there because I had my new shoes on!

Nothing came of it, thank God, but shortly after that I collapsed on the street in agony. I thought I was going to die. The next thing I knew I was waking up in my bed with a doctor sticking something down my throat, probably a thermometer or something. Then I was sitting up quick and retching into a bowl. I thought the whole of my insides were coming out of my mouth. I won't go into the gory details – I'm still here, aren't I? – but I thought it must have been food poisoning. (It wasn't until later, when we got home, that I found out I was five weeks pregnant with Benny junior.)

I think Fernando liked Benny and myself because, although we were very rich, we were just little fish compared to his wealth. I mean, by English standards we were millionaires, but by American standards we were just average. And Benny had such a liking for this man. I guess they were so alike in many ways. Fernando was about four years older than Benny, and like Benny had spent most of his life in prison and survived it. Although I was eighteen years younger than Benny and twenty-two years younger than

Fernando, I always thought of both my husband and my friend as little boys with too much money. But whereas Fernando spent his money like water, Benny of course used to iron his and was scared to spend it.

• • •

The first time I went to Miami was in the early eighties and I very nearly never got to leave the airport. After such a long flight I felt very dirty and sticky, and Benny said he'd look round the airport shops while I went to the beauty salon. It was there that I first realised just how much the Americans like the British. I was being made a right fuss of by all the staff; they were giving me cold drinks and chocolate like it was going out of fashion. I had my hair washed and was waiting for someone to come and dry it when this bloke, who I can only describe as drop-dead gorgeous, came over and put this hot wet towel round my face then started massaging my shoulders and my neck. Well, I shit myself – supposing Benny came in and saw what he was doing! This seemed right out of order. I was thinking, *I don't remember asking for a massage, and can't he see I've got a wedding ring on?* I promptly jumped out of the chair and kicked him right in the balls, and he went down like a sack of spuds. I remember everyone in the salon looked really shocked and the police were soon called. I told them what my problem was: that I found it offensive, this guy rubbing my shoulders and my neck, me being a respectable married woman. Well, the salon owner just burst out laughing, and so did the policemen (though the guy I'd kicked didn't laugh). That was when I found out that that's just the way they do it in America. It's all part of the service and everyone gets the same treatment, even men. I just wanted to die of shame. I'd really thought this bloke was trying to pull me. I remember the policeman telling me that he was only letting me off because I was English. Of course, I said a big sorry to the bloke I'd kicked, and I gave him $200 and told him to take his bird out for dinner. And then the manager promptly told me, 'No worries on that score, ma'am, you were never in any danger. He's gay!'

Benny fell asleep during the drive from the airport to the hotel on Collins Avenue but I stayed very much awake. *I'm in America! I can't believe it – me, Joan Hannington from an ex-council house in East Acton. I wonder if I'll see Muhammad Ali. I wonder if we'll have time to go to Disney World and see Mickey Mouse.* I was so overwhelmed by it all. I'd dreamed about this country all my life, never ever believing I would be there one day with lots of money in my pocket. I was as high as a kite. The sun was shining, the sky was so blue, the air was clean – I just knew that Miami would be everything Fernando had said it was. I've been back to America many times since then, including to New York, but I'll always remember that first trip as being the best, and I think that throughout my marriage to Benny this was my happiest time. Life couldn't get any better.

We spent the next three weeks drinking, eating, clubbing, having sex and hanging out with Fernando and Eudelia, who lived in the best part of Miami. His office was on the bay and he took great pleasure in telling us he sometimes went there from home by boat, which to me was really funny – nobody goes to work on a fucking *boat*. He took us to a restaurant one of his father's friends had built, which was exactly the same as one he'd owned in Havana years before. Most of the people eating there were Cuban and they treated Fernando with such love and respect. I don't think it had anything to with the fact that he was a rich man, or even a drug trafficker. These people loved him because he'd fought Castro; although he hadn't won the revolution, to them he was a real man of the people.

To this day I feel humbled by the thought of Fernando's presence. It doesn't trouble me that he became what he did when he left Cuba. Fidel Castro robbed him of the right ever to become a father, just as Eudelia was robbed of her chance to become a mother. When Fernando was in prison he didn't see his wife for twelve years, during which time she was also a political prisoner, and by the time they were both let out she was too old to have children. Any other man would probably have had a child with another woman, but Fernando didn't. And in turn his wife stood by him all through his life.

CHAPTER THIRTY

Trophy Wife

When a member of my husband's family went to prison and we first went to see him, Benny was almost proud of him, like a 'chip off the old block' type of situation. A lot of what the bloke knew, my husband had taught him. And look where it got him. To Benny it was a case of, *Oh well, at least he's not a grass; he's doing time . . . Well done, my man!* But to me it was a sad day, getting up and leaving this guy behind in a stinking prison. I remember walking out of prison that day with my designer clothes and diamonds on every finger, about to step into my brand-new white Jaguar and drive home to my beautiful home full of antiques, and I felt like scum. It seemed all of a sudden to put a barrier up between me and my husband.

By this time, Benny junior – or Ben, as we used to call him – was one year old, and worth more to me than all the diamonds in Cartier's main safe. Even though I was a criminal and was married to a criminal and spent a lot of time with criminals, as a mother I didn't want to bring him up to believe it was right to go down the road I went down. I couldn't bear the thought of him spending one night of his life in a prison, where he would be so vulnerable. Supposing some big nonce case got hold of him and hurt him? It never happened to me, but I began to think it could happen to Ben if I didn't help him to go down the straight road. It didn't matter what we'd done, was my reckoning, but we shouldn't bring our kid up to do the same. I felt that we owed it to him to give him love, to show him there was a better way of getting money than nicking it. I didn't quite know what that 'better way' was, but I just knew it had to exist.

• • •

Round about this time, when Ben was a young toddler, I relaxed in myself and became more content – and consequently I put on a lot of weight, about three stone. I carried it very well because I wore the right clothes: loose tops, long skirts, whatever. But I was aware of it when I undressed and so was Benny. He was going on about these doctors that everyone's wife was going to – it was always 'everyone's wife'. I knew what you were supposed to do to lose weight – exercise and cut down on certain foods – and I've always been very anti-drugs, pills and stuff, but Benny insisted I went. You could say, 'But Joan, you didn't have to go.' Quite right, I didn't have to go, but I went because it would keep him happy.

Be slim, you know, stay slim. And I did.

I used to have to go to this diet doctor once a week for an injection and within three months I'd gone from a size sixteen to a size eight. I'd gone from about eleven and a half stone to seven stone. I looked a million dollars because I never lost the bust; I had a bust at that time, after being pregnant, so I looked amazing. I was having to take tablets as well, amphetamines, and the last thing someone like me,

who's high-strung anyway, needs is to be taking amphetamines, which is speed of some description. And then to
counteract the speed so you can sleep at night, you have
the beta-blockers to knock you down. So you've got something to wake you up, so you're buzzing like a fucking bee,
and then you've got something to knock you out. And
that's the way it was. But for me, because I had loads of
energy anyway, being on speed made me feel like I was off
the planet.

I used to tell Benny I felt dizzy, or hyper, and then
when the injections were wearing off I'd get irritable. I
knew this wasn't right; I wasn't right in my mind. To me, it
was like being a junky. And basically that's what I was. I
could go out in the day and earn £10,000, kiting again.
The problem was that I'd be losing myself: at home I was
Joan Hannington but out there I'd be Barbara Smith, say,
a Scottish bird, so all day I'd be speaking with a Scottish
accent, and then for another four hours I might be Susan
Brown from the US. And it wasn't easy, you know,
because – whether you approve of the job or not – when
you're doing that sort of work you have to be sharp. You
can't afford to slip up.

Then when I'd go home and dump the bags – yeah, I'd
have lots of money, I'd got away with it, but I wasn't switching off; you don't, from that. I'd be still going, not able to
come down.

Benny's idea of coming down would be to drink and
take weed. I would never do it on drink; I couldn't get on
the drink buzz. And if he didn't have weed there'd be these
amazing mood swings. If he didn't have it, even for a day
or so, he'd go insane. Sometimes I'd have to get up and
drive down to Dalston at two in the morning to get weed.

Maybe understandable for someone on heroin or charlie, but my husband didn't come from that generation. Even so, after twenty-eight years in the nick, he was used to rolling his little spliff every night. And I now realise – as a person who's smoked weed – that you pretend it doesn't have much effect but if you smoke enough of it you do forget things, it kind of slows you down.

Anyway, eventually I stopped the pills and injections because I was going off my nut.

Benny was in his forties and, let's face it, not exactly good-looking. Right up until I was twenty-eight, twenty-nine, I was slim, pretty, game, kept my mouth shut. But even when I was in my mid-twenties and punk rock was in, he'd want me to have a bouffant or something, a beehive. I mean, *I'm twenty-five, not fucking forty. I don't want to look forty.* I realise now that I was far too young to be wearing mink coats; I should have been wearing jeans and a denim jacket. That's how I should have been dressing, and that's how I wanted to dress.

But Benny would say no, so-and-so and his old woman are coming.

I've done a big dinner, I've done all the cooking, and I've got to sit there in the stiletto heels, the blouse, the jewels, and he's coming over and whispering in my ear, 'Your lipstick's coming off. Go and put some more lipstick on.' And I'm in my own house; I can't even kick my shoes off. I'm on fucking parade. Like, twenty-four hours a day for twelve years I was on parade.

I wasn't a wife; I was a trophy. I was a fucking trophy.

We'd go to restaurants and I'd order off the menu. I knew how to use my knife and fork, and what went with what, but sometimes I wasn't sure exactly, with all these different menus. So I'd look and I'd say, 'Oh, right, I'll try that.' And of course sometimes when it came I wouldn't like it. Any normal person would say, 'Well, don't eat it, babes, if you don't want it.' Not Benny. He'd say, 'That's fifteen pounds,' or that's a tenner or whatever, and I'd say, 'Yeah, but it ain't really because we ain't paying for it, it's free.' You know, like – does it matter? Our money's never really our money. But because he'd paid for it he'd make me eat it. And me like a mug I would eat it; just for peace I'd eat it.

So on the one hand he was telling me I shouldn't get fat, then when we'd go to restaurants he'd insist that I eat whatever I'd ordered, even if I didn't want it. He could reduce me to tears. I'd be sitting there thinking, *This ain't right. One of us is not well, and I'm fucking sure it ain't me. But why am I the one sitting here feeling like shit and crying? No, he's not hitting me; he's not doing anything like that. He don't play away with other women. Yet he's this monster who took over.* All he wanted was to control me: what colour hair, what shade of lipstick, what to wear, what to say . . .

We'd be in the house for weeks at a time without having a conversation. He could sit in his chair night after night after night and not talk to me. In the same bed, having sex – you know, roll me over in the night, give me one and roll back.

After I stopped the injections and the pills, and because I wouldn't go on a diet, the weight started to go on again. And the more someone tells you you're fat, the more you find you're getting fatter. And it was always psychological abuse with Benny; it got to a stage where he'd be saying: 'You're too fat, I don't fancy you any more.' And that was a killer. Even though in my heart I didn't fancy him either – not that he knew that, of course – it still hurt.

Benny was still out thieving at night and I'd be kiting in the day. He had bundles of money – he was, as I've said, a millionaire, much richer than me – and yet he didn't spend any; he was the meanest, meanest, meanest man I've ever met. If he was your friend, you wouldn't have found him that way. But as his wife, well. I don't ever remember getting housekeeping off him. I bought the furniture – though not the antiques, obviously – and all the other stuff for the flat. He had the shops and yet my name wasn't on any of them. Everything seemed to be in his name or he'd have access to it, or he'd have the keys or he'd have the account books. Of course, he used to tell me that if he died it was mine, I'd get it all, but I never felt secure. I just felt, like happened with Ray Pavey, that any day he could up and go and I'd have nothing. Which I thought would have been a bit unfair. So over time I became quite dishonest with him, if that's what you want to call it. If I went out and earned thirty grand I'd come home and say I only earned ten, and I'd put the other twenty away – hide it or whatever.

They say crime doesn't pay. Well, I'd say that it does, but only as long as you're prepared to pay in other ways. Crime pays very big financial dividends but there are a lot of hidden costs along the way.

It was always big money. I wouldn't get out bed for little money. I always worked on the basis that if I got caught I was going to get bird, and I might as well get bird for some creamy crime, not because I didn't have a TV licence or for nicking out of Woolworths. Never saw the sense in that sort of thing. I can't sit here and write that Benny made me do it, forced me into it . . . He did, to a degree. But I also liked the nice homes, I liked the nice restaurants, I liked the nice side of what money could bring.

What I didn't like was the arseholes I had to deal with, the two-facedness, and sometimes the violence. The truth is that I enjoyed the buzz. Thieving made me feel alive; it was my sex, my drug, because it gave me good self-esteem. Because it was the only thing I felt I was any good at.

Most people when they do something will always ask, 'Did I do all right? Am I good? Do I look OK?' When it came to being a thief, I never had to ask anyone. I knew I was good. That's a terrible claim to fame, but I know I was good at what I did. Probably if I'd had the right channels and the right, you know, background, I could have done anything I wanted to do. I realise that now. But that's *if, if, if.* I didn't do anything else. I was a thief.

Another thing Benny would suggest from time to time was that I should get involved with certain people to find out information about their bank account or to burgle them or whatever. He wanted me to do the dirty deed just so he could rob them. I always refused to do it. The idea was for me to get into some bloke because hubby wanted to get the deal going. And they always fancied me. I'm not trying to build myself up to be something, but I was lovely when I was young, and the blokes he did business with were forty, fifty years old, and I was in my twenties with blonde hair down to my arse.

That's when you step back and start to think. Benny was worth literally hundreds of thousands in cash alone. He had shops, lock-ups, cars; he was involved in bonds and all that on a very big scale. He had money in America, Spain, Germany, bank accounts in the Cayman Islands. In other words, he had bundles. So why did he want me to sleep with some old bastard just so he could do him over? I could never and will never get my head around that one.

And so I began to hate him, and he knew it, and then I couldn't have sex with him any more.

The day eventually came – and I suppose it had to – when he said to me, 'Do you want out of this marriage?' and I said that yes, I did.

He said, 'Well, you can pack your bags and go.'

I'm like, 'Excuse me, mate. This is *my* fucking house. This was my house before I met you. It was my house, it's still my house, you know it's my house. You go and, you know, take your fucking antiques with you.'

Take the ones I've nicked as well.

I never thought I'd see myself on that level, when you come to carving it up – this is yours, that's mine. I couldn't deal with that; I can't. I'd rather let the other person have it and walk away. I couldn't argue with Benny about it, but that didn't stop me thinking, *You cunt, I've been grafting for ten years here. I've suffered every piece of shit you've thrown at me, I've looked after you when you're in the nick. I've been loyal, I haven't got a lover, I just want to be free from this shit.*

In the end we didn't split up because I didn't want to raise my son on my own. The truth was that I'd always thought that once we had money we'd go into business and that would be the end of the dodgy lifestyle. We'd become nice people, straight people. (Yeah, we are nice people and we have got shops but we're still criminals.) Benny couldn't come out of that; he wouldn't let us, as a couple, come out of it. The way I saw it was that when you've reached a certain level and you've got a lot of money, *you don't need to be doing this.* Benny couldn't see it that way. I had to go to work every day – it didn't matter if I only brought a hundred pounds' worth of goodies in. If I didn't go to work every day he'd have the hump and he'd sulk for weeks.

Like the time I used to buy paintings and antiques off the Irish underground. I just thought Benny was so shit, because he'd send me out there but he never had to deal with them, it was always me. I'd have maybe £300,000 in my pocket and no one watching my back. I'd be going up the road to meet this Sean and this Michael; and all right, they're IRA, but I didn't know everybody in the IRA. And 300 grand was – is – a lot of money. I'd be thinking, *Supposing I don't come home, supposing they kill me?* 'I don't want to go,' I'd say. 'You go.'

'No, you go. They know you; they trust you, you're one of them.'

Thinking about it now, he was as cold as he had to be when it came to money. He was from a different generation to me. I suppose it was the generation that came from nothing. And, although he never went without during the war or after, he couldn't change. That's why he was the way he was.

One thing about Benny, though, was that I never had to worry about other women. He'd be out all day and perhaps back tonight, perhaps not; either way, I wouldn't worry. I didn't know where he'd gone or what he was up to. He'd just say, 'Don't have anyone in, because I don't know when I'm coming back and what I'll be bringing with me.' I always knew he wasn't unfaithful because when he'd come back you could see where he'd been: he'd be tired, hungry, covered in shit, and happy 'cause he'd have all this gear he'd just nicked.

One time he'd been off on one of his jaunts and came back with a million pounds in cash.

He'd been up to something (I didn't have a clue what and knew not to ask) and had been away about three days.

I was in bed asleep when he came into the bedroom and told me to get up and close my eyes and not open them till he said. We had a big Victorian brass bed, and he laid all this money down, covering the bed completely. He told me to keep my eyes closed, and of course I didn't. I had my hands over my face but was looking through the cracks in my fingers. I nearly creamed my knickers at the sight of all this money. I mean, I was a good thief myself, and had had some nice touches, but I'd never seen as much in my life before. It was all over the bed, on the floor – and to think we only lived about 200 yards from Holloway Police Station. The buzz was mind-blowing.

Standing there like a little boy waiting for some praise, Benny told me to open my eyes. I made a show of looking at the money, then promptly turned to Benny and said, 'I hope you don't think I'm going to fucking iron that, babe.'

'No,' he said, 'you're going to get your drawers off and come here' – pulling me down on the bed. We fucked like rabbits on top of all this money and when Benny was ready to come his lot he shouted out, 'Queen Elizabeth, this is for you, darling,' which I thought was really funny, because he knew I hated the Royal Family (apart from Diana of course).

I don't care what normal people think of that, because only a criminal's wife knows that feeling. It's a rush that no drink or drugs can give you. It's just pure adrenaline. Little did I know that night that Benny would be dead in two years, and Fernando doing thirteen years in a Florida jail; but at least my husband never died in one of Her Majesty's prisons.

CHAPTER THIRTY-ONE

An Ordinary Friendship

I can't remember how I found out Fernando was in jail in Argentina. Back in 1986, Fernando and Eudelia were coming to London to attend my son Ben's christening. They were to be his godparents. Fernando was really pleased we'd asked him, yet I felt the honour was mine. I phoned them up about a week beforehand to make final arrangements, but their home number was out of order. At first I wasn't too worried – I thought he probably changed it every three months anyway – so I phoned his office, his car phone, his personal secretary and a load of other people. Every number was unobtainable. I knew then that something was wrong. I'd sussed out within a few months of meeting Fernando that he was a big-time drug trafficker, so I just assumed he'd been nicked. I knew he'd contact us eventually. All the same, in my heart I was really worried. Benny was very upset because he had such a liking for this man.

We went ahead with the christening. I had Ben's gown and long coat and bonnet made in ivory silk, all by hand, by my friend Krisha. He looked like a prince and never cried once during the service. We took him to church in a vintage Rolls-Royce – it was a really good day for me.

As I mentioned, I'd begun to change my way of thinking a bit when my boy was born. He was such a wanted child by both his parents, and I just wanted to stay home all the time with him. I think I was frightened of missing out on something.

The following year, when my son was about fourteen months old, Benny and I decided to go to Argentina for Christmas, because we'd had contact with Fernando by then and knew what jail he was in. Neither of us really wanted to go – English people weren't exactly flavour of the month after the Falklands War. The first thing we saw as we went through passport control was a big banner that read 'The Falklands Belong to Argentina'. We just looked at each other. We didn't say anything, but I knew we were both thinking, *What the fuck are we doing in this country?* My priorities were with my baby, Ben, all the time. I just wanted to get back on the plane and go home. I hated this country even before I left the airport.

During our journey to the hotel I couldn't help but notice all the cars. I'd never seen so many old bangers – only they weren't really bangers; they were in mint condition, from the fifties and sixties. Those cars would have been worth a fortune in that condition back in England, and I wondered how much it would cost to ship them over. We could make a killing and it would be legal.

When we got to the hotel they obviously knew we were English and we had to carry our own luggage up to our suite. Only it wasn't the two-bedroom suite we'd ordered, it was just a room with a double bed and no cot for Ben, no air conditioning, and full of flies. Not to pull any punches, it was a fucking pisshole, yet it was rated as 4-star. Ben was hungry and started crying so I rang for room service, but no one spoke English. And if that wasn't bad enough, I'd lost Eudelia's address and didn't know how I was going to contact her. We tried to phone someone in America but were then told that all the hotel phones were out of order. I swear, if anyone thinks Fawlty Towers was a joke, they should try the Hotel de las Americas.

Because the conditions in the hotel were the pits, Benny and I decided we'd stay for one night only; I don't think we even had anything to eat there. It was quite obvious that the staff didn't like the English, and we thought they might spit in our food. So we found another hotel to stay in for the rest of our visit. Eventually we got Eudelia's address and went to see her. She was on her own with a maid, Monica, who couldn't speak a word of English, but she made us very welcome and more or less kidnapped my young son.

We were in Argentina for three days before we got into the prison to see Fernando. The day before we did, I remember we got up early and turned on the TV in our room. And of course every channel was in Spanish, but even though we didn't understand what was going on we could just sense there was something wrong: on all the channels there were pictures of soldiers and military vehicles. I decided to go downstairs and make enquiries. I was told to go back to my room, I wasn't allowed to leave the hotel. I thought it was a joke but it wasn't. I told my husband what had happened, and we decided to go out for a walk. But when we got downstairs with baby Ben in his buggy, the people in reception still tried to make us stay inside. Because we didn't speak Spanish and they didn't speak much English, we didn't really understand what they were telling us, so we just walked outside.

There was no one on the streets, no cars anywhere, and all the shops were shut. My bottle started to go when we heard shouting and gunfire, and all of a sudden there were soldiers everywhere. But what was really scary was that they seemed to be running towards us. I remember saying to Benny, 'Don't worry, it's not us they want; they'll probably run straight past us.' I was wrong. It *was* us they were chasing after. We just froze on the spot. We had guns shoved under our noses and were forced to stand against a wall. Baby Ben was in his buggy, chatting away in some mumbo-jumbo language, like babies do, and in a panic I bent down to pick him up; then this soldier – I don't know what he thought I was going to do – literally put a gun to my head. I just closed my eyes and stood there holding my baby, thinking this man was going to blow my brains out.

When I opened my eyes the gun was still pointed at my head, but I think the soldier must have realised I was only concerned about my baby and he moved back. They were yelling at Benny to put his hands on his head, and when he wouldn't they kept shouting into his face and poking a gun at his chest. Neither Benny nor I said a word; I think we were both so frightened we just couldn't speak, and we were totally in the dark about what was going on. I mean, we'd only arrived in the country a couple of days earlier and hadn't left the hotel apart from when we went to see Eudelia – and everything had seemed OK then. So why the fuck were soldiers suddenly chasing us up the street and threatening to kill us? None of it made any sense. And the really scary thing was that there wasn't another human being in sight, not one person around apart from us and these poxy soldiers.

After what seemed like ages we started trying to explain that we were staying in a hotel and were here on holiday. At first they didn't want to know, but then I think they finally realised we weren't from Argentina and didn't have a clue what was going on. I can't say they were violent to us; they weren't, but my poor husband's complexion was going from white to grey and his lips were going purple. I thought he was going to have a heart attack. I have to laugh about it now. It turned out that we had arrived in Argentina during a military coup. Basically the army tried to overthrow the government or something like that, and apparently what we'd been watching on the TV was an announcement telling everyone they weren't allowed out on the street because the government had called a curfew after midnight. Well, we didn't understand the language, how was we supposed to know? We asked the soldiers to take us to the British Embassy. Then Benny suddenly realised – if the Embassy run a check on him they might find out that he shouldn't have left England in the first place. He was on bail for receiving, and one of his conditions of bail was that he wasn't to leave the country, so how could he explain that?

God, I thought, *supposing he ends up in a fucking jail in Argentina like Fernando, waiting to get extradited back to England?* I couldn't see myself lasting too long alone in this country.

We were eventually taken to the Swedish Embassy, because at that time, even though the war was over between Britain and Argentina, there were still no diplomatic relations between the two countries. However, it was good to be in the Embassy: for the first time in two days we got to speak to someone who could speak English, and it didn't take them long to explain our situation to the soldiers. After a brief lecture from the authorities we were taken back to our hotel and all was well again.

Benny started making a right big fuss of me and baby Ben, promising me that once we'd seen Fernando he'd take us straight to Brazil for a proper holiday. I think this little episode shook my husband up a bit. He really thought the soldiers were going to blow my head off when I bent down to pick baby Ben up, and for the first time in his life he felt utterly helpless. He said that all he could think of at the time was that old habit of mine of laughing whenever I get nervous, and he'd thought that if I'd started laughing then they'd shoot me for sure. But what's funny about having a gun put to your head when you don't even know why? Even I knew not to laugh at that point.

I have to say that at thirty years of age I thought I'd seen it all and nothing could shock me in life; that is until we arrived at the jail where Fernando was staying.

The first thing I noticed was there was no windows in this building. I couldn't even put an age to it, other than it was very old. As I stood waiting to go in with Benny and Benny junior, all I could think of was the film *Midnight Express*. Imagine the prison in that film, then imagine it a thousand times worse. As I stood in the filthy waiting room, a rat ran across my foot. There wasn't anywhere to get a cup of tea. Not that you'd drink it – the first thing you noticed was the smell of piss, then the rats, then the damp, the broken pipes everywhere leaking sewage. The guards were the dirtiest, filthiest pigs I've ever come across. I wanted to just turn round and get out of there, but we'd come so far already to see our friend and he knew we were coming. If ever my friendship or loyalty to someone had been tested, this was it.

I mean, in all the time we knew Fernando we never asked him for anything. Even though he pointed out on so many occasions when we went to America that we were his guests, we always paid our way. For us proud Brits, it couldn't have been different. If he paid one time, Benny paid the next. We weren't as rich as him but we certainly weren't poor – and why ponce on someone else just because they're richer than you? Also, for me, I didn't like accepting anything from anyone. A strange attitude for someone who spent half her life being a thief, I know, but I was independent to the core and never wanted to owe anyone anything, not even my husband. I think it was my safeguard: you know, go and get your own and don't live off other criminals.

Our friendship with Fernando wasn't about what he could do for us or what we could do for him. We didn't do business with him, apart from the odd antique here and there. Ours was just an ordinary friendship and a genuine one, and that's how I found myself, my son and my husband halfway across the world in this dirty, filthy pisshole of a prison. I couldn't help remembering the last time I'd seen Fernando Pruna, in Miami eighteen months before. We'd all had dinner in Raguns in Coconut Grove, and he was the investment banker. Now I was seeing him as the big-time drug trafficker. I wasn't shocked, and I didn't think any less of him. He was still my mate. As far as I was concerned, anyone who was prepared to spend one night in this hell of a prison, in virtual darkness for the next four years, I could only respect. He knew the risks and took them and bloody good luck to him. I just hoped that in the not-too-distant future they'd send him back to America, where the prisons were easier and cleaner.

After much waiting around we were eventually marched off to where the visit was to take place. On the way we passed this cage made of metal bars, nothing in it except a man with no clothes on who just sat there, rocking backwards and forwards, totally off his nut. I was beginning to feel a nervous laugh at the sight of his willy on full view. Not that it was funny or anything, I thought it was a bit inhumane, but I was so much on edge. (I later found out from Fernando that this man was a rapist and that's why they made him stay in this cage on full view. I must admit I was a bit shocked when Fernando also said that the man hadn't even been found guilty yet – but they were still treating him like that. I promised myself I'd never get nicked in Argentina.)

Considering the barbaric conditions of this prison, I was amazed when I finally saw Fernando. He looked like the fucking prison governor. Everyone around him – prisoners and guards alike – were absolutely filthy, unshaven pigs. And there, at the end of this room, stood our friend, looking like he'd just walked out of a barber's shop, all groomed and clean-shaven, wearing a clean white shirt and pressed trousers. It was so amazing I just burst out laughing.

Fernando explained to us that unless you had friends or family to bring you food, clothes or a mattress, you just went without. Apparently the prison authorities didn't legally have to feed them or give them a mattress, so they didn't. (There were 900 men using about three toilets,

Fernando said, and paper was a luxury.) Fernando was lucky; he had his wife to bring him food and clothes. He also had the best lawyer money could buy and was constantly in touch with him – although at the time he had no idea that he would be in that prison for four years before getting extradited to America to stand trial. (After which, in 1993, he was sentenced to thirteen years in a US jail.) It seemed as if they did just what they wanted with you in Argentina, guilty or not.

Fernando even managed to find humour in the whole experience somewhere. I think it was because my friend was so mentally strong. After he'd survived Castro's prisons for seventeen years, this seemed like a doddle to him. The young villains of today probably couldn't survive in a jail like that; they'd end up topping themselves.

We visited Fernando several times, and eventually we stayed on in Argentina for a holiday. We took a short plane journey to a seaside place called Mar del Plata. The people were much nicer and we never saw any soldiers there. But I have to admit it was one country I was pleased to leave with not too many intentions ever to go back.

CHAPTER THIRTY-TWO

22 November 1990

Coincidentally, this was my daughter Debbie's sixteenth birthday. Benny came in from work at the usual time, about half-past six. He emptied all his pockets on the table: a few cheques, three or four grand in cash, shop keys – apart from the big money, all the gear you might find in your pockets. It's what he did every night, and then he'd go upstairs, strip off, take a quick shower and put on a pair of tracksuit bottoms and leather slippers. He did this, as usual, then came downstairs, had a malt whisky and rolled a joint. After he'd had his dinner he said he had to pop out later on a bit of business. 'Nothing wrong; just to do a valuation.' He told me a man was coming round to pick him up. 'If I'm upstairs let him in, babe.' And I told him no problem.

So, about eight o'clock – it was after *Coronation Street* – Benny was upstairs tarting about when there was a knock at the door and I let this man in. As I'm letting him in Benny's coming down the stairs: 'Oh, hello, mate, go on through.'

The man was about five feet ten, swarthy-looking. I didn't know him but I knew he was an Egyptian and that he had a rug shop down Portobello somewhere. He came in my front room and I picked up on his vibe straight away; I just picked up that there was something not right about this geezer. Benny went back upstairs, and so I told this guy to make himself comfortable, invited him to sit down, you know, and then he saw there was a little child there. Benny junior was about four, so beautiful you'd want to take a bite out of him, and even if you didn't like children you'd usually try to make some sort of conversation – 'Oh, what a lovely little boy.' But this guy didn't.

We had this Sheridan wall cabinet with cupboards and leaded glass along the top, and it was filled with porcelain and China and Tiffany crystal and everything. And instead of sitting down this guy kind of stood with his back to me, looking at the unit. I got the impression he didn't want me to see his face, and I remember thinking, *That's a bit ignorant. You don't even know me, you've come into my house, me and my baby are here and you ignore us, looking at my things.*

Benny come back down and said to me, 'We're going, babe. We'll only be about two hours . . .'

Then guy said, 'No, no, no, we'll be a lot quicker than that, maybe an hour.'

'Well, depending on traffic,' Benny went.

I said, 'Shall I put Ben to bed?'

'No, babe, keep him up and I'll bring him some pop back.'

He gave me a kiss on the cheek and walked out.

I don't know what I was thinking but I had a funny feeling, strange enough for me to run upstairs and look out the bedroom window to see which way he went when he left the house. Which I'd never done before. I'd never questioned him; I never had any reason to. But there was something not right in my head. I looked out and couldn't see them, so I came back downstairs. The way he'd acted was perfectly natural. He'd left the three grand, his keys, he hadn't even smoked the joint – he'd rolled it but didn't have time to smoke it – it was all there on the table. So I knew he was coming back soon.

By ten o'clock that night I'd put Benny junior to bed, but I hadn't got the hump, I just thought my husband had been delayed. I just sat there watching the telly (a new one, about three days old) with our dog, Lulu. Well, Benny's dog; she was about thirteen at the time. Then Lulu suddenly got off the chair and for no reason made this howling noise, like a wolf. It was awful. I'd heard it before, as a child, probably in a film on the telly, and I related it to a death call, when a dog knows his master's dead.

But I didn't get upset or worked up or anything – after all, it was only what I knew as a kid, something on the telly. So I didn't get the buzz.

While the dog was going off her trolley and I wasn't sure where she was coming from, my television blew up. The plug shot out of the wall and the telly conked. Of course I got frightened, and I went to wherever the main box was, switched everything off and then switched it back on again. Everything seemed normal again, so I turned on the ten o'clock news, and there was an item about this explosion, suspected IRA, that'd happened. I can't remember the exact details of what they were saying, but it was in west London, and there was darkness and a building lit up and fire engines everywhere. (Later I learned the blast was heard from half a mile away, and it demolished a house on the corner of Inverness Street and Bayswater Road.) I saw them bring the body-bag out and they said there'd been one fatality. I still didn't think anything was wrong.

By about twelve o'clock, I was getting tired and I wanted to go to bed; but I had to wait for Benny.

I sat up all night. He didn't come home.

By half seven in the morning I was thinking, *Bastard, he could have phoned.* Then, *No, he was obviously on a bit of work; he's probably in a gaff somewhere, no problem. Today I'll get a phone call.*

I waited all day, but no phone call.

By night-time I was getting a bit edgy. It was still only twenty-four hours since he'd left, but I was getting nervous. I didn't know who to phone, couldn't phone anyone, didn't dare phone anyone. And I now knew there was something wrong. I didn't know he was dead; I just knew there was something wrong.

I knew that we didn't have any enemies, because we didn't get enemies; we didn't cause trouble with anyone. So obviously I knew he'd not been murdered . . .

Then I thought, *Well, hang on, he could have been taken away because it's known that we've got bundles. You know people, they gossip – maybe he's been kidnapped. But do they know there's money under the floorboards in his shop? Is that why they kidnapped him? Fine, then go to the shop.* I had the keys, so the next day I went where the money was, in the warehouse at the back, and it hadn't even been disturbed. I went into the shop area, which was done out like a front room, with furniture and rugs, the idea being that people would come in and sit down and think, *Oh, this is comfy,* and end up buying the chair.

I lifted up the rug from where his table was and I pulled out about £8,000 in cash, which I assumed would have been the day's takings. I took that money and brought it home and put it on the table, thinking that if he got angry I'd just tell him I'd got panicky and went to check it out; he wouldn't have minded.

Of course, he didn't come home that night either. And I was telling myself I had to think logically. He wasn't a womaniser; he wasn't one for going out; he was always home. For ten years I could read him like a book. The dinner was at the same time, we were very routine in our life – that's why our marriage survived, because it was such a routine. And all of a sudden that routine is broken.

We hadn't had a row – we didn't row, really – and from this point on I thought, *He's obviously got to be dead then. He's dead.*

Well, no, maybe not – if he's dead I'd have been told by now. If he was in a car crash they'd have told me. He's been nicked. So the rule is, if he's been nicked I'll know in three days. The first day, you don't tell them who you are; you get locked up in the cell overnight, you go to court the next day – that's day two. The magistrate will pass an order that they can take your prints off you by force, and even if you've given them a dodgy name they've got your prints. So I was thinking, *If he's been nicked and given a dodgy name, he's got people he can contact. I'll know by the third day.*

On the third day, I waited until about eleven o'clock in the evening and nothing happened. I didn't know he was dead. (Well, I *did* know he was dead, as it happens, I just knew; but I told myself he wasn't.)

So finally I phoned up my friend Mick, a copper, and I told him the story. The long and the short of it was that Mick said he'd try to tell me by the end of the night if Benny was nicked or if he was dead. Mick asked me if I'd officially reported Benny missing, because he'd been gone three days. I said no, of course I hadn't; Mick should know we wouldn't do that. 'We'll give it another day,' he said. 'If I can't tell you something by tomorrow we'll think about Plan B.'

Obviously, with all this happening, all this not

knowing, I was going off my rocker. I hadn't eaten, I hadn't slept, I was crying, worried, scared.

I phoned my stepson Buster and he came and took Benny junior back to Brighton to stay with him and his girlfriend Sara, just to give me a bit of space. He didn't think his dad was dead; he just thought he was on a bit of work. But he could see I was worried.

The next morning (the fourth day), Mick phoned me back.

'Joan, I can guarantee you he's not in prison, he's not nicked. He's not in hospital and he's not in prison under that name, this name, or any other name.' Then he said to me, 'Now come on, Joan, have you and Benny had a row with anyone? Is he involved in the drug world?'

In 1990 the drug world proper had only just hit London, and I said, 'No, no. Leave it out.' But he'd only asked because he knew about our connection in America with Fernando and all that. I told him, 'Please, don't even think it. I'm not hiding anything—we are not involved in drugs.'

No one had killed my Benny for that, as far as I knew.

Mick went on: 'Well, I think now you'd better go and make it official.'

So I called Holloway Police Station and said I wanted to report my husband missing. At first they didn't seem bothered, like, 'Oh yeah . . .' Then they said, 'What's your husband's name?'

'Donald Thomas Hannington.'

They were there in two seconds. I lived opposite the police station so they only had to walk across the road. And because they knew Benny to be a big-time villain, they thought, 'Let's go, it could be murder.' Yeah, they loved it.

As soon as this cosser walked through my front door I

knew him. It was a guy called George Couch. I didn't know from where, but we established we knew each other. He said, 'I know this is going to be painful, but you've reported him missing and I've got to ask you: have you got a lover?' Even though it was an awful time for me, they were saying things like that. 'Well, Joan, you're twenty years younger than your husband, you know, and you're a good-looking girl.'

I got very defensive with the police. 'If that's how you're gonna start, no, I ain't got a lover. I married this man because I loved him. Forget age, forget money, he's the only man in my life, and if you want to start with that you'd better fuck off.'

So then this copper went, 'You know, Joan, you're no different than anybody else. We have to ask these questions. You'd be surprised how many young women marry older men and get them bumped off.'

I said, 'This fucking bird ain't one of them, 'cause she's got her own dough.'

Anyway, it was official now – description, what was he wearing, when I last saw him, etc. Then we went to the shop and they searched it. I didn't know what they were searching for; a body, I suppose. But there was nothing there, nothing suspicious, and that's all they could do for now: 'You've reported it, and if you hear from him obviously let us know.'

I don't remember exactly when I found out Benny was dead. I do remember being at home, crying all the time, smoking cigarettes and drinking coffee non-stop. I'd hardly been to sleep, I was smelly, my mouth dirty, but I didn't care. Thinking things like, *Just because you don't love him doesn't mean you want him dead. Wanting out the marriage don't mean I hate him enough to wish him dead.*

There was a knock at the door and it was Mick. I didn't know what to say and I must have been stinky, not caring how I looked. He'd phoned me up about an hour before and asked if I was all right. And when I'd said, 'Yeah, I think so,' he'd said he'd pop over. So I thought he was coming round for a cup of tea, you know, see if I was all right, see if he could find anything out. So there was Mick at the door and with him another man in plainclothes and a policeman in uniform – and I remember that when that one saw me he took his cap off. I said, 'Oh, fuck me, don't tell me you've come to tell me I'm the Merry Widow.'

The guy in the uniform sort of reacted, stood back. It was all so quick. They came inside, and I now knew why they were there. I knew what they were going to tell me but I just didn't want to hear it. I was fart-arsing about, asking if they wanted a cup of tea, and as they were trying to tell me I was off in the kitchen putting the kettle on. Mick came in and he said, 'Joan, you're going to have to come in the front room. You know I have something to tell you, and I've got to tell you.'

Mick was a bit older than me, a hard bastard, but he was all right. He'd been a policeman for fifteen or twenty years, been on armed robbery and murder cases, there's nothing he hadn't seen, but in all his career he'd never had to go and break the news to somebody that their husband was dead. He'd never had to do it.

'There was an explosion in west London and your husband's in a bad way.' It turned out that the police were watching my husband the night he went out. They knew more than I did, these policemen, knew he went out in a red BMW and followed him to this address in west London. Benny hadn't disclosed any of this to me. They saw him go into the building on Bayswater Road but they had no more idea than I did that he was going to commit arson. That wasn't what Benny was about, arson. Except on this one occasion, when him and his accomplice were torching the building so somebody could cop the insurance. After he disappeared inside the police drove away, apparently, because they knew where he was, and where to look if the place got burgled. Which it didn't. It blew up.

My husband was on his way out – had actually left the premises – and as he shut the door the place went up and took him with it.

I had to go down to Horseferry Mortuary to identify the body. The lady pulled this screen aside and the first thing I saw was my husband's tongue. All I could see of him was the lower part of his face, from under the nose to the chin. The rest of it had been blown away. He had no eyes. No nose. His head was to one side on his shoulder. His lips had expanded in the heat and his tongue was hanging down – it seemed to come right down onto his breast. I'd never realised how long a human tongue was before.

I don't know what made me say it. I wanted to scream and cry but I knew I couldn't drop my guard. I remember saying, 'Blimey, you could give good plate with that tongue, Boisie.'

The copper behind me just couldn't believe what I said. But I had to find humour. I could feel my legs going. I couldn't move. I thought, *If anyone tries to move me I'm going to fall over.*

He wasn't buried, he was cremated. I mean, he'd already cremated himself before he went anyway. Boisie's number was up.

CHAPTER THIRTY-THREE

Payback Time (1)

My husband blew himself to bits. There was no visiting him at the hospital, just the knock at the door to say he was dead. You never get over it; it's a shock that stays with you for years. Even now if there's a knock on my door or a phone ringing after ten o'clock at night, I won't answer it in case it's the police with bad news; I don't want to hear it. But I'm big enough to know that if you live by the sword, you die by the sword. My husband knew what he was doing. The fact that it went wrong and he blew himself up is life, and I didn't want anyone's sympathy and my husband would have agreed with me.

Looking back now it's easy to say 'I shouldn't have done this, I shouldn't have done that', but death affects people in different ways. I'd never really experienced emotional grief before. My dad's death ten years earlier hadn't upset me that much. I hated his guts all my life and those feelings didn't change when he died. Because my husband was eighteen years older than me, I'd always expected that I'd outlive him; I didn't think he'd be dead at fifty and I'd be a widow at thirty-two with a young son, though. The fact that he left me so much money and possessions and property didn't come into it. I think I was scared because I'd been with a man since I was fifteen, and although I'd lived on my own for a little while after I left Ray but before I met Benny, I hadn't had much experience of it. I hated it. It had nothing to do with sex. I mean, you can get that anywhere – and besides, I was always much more happy out thieving than pulling blokes. When I met and married Benny it wasn't hard to be faithful or loyal. He was a good bloke. We were together eleven years before he died, and apart from me going to jail for two years and him doing ten months of a four-year sentence, we'd not really been apart. I knew I was going to find it hard on my own, especially as I had so much valuable property and three shops. I knew I'd be a target for robbery.

The security in my home was the best money could buy; every window had grilles on it, all the doors had locks. But I'd been married to one of London's most professional and successful burglars, so I knew that nothing was really impossible. If someone really wants to get in your home, then they'll get in. And for me, it started four days after I heard about Benny's death, with someone trying to break through my back gate at about two in the morning. But right at that moment, I wasn't too worried. I knew he couldn't see me sitting there in the dark, watching his every move. First he tried to break the glass of my sitting-room door so he could cut the grilles and get to the locks. Under normal circumstances I would have been asleep at that hour, but I wasn't. I'd found that after reporting Benny missing and then finding out he was dead, I couldn't stand to go upstairs to our bedroom. So I would put Benny junior to bed and go back downstairs and sit up all night, thinking, crying, talking to myself, getting angry – all sorts of things would be running through my mind. And now this bloke was trying to get into my home, not realising that I was only about eight feet away from him, lying fully clothed on a chair. I can't say I was frightened. I knew that if he was lucky enough to get the door open I'd have been off that chair like lightning, smashing a big bronze statue over his head, so either way I couldn't lose.

I could have phoned the police and they'd have been there in seconds but that wouldn't have been right. How could I have phoned the police and told them my home was getting burgled when I'd been married to a burglar most of my adult life? That to me seemed wrong. I just wouldn't have had the cheek to phone the police. And I wouldn't have wanted this bloke, whoever he was, to get nicked because of me. Plus, of course, he had much more to fear than me, only he didn't know it.

I let him fuck about outside a bit longer, then I just jumped up, ran to the door he was trying to get in and pulled the curtain back. Well, he got such a shock. I was shouting at him through the glass: 'If you ain't got in yet, you cunt, then you're never gonna get in, and when you do I'll be ready for you.' He may have heard the first part, but by then he was up and back over the garden wall before I could do anything more. So with him gone I just went and rolled a joint and laid back on the chair. I remember thinking to myself, *Well, Joan, you'd had it very good this past ten or eleven years. Now it's payback time.*

And payback I got.

I organised Benny's funeral myself. We had sixteen stretch limos, six bagpipers and a horse-drawn hearse with huge wreaths either side. Not long afterwards I found out I had to go to Southend and collect a lorry-load of antiques up from the police station. Benny had been arrested a month or so before his death for receiving stolen property. He was later charged with other offences, one of which was burglary. At Benny's age, you don't need charges like that, especially when most of the twenty-eight years in total that he'd spent in prison were for the same offences – he knew that if he got found guilty he was facing ten years. He wasn't actually caught on any burglaries in the end, but the police had arrested someone Benny had bought gear from who lived in Southend. They struck up a deal that if this bloke told them who was buying the gear from him they wouldn't charge him, because at the time there were no prizes down at the nick for catching burglars. It seemed like the police were only interested in the receivers. But this person then informed the police that Benny had also been on some of the burglaries with him, and that it was Benny who'd told him which houses to burgle.

They remanded him in the nick to see if Benny would visit him, which he did. He met this bloke's mum at South-end train station and they went to the prison together. What Benny didn't know was that there was a tape recorder stuck under their table during the visit, and that everything said could be used against Benny at a later date – which it was. That's how Benny came to be on bail for receiving and was facing at least six to ten years at the time of his death. He was due to go for trial in 1991, but now that he was dead there was no case against him and the police had to hand all of Benny's property over to me. There were hundreds of pieces there – furniture, paintings, books, China, porcelain and loads of other stuff. To me it was a pain in the arse, right after his funeral, and I have to admit

I wasn't looking forward to going to Southend nick: I'd once upset one of the coppers down there big-time.

Benny and I had been taken to one of our shops so that we could witness the search and the removal of property from the premises. I remember overhearing some of the cossers laughing because the first thing they'd come across in the warehouse at the back of the shop was a big spider. It wasn't real – it was all furry and rubbery – but it looked real. They were larking about, throwing this spider at each other. But when they threw it at one of their mates he nearly passed out, and I knew straightaway that he had a phobia about spiders. Normally I wouldn't have noticed; it was just his reaction when this thing was thrown at him.

Not long after this, the copper in question happened to upset me, and when he did I decided to settle the score. For fear of incriminating myself I've decided not to tell the whole story, but let's just say I found a way to take the piss before the trial. And this copper found a real live tarantula in the top left-hand drawer of his desk at Southend Police Station . . .

I wonder if he ever discovered how it got there?

In the months after Benny's death the shops were broken into three times. I knew one robbery was down to someone – I'll call him Chaz – who used to work for my husband. The day I walked into Hornsey Police Station to report it, who should I see there but this bloke Chaz. I'd always hated him anyway – he was one of the Yes brigade. I have no idea what he was doing there, but I do know that this was the first time I'd seen him since finding out he'd robbed my shop a few nights earlier. The minute he saw me he jumped over the counter to get away. I jumped over after him. I was going like a fucking nutcase, head-butting him – and down he went like a sack of spuds. I got him round the throat and I wouldn't let go. The fact that I was in the police station didn't worry me. I wasn't going to grass him to the police, but to me he took a liberty. My husband was always good to him and never treated him bad. In fact Chaz was at Benny's funeral – he *cried* – so how come he felt the need to rob my shop? It was a slag move by anybody's standards, and even if it got me arrested I wanted to make sure this mug got his nose broken.

All hell was let loose – the uniformed police were trying to restrain me, but every time they had me face down I got this surge of energy, jumped up again and lunged at this bloke. Eventually they hit me across my elbows with a truncheon and my arms went weak, but such was my anger I wouldn't go down. I couldn't go down. I just felt that in the world I lived in, we didn't rob each other, we didn't rip each other off. I never stole from other criminals. I wasn't on that wavelength. But after Benny died it seemed like too many people thought they were going to have a piece of me. And I just thought, *I don't think so, mate.* I just wanted to go about my business and not get involved in other people's business, but I was learning fast that without a man like my husband behind me life was very hard. I wasn't weak; I'd just have to keep standing my ground.

I remember waking up in a cell a short time after with blood all over my face. I can't say I blame the police, especially as it took four of them to hold me down. After all, to them I was a nutcase who'd just come in and started going berserk.

I was never charged. The police later told me that the bloke I attacked didn't want to press charges, and that because my husband was not long dead it was obvious I

279

was still grieving. They were prepared to overlook the fact that I'd caused such a scene, but they said I'd be charged if I got nicked again. Just as I was leaving the station, some DI called me back and took me into a room. I thought to myself, *Fuck me, not again, now what am I supposed to have done?*

But he said, 'Don't worry, you're not in any trouble. I just want to talk to you.'

I told him I didn't mind talking to him but that I wanted the tapes on. He said there was no need for tapes, it wasn't about crime, but I insisted: I wouldn't talk to him unless it was on tape. He started by telling me that if I didn't slow down I was going to end up dead or in prison for a very long time. I told him I didn't know what he means. He said that even though I wouldn't talk to the police, they were aware that I was getting ripped off by Chaz and others. He said that they knew I was trying to deal with the situation on my own and that it was common knowledge that both my late husband and I knew some pretty heavy people in the IRA and other criminal sources. At this stage I began to think that he was just trying to find out about the IRA, so I told him I wouldn't talk to him about that subject. He told me he wasn't asking for information, he was just curious. I seemed to be having a lot of problems; I could have called on a whole number of people to deal with these scumbags, so why was I taking so much on board?

'We know you're not short of a bob or two; why don't you move abroad? Why are you still working six days a week when you could be sitting on a beach with your son somewhere?' I remember him saying, 'If I had your kind of money, Joan, I'd be out of this job as quick as a flash.'

I said, 'Just because I've been having problems don't

give me the right to go to the IRA or any other criminal for help. I'll get myself out of this mess without trying to play the gangster's moll bit.'

I guess that over the years I'd seen so many criminals go to the aid of another criminal, on request or out of loyalty, and watched it end up nine times out of ten with someone getting hurt or killed. I didn't feel I had the right to ask or pay someone to deal with my problems. These scumbags thought they could move in on this woman on her own, but they never expected me to fight back. They thought I'd wither away, all broken-hearted like some pussy. This was my problem and my business. I wasn't the head of some fucking crime family, even though the police would say different. I was a young woman whose husband had died on a bit of business and left me all his money and a kid. The only bit of advice I took from the inspector that day was not to get mad any more – but to get even.

CHAPTER THIRTY-FOUR

Payback Time (2)

For the next eighteen months I don't think my feet touched the ground. I got very involved with Ricardo Negro – or Dick, as I liked to call him. Basically, Dick wasn't really the big high flyer he professed to be. He was a skint member who used to make his money by ripping people off on some moody scam or other he'd made up. I fell for it hook, line and sinker. And for Dick too, and lost not much short of £2 million.

Given that someone had tried to break into my house when I was alone there with baby Ben, I'd decided that I should get some of the more valuable stuff into storage, particularly a couple of paintings Benny had acquired just before he died. A friend gave me the phone number of a storage company that they used, and then went on to say that I'd met the bloke who ran it. When I said I couldn't remember, he said, 'Yes you do, his name is Ricardo Negro. He's the one with the gold Bentley.' I then realised who he was talking about.

It had been a few years back. I was sitting in the pub one day with Benny when a bloke pulled up in a gold

Bentley. To be honest, I didn't notice the bloke getting out; I was too busy creaming my knickers at his car. It really was a tool. It had an open top and leather interior. I told myself it was about time I had another car like that. He knew Benny, who then introduced us. He had a nice body, lovely face, but I couldn't help but notice his terrible teeth. On the other hand, I had no room to talk. I'd just come back from an auction and was wearing scruffy old clothes and was filthy dirty from head to toe – and parked outside was a hired Transit van I was driving.

I put my hand out to shake his, and Dick says to me, 'What's it like to shake hands with someone who owns a Bentley?' Well, that was enough for me: I got the strength of Dick Negro there and then. And I remember Benny saying to Dick, 'Don't take no notice of the way she's dressed. She could buy and sell you ten times over.' At this I laughed and left the pair of them to have a drink together. I saw Dick sometimes and Benny used to talk about him, but that was it.

Benny's funeral was to be on 8 December and I wanted it sorted before then.

People kept stopping me to offer their sympathy. I didn't want to talk to anyone. After all, what could they say to me? What could I say to them? I was a loner. I didn't trust anybody, but I'd trusted Benny Hannington with my life. Also I hate drama, I hate tears, and I knew that if I got into conversation with anyone I might start crying. I always saw tears as a sign of weakness and this was no time to be weak. I had a child to bring up. How I felt about Benny being dead had to be put on hold until I was on my own. And not all of the people talking to me were genuine: some were arseholes who just wanted to say they'd seen me.

I decided to go in person to Dick's company and ask him to arrange the storage now, whatever the price. I had the address and found myself walking down Kennington Road towards Brixton. I hadn't had a proper wash or even changed my clothes for two weeks. I remember it was freezing cold, so I did put a mink coat on. I could have driven, but my nerves were gone and I knew I'd probably cause a serious accident. Plus it was the first time I'd gotten any fresh air in weeks, because when Benny went missing I never left the house.

By the time I got to Dick's office I was exhausted. It took all my energy just to walk up the stairs to reception. I walked through the door and recognised him straightaway, but he didn't recognise me. I introduced myself and told him my husband had just been killed and asked him to get things sorted. Well, unlike the Dick I met a few years before, he seemed very polite and sincere, and he said he'd make sure it got done. In fact, he came round the desk and up to me and very quietly said, 'My car's outside. Come downstairs and I'll drop you home,' and that's exactly what he did. Before we drove off in his new Lotus Elise he asked me if I wanted to have something to eat or drink before he dropped me off. I didn't feel clean and hadn't changed my clothes, so I said no, but I said I'd phone him the next day and maybe we could talk a bit of business. He dropped me home, we shook hands and I went indoors, thinking I'd made a right move going to see him in person rather than talking on the phone.

My intention was, after my husband's funeral, to close the three shops we owned, and I told Dick I would rent another storage unit from him. My husband and I had property – mostly antiques and fine art – stored in about eleven different places and I wanted to get everything, including the stuff in our shops, under one roof. I was very direct about what I wanted, and to me Dick seemed very professional; I felt he was an OK kind of bloke. He introduced me to his partner, Bernardo Vialli, who shared the same business manner as Dick and also drove a new Lotus.

I was having difficulty getting a couple of tapes I wanted played at Benny's funeral service: 'Ben' by Michael Jackson and 'The Power of Love' by Jennifer Rush. Dick told me he'd send this girl Sal, who worked in the office, out to the record shop to get me them so I wouldn't have to worry about it. And sure enough he sent her round to my house with them later.

I'd had the good life with Benny. I was financially secure for life, but I wanted to carry on working and see if I could turn my late husband's businesses into straight companies. I'd had enough of flying round the world and living close to the edge. Now that Benny was dead I knew I'd go straight. I'd have been a mug not to. I worked hard all day and went to auctions two nights a week. The only time I went out was for a meal, and then I always took my boy with me. On meeting Dick Negro I thought I'd made the right choice. How wrong I was.

I wouldn't have minded if I'd treated Dick like a mug, but I didn't – far from it. In the first six months of knowing him again after Benny's death, I bought him a couple of new cars, including a Lamborghini, for £120,000, and spent thousands more on clothes because he had no dress sense. I personally lent him about £300,000. I bought him a 4-carat diamond ring, a couple of watches (twenty-eight grand the pair, dealer's price), a Louis Vuitton briefcase and much more stuff. I ploughed well over a million pounds into his companies. Only by the time I got suspicious it was too late, the money was gone. But to me it wasn't about money in the end. What mattered to me was his lack of respect and loyalty.

This really showed itself in 1991 when I had to go to Brighton Police Station to pick up a suitcase full of jewellery and cash that was valued at about £750,000. Dick and I drove down there in the Lamborghini, and when we got to the station I was taken into a room and shown this property. Even before the police opened the suitcase I was describing in detail what should be in there. A load of property had been returned to my husband just a few weeks before he died, because the police couldn't prove it was stolen. I knew it was in plastic bags the same as the ones they were now showing me – and that Benny had buried the jewellery under the floorboards in one of our shops, along with some diamonds, which were ours, and about £300,000 in cash.

I told the police that someone had broken into my shop a few months earlier and nicked the bags from under the floorboards. I knew who it was, but didn't say. After sorting through the property, the police handed it over and I signed for it. I left the room and was just about to walk out the station when a plainclothes officer came up and said to me, 'Are you Joan Hannington?'

I said, 'I hope so, mate, because I've just been given £750,000 worth of jewellery belonging to Joan Hannington,' and started laughing.

The smile was soon wiped off my face. He told me I was under arrest on suspicion of a £1,000,000 antiques and jewellery robbery from somewhere in Bond Street. I was a bit shocked. I really didn't know what he was talking about. He then asked me if the yellow Lamborghini out-side was mine and I said yes.

'We're going to search it. Do you mind being present while we do this?' I said no, I didn't mind (like I had a fuck-ing choice), so they handcuffed my hands behind my back and took me out to the waiting room where Dick was sit-ting. He turned white. 'What's she done? Why's she in handcuffs?'

They told him I was going outside with them to search the car. Dick jumped up. 'Well there's nothing stolen in this car. It's mine, it's registered to me; she bought it for me. You ain't gonna take the car, are you, mate?'

And I remember thinking to myself, *Fuck me, is that all he's worried about, a poxy car? I've just been nicked for a million pounds' worth of stolen jewellery and all he can think about is the fucking car.* The police found nothing but then told me I had to be kept at Brighton Police Station until officers from the Flying Squad came down to escort me back to West End Central Police Station in London. I can't say I was honestly that bothered. When you know in your heart that you haven't done anything, it doesn't trouble you to get nicked. You know they'll put you in a cell, play mind games for a few hours, make their enquiries, maybe keep you a couple of days, then you're let off. That's if you're innocent, and I was. I had no choice but to go through the motions. I've always known not to try to resist arrest, because you're still going to get nicked in the end. It doesn't make sense to start shouting and screaming, because you aren't getting out till they let you out – so why wind yourself up? They expect you to start crying and kicking at the cell door to get out. It's when you don't do what they expect that they can't figure your mind out.

I turned to Dick and told him to take the case of jewellery to my solicitor and get him down to Brighton. What I didn't tell him to do was keep the jewellery, go back to London and not get me a solicitor and not tell anyone where I was – but that's exactly what this piece of shit did. He watched me get taken back inside, then he put my jewellery in the car and pissed off back to London without leaving me so much as any money or food or fags. Only I didn't know this at the time, of course. I was quite happy to go to sleep in the cell, knowing I'll have a solicitor there in a few hours.

At about three o'clock in the morning my cell door was opened and I was handcuffed to two officers, a woman on one side and a bloke on the other. I remember thinking to myself, *How come Dick hasn't sent a solicitor yet? How come he ain't sent me in no food or clean clothes? What the fuck is going on?*

I was taken back to West End Central Police Station, put in another cell and left alone. Eventually I was interviewed on tape about this robbery in Bond Street. It turned out that a member of my husband's family who lived in Brighton was stopped by the police and found to have a load of jewellery hidden in the boot of his car. Then I remembered that in Brighton the day before, the police had showed me some other jewellery apart from my own. I'd picked out all that belonged to me, and I'd told them straight that the stuff I didn't recognise wasn't mine. Thank God I had.

What I didn't know was that in the meantime Dick had done a disappearing act, sold all my jewellery, blew the money on charlie and heroin and paid off his debts – while I'm rotting in a police cell. I mean, you just don't do that to people if you're in the criminal world. Whether it's your lover or not, if one of you gets nicked the other one should do right by you and get you a solicitor and make sure you have food and newspapers.

• • •

It was going on all around me yet I knew fuck all about it, because to me a drug addict was someone who was dirty and slept rough and would rob old ladies or rip chains off people's necks just so they could get their next fix. Dick wasn't on that level. He was thick anyway, a bit slow, and so the fact that he was always wiping his nose didn't send any warning signs to me that he was sniffing charlie. As I mentioned, when Benny was alive we'd both dabbled in it but it wasn't for us. I never even got suspicious if Dick said he'd got another cold or the flu – he was basically a wimp in a bodybuilder's body anyway.

And by the time I found out, I had so much money wrapped up in him and his companies I couldn't walk away. But not only did Dick Negro get in my business, he also tried to take it over and get rid of me in the process.

He'd tell me the money was being invested in properties all round south London. He would show me the properties, I'd pay him the money, and he'd blow it all. The property deals didn't exist. He wanted to be in the big boys' league, but up until he met me he didn't have the money: he and Bernardo might've owned stuff, but only on paper – there were court orders flying all over the place. They didn't even pay the little people who worked for them. And yet they managed to lead a very good life, on my fucking money. Well – they did before I took them both to the edge.

Dick thought I was as thick and as weak as he was. He hoped that the fact that he strangled me twice and left me for dead would be enough. And when it wasn't, he tried to kill me by stabbing me with a needle full of heroin, knowing I didn't use drugs, and while I was still conscious he tried to get me to sign a will leaving everything I own to him, including custody of my son. I didn't tell the police or run to anyone. *I got into this mess. I'll get out of it.* Although I hadn't told anyone I was having major problems, I think it was becoming obvious, and people who shall remain nameless, but were very good friends of my husband's, kept coming to the house offering to deal with it. But for a start, I wasn't ever afraid of Dick. I was a bird with a kid and I just happened to have gotten involved with a couple of plonkers. But was I going to cut my losses, keep quiet and accept that this arsehole crack addict – who'd never done any great bird or ever earned any major amount of money committing a crime – was going to blow £2 million of my money on poxy drugs? Was I really that stupid? I don't think so.

Then Bernardo started going behind Dick's back. He started telling me that not only was Dick ripping me off, he was also spending my money on other birds and even letting some bird drive my Lamborghini. And if ever I was prepared to die for my pride it was then.

All of Dick's little tricks and cons were now blowing up in his face and he could suddenly see an end to the good life: his money tree stopped giving him money. Although he may have 'fucked my arse', as he put it, for £2 million, he was going to have to put it back. This crack addict, ex-business partner, ex-lover was beginning to realise he'd picked the wrong woman to cross. There's a limit to what I'll stand for and what I won't, and what I won't stand for is a man or a woman that I'd been very good to trying to pull one over on me. I'd never asked Dick Negro for any-thing. I'd never stolen anything from him. I'd only ever tried to help him, and he thought I was going to take this latest turn of events on the chin. I just thought, *I don't fuck-ing think so, mate. You are going to pay.* And pay he fucking did. Big-time.

But not straight away. I was in my bed one night, fast asleep, when I was woken up by something in my left ear. It was right hurting me. I jumped up in bed and saw this shadow in front of me and I realised it was Dick. 'I'm going to blow your fucking Irish brains out,' he said. 'Why can't you back down like a good girl?'

There wasn't time to be frightened. But I knew I wasn't going anywhere, not with a .45 sticking in the side of my head.

That I wasn't showing any fear seemed to make Dick more angry. 'Either pull the trigger,' I remember saying to him, 'or fuck off.' I wasn't being hard or flash or anything. I just knew that if he was going to pull the trigger he wouldn't have been telling me about it, he'd have done it. That's the way I saw it at the time, and in my position I didn't have a lot of choices, so I told him again: 'Pull the trigger or fuck off!'

Well, he didn't pull the trigger. Instead he tried to drag me out of the bed, but I was too quick. In the dark I jumped over the bed and managed to get down the stairs with Dick close behind me. We ended up in a nasty struggle in which Dick nearly went through the glass door of my sitting room and I managed to get the gun in my hands. I remember staying very calm; I knew the gun was real, but I didn't know if it was loaded or not. Dick had his back to the glass door and was coming out with some right old bollocks – he was only joking, he would never hurt me – it's just that he gets all wound up and lashes out sometimes – 'You know I love you.'

Honestly, I nearly started laughing. Was this the same bloke who'd cheated me out of £2 million, had beat me up and tried to kill me more than once? And now he was begging me not to shoot him! It was never in my mind to shoot him. I just didn't want to give him the gun back in case he panicked and really did shoot me. I remember looking at him, sweat pouring from his face (obviously in need of a quick line of charlie), and thinking of all the terrible things he had done to me. Like the time he beat me up and I had to stay in bed for six weeks. My ribs were cracked and bruised, my head was twice its normal size; I was in agony. But I never told the police, I never told anyone. I just stayed in my bed, knowing I was going to show Dick Negro the true meaning of the words 'getting your arse fucked'. In fact, in a sick way, it was the only thing I made myself get better for, because mentally I was drained, physically I was exhausted; and this was all within twelve months of my husband's death. And now, for one brief moment, I seriously considered pulling that trigger. But he wasn't worth it. I had my son to think about. What would happen to Ben if I went to jail? He was only little and him having to live without me didn't bear thinking about.

It wasn't a case of wanting to kill Dick Negro. I didn't want to. But he'd put me in a position where I could either shoot him, call the police or give him the gun back. And yet my legs wouldn't move. I was frozen to the spot – still pointing the gun at Dick, who didn't know what I was thinking and was by now crying like a pig, begging me not to shoot him, promising he'll pay me back my money . . .

He was pathetic. And to think I slept with this big heap who's now just a wanker in my eyes.

I wasn't ready for it when all of a sudden Dick leaped at me and grabbed the gun; it went off, but the bullet wasn't in that barrel. He got the gun full off me then, and ran out of the door, yelling that I was dead, that it wasn't finished with yet.

So this war still wasn't over. *What have I got to do to get this bloke off my back?*

• • •

Eventually I got away from Dick Negro. And I had my revenge – both on a financial level and on a personal level. It was the ultimate payback for someone of my mentality.

Some time after I'd parted company with Dick, I had to go to Spain on some business of my late husband's and, although for one reason or another I kept putting it off, I thought it would be good to take a break. I'd lost a lot of weight since Benny died and was having problems with my stomach, so I figured I'd do what I had to do in Spain, then stay on and have a holiday. Benny junior was going to Cyprus to stay with my husband's sister. The day before I left, I had a couple of girlfriends round my house for dinner. They bought me a present, and told me it was just what I needed and not to open it till I got to Spain. When they left that night, of course, I did open it, and I couldn't stop laughing. It was the biggest vibrator I'd ever seen. I think it was the first time since Benny died that I actually had a proper laugh.

Anyway, I didn't take this thing to Spain with me (I'd have died on the spot if Customs opened my bag and found that in there – it wouldn't have done a lot for my ego to have to resort to a vibrator, let alone to get caught with one). But I stayed in Spain a couple of weeks and felt very healthy and fit by the time I got home. I'd more or less decided I was going to sell up and move to Miami, which is what I should have done straight after Benny died.

I'd been home two or three days, and still had a really good suntan, when there was a knock at my front door. It was Dick Negro. It was several months since I'd seen him last, and over that period he'd been paying my money back, bits here, bits there. On this day he must have had a touch, because when I opened the door he was all smiles, obviously high on drugs, and shoved a bag in my hand and said, 'I'll give you more in a couple of weeks.'

I remember there was £20,000 in the bag, all in bundles of £500. I must admit I was a bit shocked, especially as we weren't even on speaking terms when we'd last seen each other. I just stood there and didn't know what to say. Dick was going on about how sorry he was and maybe we could be friends, but no way did I trust him. Even him paying me back every penny he owed me wouldn't take away what he'd done to me. He was bad news and I wanted him away from my door. But because he was off his nut on cocaine he couldn't stop fucking talking, still standing in the hallway of my home, going on and on. Then he said something like, 'Bernardo fucked your arse, Jo, not me,' and I couldn't get past those words. Of course, when people use that expression they don't mean it literally – they mean that they'd had you over or you got a slap or they ripped you off. In my case it meant that Dick Negro fucked me for £2 million.

However, let me now say that all of a sudden I had a change of heart and invited Dick into my home. My son was still away in Cyprus, so it was just me and Dick. I opened a bottle of wine and we just sat and chatted. Everything got very relaxed, and I think Dick, being in the state he was in, started to get ideas, I guess thinking that the twenty grand had sweetened me up, which it hadn't. In my own mind I was still focused on what he'd said in the hallway, about what Bernardo had done to me. Without going into too much detail, let's just say that Dick Negro really does know the true meaning of that expression he'd used.

It is said that I lured him into the bedroom, wrapped him up in duct tape and shoved the big vibrator my friends had given me right up his arse and left him screaming like a stuck pig. It is said that I left him in my flat for a couple of days with that vibrator stuck up there, and that he was unable to move, while I went and slept in a hotel. It is said he was very sore for a while.

No, Dick, you never fucked my arse, mate, you just had my money. But me, I fucked *your* arse good and proper.

Dick Negro can be found hanging around a certain store in south London now, hoping to rip someone off or mug them for his heavy drug habit. Gone are the cars, gone are the clothes, the jewellery, the warehouses, and all that's left are his memories. I gave him one he'll never forget.

CHAPTER THIRTY-FIVE

Settling the Scores

I was asleep in my bed one night when the phone rang. I knew instantly there was something wrong, because anyone who knows me knows I go to bed very early, so no one rings my house after nine o'clock at night. And by now it was one o'clock in the morning. It was my sister-in-law Caroline, and she sounded very upset. She said she was sorry for phoning me so late, but she'd just been to see my mum in hospital and couldn't believe that none of us had told her how ill my mum was. Since my husband died my relationship with my family was non-existent, so I let her go on a bit longer and then I said, 'But Caroline, I don't know what you're talking about. You know I don't see my family.'

It turned out that my mum was very ill in Hammersmith Hospital. I can't remember what more was said between me and Caroline – I know I just wanted to put the phone down and call the hospital. I got through to the ward and was very polite to the person at the other end. I told her I was enquiring about Mrs Josephine O'Leary. She asked me who I was, and I told her: 'I'm her youngest daughter.' Then she informed me that no information on

Mrs O'Leary could be given out. 'But I'm her daughter,' I said again. But this nurse wasn't having any of it, and after much argument she hung up the phone. I just sat in the chair, trying to figure out my thoughts. It was too late to get my boy out of bed to go over there, and to be honest I thought I'd end up going into one at the nurses, so I decided to go over in the morning once I'd seen Benny junior off to school.

I remembered years earlier that my mum was paying me a compliment one day and said that she liked me best with no make-up on and my hair in a ponytail with a base-ball cap on my head, so that's exactly how I dressed to go and see her. Just as I was.

As I walked along the corridor to her ward, the smell in the air was a typical hospital smell; you know, death, anaesthetic. I hated that hospital. I've since lost a few of my mates and they all died in that hospital (so did my dad) and it wasn't my favourite place that day.

When I got to the ward I was told where my mum's bed was, but when I went down there I couldn't see her. Then all of a sudden I hear this voice: 'Joan, Joan, I'm over here.' I turned round and saw this tiny little woman sitting in the corner by a bed. I couldn't believe I hadn't recognised her. She was trying to get out of the chair to come towards me, but couldn't quite make it. I felt rooted to the spot, thought my legs were going to give way. She was so thin and her hair was cropped short and her face was so badly bruised; she looked like she'd had a terrible hiding. I have to admit that for the first time in years my bottle had gone. I was in a situation I couldn't handle. I wanted to run away and hide.

This was my mum – and she looked like a broken old

doll. Gone was the beautiful woman with the lovely body, always so immaculately dressed, who when she came to England all those years earlier was spotted by a photographer and had her picture on the front of the evening paper because of her stunning looks and her beautiful smooth Irish skin. And now look at her. Bony and weak, with a face so bruised that it looked like someone must have hit her.

There she was, looking straight at me with a smile that told me she was happy to see me, her arms outstretched as if to invite me into them. I just sank to my knees and put my head on her lap and started crying. She pulled the cap off my head and loosened my hair out of the ponytail and sat there stroking my hair. It was such a wonderful moment. I remember thinking how lovely she smelled. Then she lifted my face up and told me to stop my tears. I can remember saying, 'I never knew you was ill, Mum. Someone should have phoned me.' Because even though we were estranged, and sometimes I felt like I never wanted to see her or any of them ever again, someone should have called. Mum said she thought I knew, that someone had contacted me.

I felt a surge of anger. I felt like killing them for not telling me how ill she was till now. I picked up my mum out of the chair to put her in the bed and tuck her in. I said to her, 'You smell really nice, Mum, what perfume have you got on?'

'I don't know,' she said. 'But I know it's a good one because I nicked it out of Irene's bag the other day and none of my girls wear fake stuff.' Cunning old cow!

When I'm on my own I can smell the perfume she had on that day. I wish I'd have kidnapped her and brought her to my flat. I just wanted to wash her and comb her hair, cook her nice dinners, and maybe I'd have given her a little brandy. You see, my mum wasn't really so bad; she was just weak, and she was afraid of my dad. She didn't like fights or arguments, so she gave in. I feel sad that I wasn't mature enough to help her with her problems, but I never added to them.

It's not pride that stopped me from going to see her, it's fear that she wouldn't know who I am. I won't put either of us in that position. I'll just remember my mum from when I was about four years old, when she used to wear the big ballroom dresses. She looked so lovely. She'd make apple pies and scones and play 'From a Jack to a King' on the record player, and while she was peeling the spuds she'd sing, *'I'll take you home again, Kathleen . . .'* That's how I choose to remember her: Mary Josephine Masterson O'Leary, the pretty Irish girl from Limerick. I'm not ashamed of her any more, and why should I be? She's my mum and I really did love her. But we'll meet in another world one day and I'll take care of her, and she knows it.

When I got home I locked myself in and didn't leave the house for two weeks. I'd send Benny to and from school by cab. I got other cab drivers to get my shopping. It didn't matter what I'd said to my mum over the years; she was still my mum. Whether I loved her or not, she was my mum, and if she was dying or ill I had a right to know.

I always thought she would have a good life when my dad died. Over the years I'd phone her to see if she'd like to go to New York with me. I promised her I'd put her up in Trump Towers and buy her new clothes; she'd be right happy and excited, but she never came.

• • •

When I was little and coming home from school, we'd have to knock on the door for my dad to open and I used to hold my breath. You were never sure – if you were a minute late it would be potluck if you got a smack in the mouth or dragged in by your hair. Even if you didn't get a clump, the fear was there anyway, and even after my dad had died I'd still think he was going to open the door on the rare occasion I went to visit my mum. I didn't like going into any of the rooms in my mum's house except the kitchen. I wouldn't even go in the toilet because it was upstairs and I'd be thinking my dad would jump out and get me.

There was one occasion when I went to my mum's and was dying to go to the toilet but wouldn't. Eventually I went, but only when my mum agreed to come with me and stood outside the door. I remember her laughing, and she even asked me if I'd been smoking the funny fags again. I told her no. Anyway, I went in the toilet with its horrible woodchip wallpaper, pulled my drawers down and sat on the loo – and all of a sudden it ran through my mind that my dad might come up through the toilet and get me. Well, I jumped up, completely paranoid, still pissing, and ran out of the toilet and out of the house into the back garden, sweating like a pig, knickers round my ankles. I can't believe I was like that – after all, I was a grown woman with two marriages and a pretty good criminal career behind me and wasn't scared of anyone. Yet all those years after my father's death I felt his nasty presence every time I went near Old Oak Common Lane.

The point I'm trying to make is that I don't think it matters whether you come from a rich background or a poor background; your childhood will always stay with you all through your life. If you had a loving background and kind parents, when you grow up you will treat your children the same way.

Even though I've spent my whole life trying to hide from my childhood and from my family, I know that the way my father treated us has probably rubbed off on me a bit. I know I'm always on the defence, even when there's no need to be. The only person I can honestly say I feel safe around is my son. I know he loves me, and not because I buy him the best toys or the best clothes, or because I give him good holidays, but because he knows I'm not a wicked mum.

I have no conscience about how I lived my life, none whatsoever. God is my judge, not anyone down here. I don't regret anything I've ever done. All I would change is losing my girl and my husband blowing himself up and leaving his boy, Benny junior, without a father. If I can live the rest of my years in relative peace, I'll just disappear into obscurity.

Epilogue

4 January 2023

My book was first published in 2002. It drew a great
amount of interest around the world, and in England one
of the major papers serialised it. I was interviewed and
photographed by German, Australian, Spanish, Irish, Jap-
anese and of course English magazines. For a while my life
was crazy, appearing on the main chat shows of the early
2000s: the *Richard & Judy* show, *The Pat Kenny Show* in
Dublin and *The Montel Williams Show* in New York. I also
made a small documentary in New York, which was aired
on US television but not in the UK. *The Pat Kenny Show* in
Dublin will go down as my favourite. I was lucky enough to
be on the show for the ten-year anniversary of Riverdance,
with my fellow guest, a then slightly unknown Gordon
Ramsay. When the show was over, a couple of audience
members were picked to meet a guest of their choice back-
stage, and they chose me! We ended up drinking until the
early hours with the crew and the chosen audience members, and a great time was had by all. There's no hospitality
like the Irish hospitality.

However, my trip was not without its surprises, and not

of the nice sort. After a good night's sleep, I went downstairs into the hotel for breakfast. As soon as I walked into the dining room I got a standing ovation as the whole country watched *The Pat Kenny Show* in those days. I was well-impressed (who says crime doesn't pay!).

I had to rush my breakfast as I was giving an interview to the *Irish Independent*, and they wanted a picture. After the interview, myself and the reporter were saying our goodbyes when another reporter who recognised me came over, and was congratulating me on the book and my appearance on *The Pat Kenny Show*. She said I was a very funny woman, to which we all laughed – then totally out of the blue she asked how did I feel about my mother's death? I nearly fell through the floor. That was the first I'd heard of it, and not from family but a stranger – a journalist! I just said the usual 'no comment' and said my goodbyes to the reporters and to Dublin.

• • •

I can't say much how I felt about my mother's passing. I don't know what she died from. I know she was in a home. I think she was eighty-six. I never understood how she came to be in a home as she owned her own house. As I was not in contact with my family, I never got the answers. My mother and I had been estranged for many years, and that's where I'll leave it.

• • •

Around about the time my book was out, I appeared on a programme called *Hard Bastards*. I was being interviewed by the wife of one of the notorious Kray twins. I was the only woman ever to appear on the show. It was about people that are considered 'hard', although I never thought I was 'hard' – I always saw myself as a survivor.

It was also about a woman living in a man's world. I always found that a strange statement, as I thought I lived in my own world and didn't need any man to achieve my goals.

The programme took me back to my childhood home in East Acton. It really freaked me out as they wanted me to go into the back garden, which you could access from the side. We knocked on the door to ask permission as my family had long since moved. There was no one in, so we went around the back anyway. As soon as I stepped in the garden, I felt sick and thought my legs would buckle under me. All the horrible childhood memories came rushing back, like the times our parents sat there drinking their fucking brandy or whisky. When it ran out, I would be sent down the local off-licence, where they were well-known, to ask for credit for more. God, the shame I felt, but they didn't care as long as they had their drink.

From there we drove to Hastings to the flat that I shared with Ray Pavey. The experience was just as bad: once we arrived at the little two-bedroom ground-floor flat, I recalled the most awful sadistic abuse I was subjected to as young married mum of seventeen. I remember the time Ray stabbed me in the side, threw ammonia into my face, most of it going into my right eye. The pain and the burning sensation was like nothing on earth. Give me childbirth any day. The horrible flashbacks meant I had to ask the film crew to stop filming. I composed myself, and we drove to another location, where, in the late seventies, Ray took Debbie and myself into some woods. For the next two hours I had to dig my own grave with my bare hands. Ray told me he was going to kill me and bury me in those woods, and no one would find me.

After a short while, I decided enough was enough. I told the film crew I wanted to go home, and we all came back to London. We finished the filming in my local pub, which was a few doors' down from my home. Talk about exorcising the ghosts from your past! Jesus, I can't believe I'm still here to tell the stories. But I am what I am, and a stronger person for it.

· · ·

I hadn't seen my brother Michael for over thirty years – since the night he left home when I was thirteen – but never forgot him (I dedicated my book to him together with my son Benny). My mother and father had been on one of their regular drinking binges and had long been in bed in a drunken heap. Bugzy – as Michael was known to us – was out for the evening and when I heard him put his key in the door, I sighed with relief, as I always did when I heard him come home. I knew if my dad got up in the morning with the hump he wouldn't be able to take it out on us if Michael was there. More often than not Bugzy would come through the side entrance, go straight into the kitchen and start cooking a fry-up, which you could smell all through the house. Sometimes I'd creep down the stairs and go into the kitchen on the pretence that I wanted a glass of water and hope that my brother would give me a bite of his sandwich (which he always did), then he would ruffle my hair and tell me to go back to bed.

But on this particular night he came straight through the front door up the stairs and straight into his bedroom. I shared a room with my two sisters, Denise and Trish (my sister Irene had long since left home) and I really don't remember my brother Barry, who was a year older than me, being in the house. I could hear my brother playing a

Bob Dylan record on his record player although he wasn't playing it loud. I fell into a nice sleep humming along (even though I wished it was Bob Marley.) My sleep was soon interrupted by screaming, shouting and smashing. I sat up in a panic just as my bedroom light went on. I could see my two sisters in the hallway trying to calm my brother down, my mother was shouting, my sisters were screaming and my brother was head-butting the wall and pulling the plaster off it. It was like he was going insane. I'm not prepared to say what happened that night or who was responsible other than it wasn't my brother. He left home that night in 1970, no one went to look for him, and we weren't ever allowed to mention his name again. I tried many times to find him over the next thirty years but it was like he just vanished off the face of the earth and nobody cared.

On a hot July afternoon in 2002 I was at home, and one of my closest pals came round to ask do I want to go for a drink. I told him I couldn't because for some reason I had a feeling like I'm going to get some bad news or something. 'Oh, pull yourself together you soppy cow, what bad news you gonna get?'

'I don't know,' I said, 'but I am!' and I burst out crying. About half an hour later my front door went, and it was my friend again: 'You've got a letter at the pub,' he said. 'As soon as I walked in the governor asks me where you were and when I ask why, he told me there's an envelope with a stamp and postmark on it so it hasn't been handed in, it's been posted.'

I brought it home and opened it and got the shock of my life. It was from one of the producers at Channel 5 television (that broadcast *Hard Bastards*) saying that somebody by the name of O'Leary had seen me on this television programme and was urgently trying to contact me. Just then the door opens, and my boy Benny comes in from school. Benny rang the number from my mobile and handed me the phone. It was a woman's voice at the other end: 'Are you Joan O'Leary?'

'Yes,' I said, 'who are you?'

'I'm Carol O'Leary, your brother Michael's wife. I've been trying to find you for such a long time!'

We exchanged the usual pleasantries, then I said to her, 'I don't mean to be rude but I've waited over thirty years to speak to him, please put him on or I'll burst!'

Just then she says, 'Well I'm really sorry to have to tell you this but he died just a couple of months ago. I've been in contact with your family but they wouldn't tell me where you were.' I don't really know what else she said; I was just numb and couldn't speak. Ben took the phone and told her we'd ring her back. I waited until the next day and phoned her when Ben had gone to school. I found out that Michael had had a brain tumour and had collapsed at work the previous January (2001) and died the following April (2002). She said they had married when he was twenty-one and had been married thirty years. They had two children, a boy and a girl, and one grandchild. What really hurt me was that he worked at Great Ormond Street Hospital in London, which was about a fifteen-minute drive from my home. I got very angry when his wife said my family had known since April. I went to church the next day and lit fifty candles. I prayed that he didn't suffer, I prayed for our lost years. I'm not one for going to church but I must admit I got great comfort that day.

I've had several phone conversations with my brother's wife since then and am happy with the knowledge that my brother wasn't a drinker or a smoker and never raised a hand to his wife or his children – in fact they adored him. She told me that in all the time they were married he never spoke about his mum and dad other than to say he hated them. She told me he couldn't watch a programme on television if it had anything to do with hurting children. When I asked her what her reaction was when he was told through the grapevine that his dad was dead all those years before, he had just said, 'Good fucking job.' I did get some small comfort from her though, when she told me that when she was talking to him earlier on in their marriage about his family he just said one day, 'I've got a little sister with blonde hair, she's the only one I miss.' After that he never spoke of me again. My brother was tortured all his life about his childhood, just like me, and just like me he couldn't talk about it. I wrote a book about it, but I guess he chose to take the secrets of his childhood to the grave and I can't knock him for that.

· · ·

For the next twenty years my life was a whirlwind: I became homeless, I had two attempts made on my life, lost all my money, was diagnosed with PTSD, which I've been battling ever since, and I survived it all. However, I always like to look on the bright side: I'm very proud of my family – my daughter Debbie is doing well, and my son Benny – aka Benny Banks – is a very successful musician who has always remained true to himself and never sold his soul. His first song, 'Bada Bing!', was in the films *Fast & Furious 6* and *Sicario*. I'm very proud to say he's raising his daughter on his own – anyone who listens to his music will know the story of his daughter who he now has full custody of – and he's doing a brilliant job. It's her prom this year, and I'm in charge, may God help her!

• • •

The moral of the story is, whatever life throws at you, whatever your background, class, race or religion, if you want to succeed, you can, but just remember, a snake can shed its skin but it will still be a snake. Snakes come with arms and legs – your first instinct is always the right one. Also, take it from one who knows, all that sparkles isn't gold. Money can't buy you happiness, it just buys you time. And in my sixty-sixth year, let's hope there's a bit more time left in this old bag, as I'm now raising two dogs that have completely taken over my life. They have very expensive tastes so I might just have to take up stealing diamonds again.

But I'm still laughing!

THE END (for now)

ACKNOWLEDGEMENTS

I'd like to thank my son Benny Hannington aka the musician Benny Banks, and my beautiful granddaughter Olivia Hannington for putting up with me all these years, with my anxiety, my PTSD, and my OCD, my changing the sheets and towels every day, as well as my tendency to change the furniture every day. I am what I am and I'll do better if I can. Cause I am what I am as I am.

I'd like to thank my friends (in no particular order): Sharon, Jade, Savannah and Tasha – without you in my life I don't know where I'd be, 33 years of friendship and never one cross word.

To my beautiful Irish friend Patricia Sullivan who I have had many alcohol-fuelled evenings with filled with laughter.

To all my friends in Islington, you know who you are, but I can't name you because you're all crooks and as I've never been a police informer I'm not going to start dropping names now!

To all my Black girls in Hornsey (I can't name you either because you're bigger crooks than the Islington lot!), you've had my back for over 15 years, so thank you.

Thank you to Terry's restaurant on Hornsey high street, Sumac Turkish restaurant for all the great food and laughter over the years and the original Green Café for all the sausage sandwiches. In a nutshell, all the Turkish community in Hornsey, who have been my friends for many years.

To Greek Angelo from the sunbed shop in Hornsey, thank you for the laughter, you're a credit to your parents.

Big shout out to Benjamin Bees furniture shop for all the good times, the reggae music, the heated debates and helping me feed my habit of upcycling furniture. Hornsey High Street wasn't the same after you left. Special mention to your beautiful wife for allowing you to be my friend.

Many thanks to the reggae group Burning Spear for 30 years of music.

To Madge and Gus (and Theresa) – thank you for the years working as my security and for keeping me safe.

I'd like to thank my book agent, Gaia Banks, for putting up with me and my mood swings (and for me taking the cup away before you've finished your tea!). I'd like to thank my film and TV agent, Lucy Fawcett, for all the support, the hard work and loyalty over the past 17 years, and for always having my best interests at heart.

I'd also like to thank my beautiful editor, Michelle Warner, for having faith in me and always making me feel welcome. This better be a bestseller or you're in trouble! I know where you live!

A big thank you to everyone involved in the making of *Joan*, including executive producers, Ruth Kenley-Letts, Jenny van der Lande, Roxanne Harvey; director Richard Laxton; writer Anna Symon; costume designer Richard Cooke; stars Sophie Turner, Frank Dillane, all cast and crew. Thank you particularly to the production team, make up-artists and catering who made me feel so welcome when I visited the set. As well as Polly Hill and her team at ITV for commissioning the TV drama.

To Nelson Hannington, my 16-year-old cat, to Rosie O'Leary, my 9-year-old Jack Russell and to Prince Hannington, my 2-year-old miniature Pincher for the love, loyalty, kisses, hugs and cuddles I've had from you in my darkest days when suffering from anxiety. Some women need a man in their life, I just need the love of my children and my animals, which I've got. To Prince, if you don't stop shitting on the new lawn, you won't see 3! I'm a better person from having you animals in my life.

In memory of my friend Fernando Pruna who died in 2023, I'll always treasure the Argentinian, Miami and Holland chapters of my younger life. You were a force to be reckoned with. Rest in peace.

Since moving to the south coast, I've been so welcomed by the community especially by everyone at Pagham Yacht Club and Pagham Beach Club, including Nathalie and Paul, as well as a special shout out to Chris and Pam. You've made me feel right at home.

Last but not least, the biggest shout out goes to Joan Hannington for never giving up in the face of adversity, for overcoming weed addiction, binge drinking and all the negative people that said I'd be dead at 40. Well I'm 67, still here with all my issues and ailments, as well as my own teeth, hair and tits (and botox-free), and I'm still laughing. And to the haters, get a life.